FROM THE PAGES OF AMERICA'S MOST
PRESTIGIOUS MAGAZINE ON FOREIGN AFFAIRS

Public opinion experts Daniel Yankelovich and Larry
Kaagan show why the American people eagerly welcomed
a new approach to foreign policy.

Former Senator John Tower examines the complexities
of the foreign policy tug-of-war between the Reagan
administration and a sometimes hostile Congress.

Secretary of State George Shultz provides a clear overview
of the Reagan program in foreign policy.

McGeorge Bundy, George Kennan, and others question
if "Star Wars" is worth the price of successful arms
control.

These are but a few of the articles, pro and con, that
combine to give the most balanced assessment available
of—

WILLIAM G. HYLAND is the Editor of *Foreign Affairs*,
the magazine published five times a year by the Council
on Foreign Relations. Before joining *Foreign Affairs* in 1984,
he pursued a long career in both government and academic
life, including service with the CIA, the Department of
State, and the National Security Council, where under
Henry Kissinger he was Deputy Assistant to President Ford
for national security affairs. Mr. Hyland is the author of
Mortal Rivals: Superpower Relations from Nixon to Reagan.

THE
REAGAN
FOREIGN
POLICY

EDITED AND WITH AN INTRODUCTION BY
WILLIAM G. HYLAND

A MERIDIAN BOOK
NEW AMERICAN LIBRARY
NEW YORK AND SCARBOROUGH, ONTARIO

NAL BOOKS ARE AVAILABLE AT QUANTITY DISCOUNTS
WHEN USED TO PROMOTE PRODUCTS OR SERVICES.
FOR INFORMATION PLEASE WRITE TO PREMIUM MARKETING DIVISION,
NEW AMERICAN LIBRARY, 1633 BROADWAY,
NEW YORK, NEW YORK 10019.

MERIDIAN TRADEMARK REG. U.S. PAT. OFF. AND FOREIGN COUNTRIES
REGISTERED TRADEMARK—MARCA REGISTRADA
HECHO EN CHICAGO, U.S.A.

SIGNET, SIGNET CLASSIC, MENTOR, ONYX, PLUME, MERIDIAN
and NAL BOOKS are published *in the United States* by NAL PENGUIN INC.,
1633 Broadway, New York, New York 10019,
in Canada by The New American Library of Canada Limited,
81 Mack Avenue, Scarborough, Ontario M1L 1M8

Library of Congress Cataloging-in-Publication Data

The Reagan foreign policy.

1. United States—Foreign relations—1981–
2. Reagan, Ronald.   I. Hyland, William, 1929–
II. Foreign affairs (Council on Foreign Relations)
E876.R395   1987   327.73   87-15224
ISBN 0-452-00889-1

First Meridian Printing, November, 1987

1   2   3   4   5   6   7   8   9

PRINTED IN THE UNITED STATES OF AMERICA

CONTENTS

William G. Hyland

INTRODUCTION

 merican foreign policy under President Reagan has passed through two distinct phases. The first phase coincided, roughly, with the first presidential term. It was characterized by a concentration on rebuilding national defenses and advancing or preparing new initiatives, especially support for anti-communists in Central America, a new peace plan for the Middle East and a new policy of "constructive engagement" in southern Africa.

By 1984 a second phase emerged in which the Reagan Administration showed an increased willingness to negotiate seriously with the Soviet Union. The Administration was buoyed by a self-confidence that had grown out of the successful Grenada operation of October 1983, a perceived improvement in the balance of power with the Soviet Union, and the continued revival of the U.S. economy. The Soviet leaders, anticipating the 1984 election results, decided that they had no choice but to deal with the Reagan Administration. The eventual result was the convocation in Geneva of the first superpower summit since 1979. While the Reagan-Gorbachev meeting in November 1985 accomplished little, it set a new tone for American-Soviet relations and ushered in a phase of intensified bargaining over arms control.

In early autumn 1986 the Administration ran into trouble: Congress rebuffed its South African policy, the Reykjavik summit of October 11–12 ended in controversy, and the Republicans lost their majority status in the Senate in the midterm elections. Then, in early November, the scandal over covert arms sales to Iran broke. The very existence of the Reagan Administration seemed threatened.

The situation festered until February 26, 1987, when a presidential review board, the Tower Commission, issued a scathing indictment of the Administration's performance in what had broadened into a covert operation to supply arms—against congressional strictures—to the Nicaraguan contras. The report, frank and critical as it was, seemed to clear the air of the worst forebodings.[1] Just as a presidential comeback was

[1]*The Tower Commission Report*, New York: Bantam Books, Inc., and Times Books, Inc., 1987.

being predicted by the news media, the President was given an assist from an unexpected quarter—the Kremlin. On February 28 Gorbachev announced a new arms control offer: in effect he virtually accepted the American proposal to eliminate all medium-range missiles from Europe. In April Secretary of State George P. Shultz traveled to Moscow to discuss arms control and another superpower summit, this time to be held in Washington.

Thus began what appears to be the final phase of the Reagan foreign policy. If all the pieces fall into place with Gorbachev, the President could leave office in an aura of success. He could then argue that his position of strength had paid off at the negotiating table. If, on the other hand, matters again go awry, as they have so often in the past in superpower relations, the President may well be a fair target for the accusation that his two terms have been a lost opportunity.

II

Whatever the final judgment, there is little doubt that the Reagan Administration has made some major changes in both the conduct and substance of American foreign policy. These changes, as well as the elements of continuity, have been chronicled and analyzed in the pages of *Foreign Affairs* since the election of 1980.

In that year, significant shifts in American public opinion were becoming more evident. The post-Vietnam era seemed to have finally ended, and a new, more assertive feeling was spreading. The mood of America, according to public opinion experts Daniel Yankelovich and Larry Kaagan, writing in the America and the World 1980 issue of *Foreign Affairs,* was characterized by a "new, outward-looking state of mind." This new body of opinion, insisting on "bold, assertive initiatives," was ready-made for the Reagan candidacy. Some polling data suggested a deep disenchantment with the American position in the world. If Presidents Ford and Carter had overcome Vietnam and Watergate and had restored a sense of decency to the conduct of public affairs, Reagan's mandate seemed to be to revive America's global power.

Yet the mandate was limited by an important factor—the significant increase in congressional power over foreign affairs. As then Senator John G. Tower described in the Winter 1981/82 issue of *Foreign Affairs,* Congress, reacting to and taking advantage of the backlash against Vietnam and Watergate, had erected in the 1970s a new structure of restrictions and impediments to the presidential conduct of foreign policy. This pattern did not end with the inauguration of a popular new president. In fact, it was this age-old clash between the executive and the legislative branches that eventually led to the Reagan Administration's worst disaster—the Iran/contra scandal. The Administration's determination to overcome or circumvent congressional restrictions on its freedom of action seemed to bear out Senator Tower's early warning of the potential for trouble inherent in the congressional drive to harness the executive branch.

The Administration initially interpreted its mandate to require two related efforts: (1) a rebuilding of a strong national defense and (2) what the late Robert E. Osgood, writing in the America and the World 1981 issue, aptly termed the "revitalization of containment."

The defense buildup proceeded from the oft-repeated assertion that there had been a "decade of neglect" in national defense. The buildup was proclaimed to be a matter of urgency, meant to proceed even while the new Administration reevaluated matters of basic strategy. In particular the Administration rejected the doctrine of Mutual Assured Destruction, or MAD, in which deterrence of a Soviet attack rested on the Kremlin's understanding that an American retaliation could be so massive that the Soviet Union would be destroyed. As Secretary of Defense Caspar W. Weinberger, writing in the Spring 1986 issue, asked: "Is a nuclear deterrent that simply threatens the end of modern society credible?"

To avoid having to choose between suicide and surrender, the Administration stressed the development of "selective, discriminate and controlled responses." This emphasis was not in itself a strategic innovation, for it drew heavily on the prior work of targeting the Soviet military and the command and control system, ideas associated with former Secretary of Defense James Schlesinger in the mid-1970s. The assault on the MAD doctrine was also the basic motivation for the Reagan Administration's most important strategic innovation, the Strategic Defense Initiative. According to Secretary Weinberger, this idea "rendered obsolete one of the concepts of the MAD logic: the belief that deterrence must rest on the threat to destroy a certain high percentage of the Soviet population."

As for the revitalization of containment, a number of early Reagan Administration policies flowed from this broad strategy. There were intensified efforts to support the anti-communist government in El Salvador and greatly expanded pressures on the communist regime in Nicaragua. Originally a covert effort, the program directed against Nicaragua gradually became public and increasingly controversial in Congress and among a growing vocal opposition in the United States.

In the Middle East there was a search for a new "strategic consensus" against Moscow. Shortly after U.S. troops helped to evacuate the Palestinian Liberation Organization from Beirut in September 1982, Washington announced a new peace plan that reflected some difficult decisions, primarily the refusal to agree to the establishment of an independent Palestinian state in the Israeli-occupied West Bank and Gaza. Whatever promise this plan might have had was overwhelmed by the consequences of the Israeli invasion of Lebanon three months earlier and the atrocities that took place in the Palestinian refugee camps of Sabra and Shatila. Some share of the responsibility for this drastic turn of events fell on the Administration, for it had pursued "strategic consensus" to a point where the United States seemed to sanction, if not encourage, the Israeli invasion of Lebanon. Soon the United States, in order to salvage its policy, had to insert a peacekeeping force in Beirut, a move that months later would lead to a major disaster.

In Africa the new policy of "constructive engagement," first enunciated in the pages of *Foreign Affairs* in late 1980, sought to take advantage of South African fears of the Cubans to promote a settlement in Namibia as well as in Angola.[2] For some time this initiative, especially as it related to the negotiations on Namibia, seemed to be making progress; in the end it collapsed, and many observers would argue that it was a South African charade from the start.

Not surprisingly, the focus of American foreign policy was the Soviet Union. A strong anti-communism had been the thrust of the first Reagan election campaign and continued to set the tone for the new Administration's approach to superpower relations. Initially there was a general reluctance to engage in negotiations with the Soviets over arms control. The Reagan Administration had viewed such negotiations with the deepest suspicion: as one *Foreign Affairs* author noted, "Ronald Reagan entered office with a deep-seated distaste for arms

---

[2] See Chester A. Crocker, "South Africa: Strategy for Change," *Foreign Affairs*, Winter 1980/81.

control as it had been conducted in the past."[3] Washington was determined that the Atlantic alliance accept and deploy in Europe new American missiles to counter the Soviet buildup of medium-range missiles, as had been agreed by NATO in December 1979. Under pressure from the NATO allies to open negotiations with Moscow on these intermediate-range nuclear forces in Europe, the Administration proposed in November 1981 that both superpowers agree to "eliminate" this entire category of weapons. This proposal was called the "zero option." The Soviets, as expected, brushed it aside. For its part, the Reagan Administration pressured the European allies to take a stronger anti-Soviet stand, especially after the imposition of martial law in Poland in December 1981. Yet the Administration stopped short of linking the Polish crisis to the INF negotiations; nor did the situation in Poland block the opening of the new Strategic Arms Reduction Talks in June 1982. Both sets of negotiations continued without interruption until late 1983, when the Soviets finally walked out in protest over the first deployment of American missiles in Germany.

The results of this first period were mixed. The American defense buildup was an undeniable success. As Secretary Weinberger pointed out, it reversed earlier trends and was supported in Congress. The eventual goal of a 600-ship navy was clearly defined; the B-1 bomber was resurrected; the MX missile was shifted from a mobile to a stationary deployment; and the annual growth rates for defense spending increased. Yet, as Professor Osgood observed, the approach was scattershot and undisciplined by strategic guidance.

U.S.-Soviet relations during this period evolved quite differently than had been originally feared in 1980. There was a series of crises—the Iran-Iraq war, the war in Lebanon, the war in the Falklands, and the conflicts in Central America and Afghanistan—but none escalated into a superpower clash. In part this was because of the moribund state of the Soviet leadership, but it also reflected the shift in what the communists called the correlation of forces. Secretary Shultz, writing in the Spring 1985 issue of Foreign Affairs, found in this increasingly favorable trend for the United States the basis on which a new relationship with Moscow might be established. Interestingly, his apt title, "New Realities and New Ways of Thinking,"

[3]Strobe Talbott, "Buildup and Breakdown," Foreign Affairs, America and the World 1983.

preceded Gorbachev's appropriation of the phrase "new thinking" by a full year.

By the end of the first Reagan term, the trend in relations with Moscow was toward the more traditional mix of conflict and negotiations. It gradually became clear to the White House that a policy of strength could not be an end in itself.

Thus, as the second term began, the arms control talks that had been interrupted in late 1983 resumed in Geneva, becoming a symbol of how far the Administration had moved back toward the mainstream of American foreign policy. This appraisal was foreshadowed midway through the first term by one observer, who wrote: "In 1982, Ronald Reagan, testing the hard line, began to meet the real world. He met the Soviet Union over Poland, Europe over the pipeline and China over Taiwan, emerging scarred from all three encounters."[4] Two years later, in the Winter 1984/85 issue of *Foreign Affairs,* a similar summing-up was the commentary by Henry Grunwald, editor-in-chief of Time Incorporated: "The Administration started out by confronting the world with a hard-line, aggressive and Manichean set of policies, or pronouncements, that in nearly every instance gave way to compromise and at least outward accommodation."

Some observers went further: they saw the Reagan Administration in terms not dissimilar from its predecessors. In a number of areas a comparison of the Nixon-Ford-Carter years to the Reagan first term showed less change than suggested by the new rhetoric. Coral Bell, a seasoned observer of international politics, wrote that "on the whole the diplomatic bark of the Reagan Administration has been considerably fiercer than its bite." Despite strident rhetoric, the basic mechanism for preserving superpower relations had not been damaged by the various crises.

Dr. Bell observed in the America and the World 1984 issue: "A powerful sense of déjà vu hung over the early 1980s for anyone who was once preoccupied with the early 1950s," when there had been an opportunity for progress in U.S.-Soviet relations after Stalin's death, one that was rejected by Washington. Thus the seeds of a future debate had been sown. Would the Reagan era be seen by historians as a lost opportu-

---

[4]Stephen S. Rosenfeld, "Testing the Hard Line," *Foreign Affairs,* America and the World 1982.

nity? Had the Administration been correct in its determination to build a position of strength, or should it have pressed harder for negotiations with the admittedly moribund Soviet leadership?

Such a debate would be left to the historians. As the Reagan Administration entered its second term, Henry Grunwald led his article with the following assessment: "The second Reagan Administration has a rare opportunity to reshape American foreign policy." First on the agenda, as Grunwald saw it, was the "imperative" of arms control: "Its achievements in the past have been modest at best. Progress has been glacial, and exaggerated expectations have been aroused by the process. But there is simply no convincing alternative to it."

The second item on the agenda for the second term would be to repair the damage in the Western alliance, where the Administration had started out on the wrong foot with the European leaders. Third would be to move forward in the Middle East by reviving the abortive peace plan of September 1982, by encouraging Egypt and Jordan to take bolder steps in the peace process, and by recognizing the necessity of dealing with Syria.

Finally, Grunwald argued, the Administration in its second term had to sort out the crisis in Central America. While the Contadora process held some promise for a negotiated settlement, there did not seem to be much cause for optimism. "Standing on principle and playing for time may not be the worst policy," Grunwald advised.

Above all, there was the opportunity, in the wake of President Reagan's massive reelection victory, to achieve a measure of consensus on foreign policy and defense issues, especially regarding the Soviet Union. For Grunwald this was the "most important foreign policy goal for Reagan II." This was also the general assessment of Secretary Shultz, who wrote in the spring of 1985 that the immediate priority was to reinforce the trend toward the emergence of a national consensus on the main elements of foreign policy; the secretary asserted that this was the most important trend of all "because so many of our difficulties in recent decades have been very much the product of our own domestic divisions."

The tragedy of the Reagan era may well be that a bizarre scandal would thwart any effort to forge this consensus.

III

The Reagan foreign policy legacy is likely to be evaluated on the basis of its two new—and controversial—concepts: the Strategic Defense Initiative (SDI) and the doctrine of support for anti-communists in the Third World.

The Strategic Defense Initiative, dubbed "Star Wars," was announced on March 23, 1983. It was a surprise. The public had not been prepared for such a far-reaching proposal—to defend the United States against all ballistic missiles. In addition to the "very real possibility," as Secretary Weinberger put it, that American science and technology could achieve a break-through, the proposal was also motivated by fear that the Soviet Union would achieve a breakthrough in its own major research program that would tempt Moscow to break out of the Anti-Ballistic Missile (ABM) Treaty of 1972.

The President's idea set off a ferocious debate. Lines were drawn around two major issues: would the system work, i.e., could there be a truly effective defense against missiles; and what would be the strategic consequences of proceeding with the program? Four prestigious critics, policymakers in previous administrations, joined together in the Winter 1984/85 issue of *Foreign Affairs* to provide a set of strong arguments against the initiative: they argued that a foolproof system would in fact not be achieved but that the effort to do so would wreck any chances of serious arms control. "There is simply no escape from the reality that Star Wars offers not the promise of greater safety, but the certainty of a large-scale expansion of both offensive and defensive systems on both sides." The President, these authors insisted, had to choose between Star Wars and arms control.

Others saw value in the proposal, but chiefly as a major bargaining chip to be put into play at the right moment for a high price of Soviet concessions in strategic reductions. This was the position taken by former President Nixon in his Fall 1985 article advising the Administration prior to the Geneva summit. A third alternative, identified with Secretary Weinberger, emerged: that the United States immediately deploy a limited ABM system as a first step toward the full SDI program. Many argued that this would mean the early abrogation of the ABM treaty, a prospect that only intensified the debate over SDI.

Nevertheless, the debate did not shake the President's own commitment to his program. Thus, at a crucial moment in the

Reykjavik summit of October 1986, the President refused to compromise on the type of space testing that would be permitted under the ABM treaty, lest the restrictive version being pressed by Gorbachev undermine or foreclose SDI. That meeting foundered over the SDI dispute, but it was clear that the last word had not been uttered.

Indeed, Gorbachev later amended his position to include a proposal to discuss what might be permitted in space testing, and he broadened his restriction on laboratory testing to include a liberal interpretation of the "laboratory." For its part, the Administration began to consider new tests that would advance SDI at the expense of the ABM treaty. Congress debated how to restrain this effort, but by 1987 over $12 billion had been voted for the SDI program since the President's original speech. There was no prospect that the program would be killed outright in Congress.

Many observers saw in this innovation a revolutionary and indeed threatening change in the strategic relationship. But the controversy over SDI and arms control unfolded in an atmosphere that was gradually less polemical, and even, at times, more analytical. The Administration was earning a reputation for pragmatism that had not been anticipated by its critics in the early years of the Reagan presidency. Thus, the secretary of defense outlined for *Foreign Affairs* readers a series of constraints and guidelines on American policy and the use of force. His general proposition was that the United States should not resort to force without clearly defined objectives of vital importance, and without the intention of carrying the operation to a successful conclusion. "The caution sounded by these six tests for the use of military force is intentional," the secretary wrote.

This note of prudence was a reaction to the growing concern that the United States was in danger of slipping into local wars. This was the fear when the President ordered a contingent of American marines into the morass of Beirut to serve as a peacekeeping force. After the marine barracks in Beirut were attacked and heavy casualties inflicted, Washington chose in February 1984 to withdraw the force rather than plunge deeper into the Lebanese conflict. The Administration was criticized for its lack of strategy, but applauded for its prudence in withdrawing. In Grenada the Administration had achieved it aims quickly with minimum losses; in Beirut it failed to achieve its aims, but quickly cut its losses. As some observers noted, in both areas the Administration seemed to have learned the lessons of Vietnam.[5]

But in Central America the Administration was drawn deeper and deeper into a major political controversy. From the outset the Administration had singled out Central America as a special zone. Reagan's first secretary of state, Alexander Haig, had threatened to go to the "source" to control the threats in El Salvador and Nicaragua. In El Salvador the Administration was assisted by a breakthrough in the election of May 1984, which most observers concluded was reasonably fair and honest and which gave President José Napoleón Duarte a strong political position to prosecute the war against the communists and to fend off the right wing. In Nicaragua, however, the approach began to change. From a policy of applying pressure on Cuba, the strategy gradually gave way to a more direct effort of organizing, arming and advising a guerrilla army of Nicaraguans staging their own *contrarrevolución* out of Honduras.

The Administration's contra program was the most prominent feature of a larger concept, which became known as the Reagan Doctrine. As with most broad doctrines, it was not precisely defined. It seemed to mean a concerted program to counter Soviet and communist efforts in the Third World by supporting indigenous anti-communist groups and forces, not only as a defensive response but as an offensive strategy as well. The idea seemed familiar, but as it evolved the doctrine had novel features. Most of the details were surprisingly public, even though the programs were nominally secret. Thus, on the floor of the Congress the debate over support for Nicaraguan contras became an annual struggle. The practice became common. Indeed, a Democratic congressman proposed openly that aid be extended to the Cambodian rebels fighting the Vietnamese-backed regime of Heng Samrin. And it was scarcely a secret that the United States was supporting the Afghan rebels. The support for Jonas Savimbi's forces in Angola became possible after restrictive congressional provisions imposed in 1976 were openly revoked in a public vote.

Partly as a result of this unusual public exposure the policy—or doctrine—became more controversial. Stephen S. Rosenfeld, writing in the Spring 1986 issue, found that, without

[5]Leslie H. Gelb and Anthony Lake, "Four More Years: Diplomacy Restored?", *Foreign Affairs*, America and the World 1984.

conveying a clear sense of purpose, the Administration had "pointed the country more deeply into open-ended conflicts." These fears may have been justified, although within a year a U.S. invasion of Nicaragua seemed less likely. But it also seemed likely that the contra program would encounter its own troubles, given the revelations about the funding of the program in the Iran arms scandal.

IV

Throughout its time in office, the Reagan Administration has shown a far surer grasp of economic policy than foreign affairs. Yet President Reagan's economic legacy of massive budget deficits and huge trade imbalances may be the heaviest burden on his successor. Since the Second World War, wrote *New York Times* columnist Leonard Silk in the America and the World 1986 issue, the United States had been the chief provider of "international economic public goods"—supplying an open market for goods of other countries, ensuring the flow of capital, overseeing coordination of international economic policy, and serving as a lender of last resort. But "1986 severely tested the ability of the United States to provide the leadership needed to prevent a threatened breakdown" in the world economy.

According to Silk, the United States has no realistic choice but to continue its world economic leadership—no one else could do the job—but the country has to set its financial affairs in order by tackling the budget and trade deficits. He argued that for the United States to cut its spending (or raise taxes) and devalue the dollar enough to remedy these deficits, its major trade partners must stimulate their economies and drive the world growth "which the United States has spurred but can no longer sustain alone."

"There are no 'technical' solutions to the economic problems the world is facing," asserted Silk. "What is most needed is political will—the will of the United States to deal more effectively with its own problems and the will of all the major industrial countries to work together for a common end." If the cooperative will was lacking, he warned, "a crack-up could indeed come, with severe political as well as economic consequences."

Indeed, for the first time since the 1930s the Congress began in the spring of 1987 to press for outright protectionism—confirming fears that neoisolationism was gaining ground.

Until late 1986 it seemed as if the Reagan Administration would prove to be "lucky." Michael Mandelbaum, a senior fellow at the Council on Foreign Relations, concluded in his *America and the World 1985* review that the President had profited from the work of his predecessors but had added his own "adept statecraft" and had displayed an "unerring sense of just how far to go." But it was exactly this sense that deserted him, first at Reykjavik and then in the Iran scandal. And both events were in some degree related to what the Tower Commission gently described as his weak "management style."

At Reykjavik both sides seemed to lose control of the negotiations; they found themselves making offers and statements from which they were only too eager to distance themselves afterward. President Reagan in particular went so far as to offer to abolish all ballistic missiles, and Gorbachev countered with an offer to abolish all nuclear weapons. Commenting on this strange turn of events (in *America and the World 1986*), former Secretary of Defense James Schlesinger was sharply critical:

> At Reykjavik the American negotiators appeared to have been little informed either on the exigencies imposed by Western deterrence strategy or on several decades of discussion and debate regarding both the possibilities and the limitations of nuclear disarmament. . . . In Western strategy the nuclear deterrent remains the ultimate and indispensable reality. Yet at Reykjavik the President was prepared to negotiate it away almost heedlessly.

The President successfully mitigated the criticism by a skillful public relations campaign. In dealing with the Iran scandal, however, the President's touch seemed to be lacking; the scandal mushroomed. Some went so far as to predict the "de facto end" of the Reagan presidency. This was obviously not the case, but the longer-term impact on foreign policy was more difficult to judge. Mr. Schlesinger summed up the problem:

> The great accomplishment of Ronald Reagan has been much more political and psychological. He has presided over, and through the ebullience of his personality contributed to, the restoration of American self-confidence and public confidence in our institutions, particularly the presidency. Abroad he has presided over a sharp rise in American prestige (and therefore perceived power), reinforced by a sharp decline in Soviet prestige during

its recent time of troubles. These were major accomplishments, but they are now seriously threatened.

VI

No final judgments can be handed down yet about the Reagan Administration's foreign policy. Some novel approaches were tried that seemed justified but ultimately failed—e.g., the policy of constructive engagement in southern Africa. In other areas interesting new ideas were abandoned without much effort—witness the Middle East peace plan of September 1982. In many significant respects, however, the Reagan policies resembled those of preceding administrations. A suitable summary judgment was given by Henry Grunwald: "On balance, the Reagan Administration often proved itself quite capable of realistic and largely nonideological policies, but they did not fit into any unified concept."

In the pages that follow, we have selected those articles which at the time they were written aptly summed up the state of affairs of the Reagan Administration's foreign policy. There is no uniform or unified point of view expressed in these essays. The Administration is represented by articles by the secretaries of state and defense. The other articles include sharp criticism as well as praise. Special attention has been given to two issues because of their probable enduring importance: the Strategic Defense Initiative and the Reagan Doctrine.

The articles speak for themselves. They are presented in rough chronological order so that the reader can gain some sense of the atmosphere and issues at different points in the life of the Administration.

Of course, the Administration, at this writing, has more than a year left in office, and, indeed, some interesting prospects in foreign policy. Thus we cannot and do not offer a conclusive portrait or draw any historical conclusion about the Reagan era. But as the presidential campaign unfolds we offer the reader some insights into a turbulent political period in our history.

Daniel Yankelovich
and Larry Kaagan

ASSERTIVE AMERICA

Between Jimmy Carter's election in 1976 and Ronald Reagan's victory in 1980, the outlook of the American people underwent one of those decisive shifts that historians generally label as watershed events. In 1976 the nation was still in the aftershock of Watergate and Vietnam—unsure of its limits as a superpower, agonizing over the moral rightness of the Vietnam War, dreading involvement in foreign commitments that in any way resembled Vietnam, preoccupied with domestic economic problems, intent on restoring the presidency to pre-Watergate levels of integrity, and dependent on détente with the Soviet Union to lighten both the defense budget and the tensions of international relations.

By the end of 1980, a series of events had shaken us out of our soul-searching and into a new, outward-looking state of mind. The public had grown skeptical of détente and distressed by American impotence in countering the December 1979 Soviet invasion of Afghanistan. It felt bullied by OPEC, humiliated by the Ayatollah Khomeini, tricked by Castro, out-traded by Japan and out-gunned by the Russians. By the time of the 1980 presidential election, fearing that America was losing control over its foreign affairs, voters were more than ready to exorcise the ghost of Vietnam and replace it with a new posture of American assertiveness.

Americans have become surprisingly explicit about how the United States should seek to regain control of its destiny, and in the context of the disquieting realities of the 1980s, these ideas create a new, different and complex foreign policy mandate for the Reagan presidency. The national pride has been deeply wounded; Americans are fiercely determined to restore our honor and respect abroad. This outlook makes it easy for the Reagan Administration to win support for bold, assertive initiatives, but much more difficult to shape a consensus behind policies that involve compromise, subtlety, patience, restrained gestures, prior

Daniel Yankelovich is Chairman of The Daniel Yankelovich Group, Inc. Larry Kaagan is Senior Vice President of the firm.

consultation with allies, and the deft geopolitical maneuvering that is required when one is no longer the world's preeminent locus of military and economic power.

In looking at the implications of the new public outlook for foreign policy, we shall first examine how the events of 1980 transformed the public psychology. We shall then turn to an analysis of the public mandate given to President Reagan, noting its contrasts with the Carter mandate, and indicating where the current mandate encourages new foreign policy initiatives and where it hinders actions the Administration might wish to take.

II

Some elements of the change in American attitudes toward foreign affairs have been brewing for several years, but 1980 brought many reinforcing developments, all of which delivered related messages about American strength and weakness, honor, eminence and standing among nations. Some of these struck the American public with astonishing force.

Although hostages were seized in Tehran in late 1979, a 1980 overview of public reaction to American foreign affairs can be said to begin with Iran and the 52 American officials held there throughout the year. This sustained episode of national anguish, humiliation and outrage focused public attention simultaneously on the complexities of Middle Eastern politics, the ease with which Iranian militants could seize the American Embassy and its occupants, and the inability of the American government to take effective measures to secure their release. While public opinion polls taken at various times after the Embassy seizure showed no lasting consensus in support of any particular military, diplomatic or other measures, a decisive 65 percent of the public agreed that the taking of American hostages and the U.S. government's handling of the situation had "decreased U.S. prestige abroad."[1] And, an even larger 80 percent majority agreed that the Iranian situation had brought the American people together and helped unify the nation.[2]

While events in Tehran were still being digested, Afghanistan provided a new focus for public attention. President Carter confessed astonishment at the boldness of Russian aggression, and the nation watched as Soviet tanks maneuvered in the streets of Kabul. Although the President was criticized for exaggeration in

[1] *Time*/Yankelovich, Skelly and White, May 14, 1980.
[2] *Ibid.*, December 12, 1979.

some quarters, his charge that the Soviet invasion constituted the "greatest single threat to world peace since World War II" struck a responsive chord with the American public. For the public, if not for diplomats, the invasion confirmed fears that had been growing for years, fears that the Soviets were taking ever more advantage of American weakness to strengthen their position in the Middle East. Surveys taken in the aftermath of the invasion showed 50 percent of the American people concluding that "the Russians feel they now have military superiority over the United States and can get away" with such a move. And a 78 percent majority maintained that, unthwarted by American strength, the Soviets were motivated by an opportunity to gain "more influence over the oil-producing countries of the Middle East."[3]

Afghanistan represents a special type of public reaction to a foreign event. Rather than just a sudden, quickly dissipated burst of outrage, pubiic opinion following the invasion displayed a coalescence of anxieties about Soviet belligerence that had long been present, and crystallized into a suddenly "tougher" view of how to respond. The nation was ready, as it had not been for many years, to "pull together and do what must be done" to reassert American military and diplomatic credibility. The President's words were a rallying cry for this new resolve, but disappointment quickly followed. Military measures, either by the United States or its NATO allies, were ruled out, and most of the diplomatic and economic sanctions imposed on the Soviets seemed either mild or counterproductive. A boycott of the Moscow Summer Olympics and the explosion of pride at the victories of the U.S. hockey team in the February Winter Olympics at Lake Placid were an unsatisfying surrogate for an effective countermove to military aggression. The frustration was enormous, yet it neither exploded nor dissipated; many months later it found expression in the presidential campaign.

Other events erupted on a scale somewhat smaller than the gnawing hostage situation in Iran or the menace of an unchecked Soviet invasion, but sufficient to remind the public that a weak American foreign stance was humiliating, and perhaps dangerous.

Following close on the invasion of Afghanistan was what might have been a routine vote in the United Nations. When a resolution calling on Israel to dismantle its settlements in the West Bank came to the Security Council, in early March, the United States cast its vote in favor of the resolution. The uproar was immediate;

[3] ABC/Harris, January 22, 1980.

in most previous votes of a similar nature, the United States had either supported the Israeli position or abstained from voting. And when President Carter repudiated the vote two days later, and he and Ambassador Donald McHenry offered the explanation of a mistake in communication, the barrage of criticism came not only from Israel and its American supporters, but from Egypt's President Anwar Sadat and much of the diplomatic community as well. Asked for their opinion on the episode, a 64 percent majority of the American public felt that the real "mistake" had been the President's management of the vote and its aftermath. Only by a narrow 42 to 38 percent margin did Americans feel that the President was telling the truth when he said he did not know that the United States would vote in support of the Arab bloc resolution.[4]

Fidel Castro's Cuba emerged at least twice during the year, each time to pose vexing questions about American resolve. For several months after intelligence revealed its presence in August 1979, a Soviet combat brigade in Cuba had been a non-issue that still would not go away; then, in May 1980, the arrival of thousands of Cuban refugees in a "freedom flotilla" became a burning issue. In the first instance the American public was led to wonder whether the nation still had the "clout" that had successfully removed the Soviet missiles from Cuba in the 1962 Cuban missile crisis. Intelligence photographs and official pronouncements about the limited significance of the force did little to allay public concern that the Soviets were having their way with little regard for any U.S. response.

Initially, the springtime arrival of nearly 100,000 Cuban refugees in a chaotic scramble of small boats evoked a sympathetic humanitarian response. But, on balance, the episode left a negative impression on the public. Juxtaposed as it was with growing American concern about domestic unemployment and rekindled suspicion of the Soviet Union, the immigration wave aroused what Louis Harris called "a pervading sense that the United States was tricked by the Castro regime." In an ABC/Harris poll, a 62 percent majority felt that "Castro made us look foolish" by forcing the United States to accept not only large numbers of refugees at an inopportune time, but large numbers of Cuban "undesirables" as well. An even larger 75 percent majority agreed that it was wrong to admit so many Cuban refugees "when we are

[4] ABC/Harris, March 24, 1980.

having real economic troubles at home and unemployment is on the rise."[5]

More distressing than the knife-twisting which Castro has learned to administer so skillfully to the United States were the tragic, symbolic catastrophes that befell the American military, first in the aborted raid in April to rescue the hostages in Iran, and then in the disintegration of a nuclear-armed missile in its silo in September, the result of a fuel explosion. The first episode, bound up painfully with the anguish of the hostages themselves, reopened serious concern about the readiness of U.S. military forces and the effectiveness of our policy planning. Still shocked over the failure of the rescue mission, Americans were treated to the additional unnerving spectacle of a respected Secretary of State, Cyrus R. Vance, resigning in disagreement with the President. And, in the aftermath of the explosion at the missile site in rural Arkansas, controversy flared once again over the reliability and possible disrepair of America's strategic military establishment.

Over and above these military and diplomatic setbacks came an endless variety of economic bad news confirming changes for the worse in America's standing in world affairs. Serious trade imbalances, rising unemployment, inflation, recurrent slippage in the value of the dollar, and the eroded position of U.S. industries in the face of foreign competition sounded ominous notes all year. Increasingly, domestic economic problems were tied to international developments and, recognizing the difference between business cycles and systemic economic trouble, a 68 percent majority of the American people concluded that the U.S. economy was in "a real crisis," as opposed to the 32 percent who felt we were encountering only cyclical "minor problems."[6]

III

What, in the context of a presidential election year, did this stream of unsettling news mean to the American people? What were the cumulative effects of these and other events, and how did they reverberate through the body politic on election day?

In the public eye, American travails in the world arena are part of a pervasive concern about what might be labelled "loss of control." Anxiety over loss of control was an evident theme in a

[5] ABC/Harris, May 24, 1980.
[6] Penn and Schoen for the Garth Report to the New York Stock Exchange, quoted in *Public Opinion*, June 1980, p. 30.

wide variety of issues in 1980, both domestic and international. With uncertainty and apprehension, Americans anxiously groped for a vehicle to regain control.

Of the many forms of loss of control, none has more serious foreign policy implications than the concern that the nation has grown "weaker." Although not confined to a military definition, the perception of a strategically weaker America has recently grown to majority proportions after a trend of rising concern for several years. In mid-1980, a 53 percent majority agreed that "we are behind the Soviet Union in terms of military strength." Only a year earlier, citizens seriously concerned about relative U.S. military weakness were in the minority (38 percent).[7] Uncertainty about national security brought foreign affairs into new focus. As the year began, a 42 percent plurality of Americans named foreign policy as "the most important problem facing the country today"—ahead of the economy and substantially ahead of energy concerns. Not since 1972 had foreign affairs been so prominent; just seven months earlier in 1979, before the hostage seizure and the Soviet move into Afghanistan, foreign affairs had been named by only three percent as the nation's most important concern.[8]

A perceived inability to "control" our foreign policy posture, as evidenced in the hostage affair and the Afghanistan impasse, left the nation frustrated and angry. The perception that America's concern for human rights had permitted us to be tricked, "used" and inundated by Cuban refugees was particularly galling. Even American potency in the world marketplace was regarded with apprehension. As an example, the perception that Japan and other countries had set up trade barriers to the disadvantage of U.S. products was held by over a 60 percent majority of the public in 1980.[9]

Concerns over loss of control not only had their impact on matters of foreign policy, but were pervasive in the daily lives of Americans. Each year more Americans are growing worried about their inability to save for the future (57 percent in a recent study),[10] and majorities are now expressing serious concern about paying the rent or upkeep on their homes. This sense of control slipping from the grasp of even the most responsible citizens is underscored by the fact that while 50 percent of American families

[7] YSW Survey, 1980.
[8] CBS/*New York Times*, January 9, 1980.
[9] YSW Survey, 1980.
[10] *Time*/Yankelovich, Skelly and White, May 1980.

could afford to buy a median-priced home in 1970, only 20 percent could do so in 1980.[11]

Beyond household economics, the growing impact of taxes, invasions of privacy, and changing social morality all raise images of things gone "out of control." The fusing of political conservatism with religious fundamentalism reflects a deep distress among Americans that the nation's family life, sexual morality, and social norms are as out of control as our foreign policy or our inflation-riddled economy. Sociologist Richard Sennett has described movements such as the Moral Majority as representing people who "feel dislocated in America now, who fear the society they were brought up to believe in is disappearing or has disappeared."[12]

Buffeted by concerns about personal and national economics and alarmed by international tensions, Americans who feel that the country is "in deep and serious trouble" reached an unprecedented 84 percent in 1980.[13]

IV

At the end of 1980, the American public's outlook had crystallized into a form that was troubled, aggressive, tough and resentful. For good or bad, the Soviet Union could take much of the "credit" for the change. Soviet leaders planning for the move into Afghanistan—relying on the calculus of raw power—probably did not give much weight to the opinions of the American public. Their calculation was based at least partly on the judgment that, in relationship to the United States, they had little to lose. They feared no great punishment, since they knew that the United States was severely limited in the pressures it could mount against them; conversely, they saw little to gain from restraint since they had already been denied crucial trade preferences, large-scale American technological assistance, or the likelihood of the Senate ratifying the SALT II arms limitation agreement.

After the Soviet incursion it became U.S. policy to convince the Soviets that they would have to pay dearly for their aggressiveness, so dearly that the penalty would be greater than the reward. But to date, the Soviets have suffered only the most minor inconvenience. Western Europe's relationship of détente with the Soviets

---

[11] *National Tax Shelter Digest*, quoted in *The New York Times*, January 1, 1980.

[12] "Power to the People," *The New York Review of Books*, September 25, 1980; for a fuller discussion of this theme, see Daniel Yankelovich, *New Rules: Searching for Self-Fulfillment in a World Turned Upside Down*, New York: Random House, forthcoming, Spring 1981.

[13] *Time*/Yankelovich, Skelly and White, March 1980.

has, for example, hardly been ruffled. In fact, as our relatively small trade has declined, Western Europe's much larger dealings have increased. But from a longer term perspective, history may show that by arousing the enmity and resentment of the American people in a manner that will not soon subside, the Russians paid a steeper price than they may have realized.

The skeptic may ask, "So what? What difference does the mood of a volatile public make? The public does not make foreign policy. Anyway, its opinions are not really its own; they are manipulated by the press or influential elites." For several reasons, this viewpoint—the conventional wisdom in some U.S. foreign policy circles as well as abroad—is a profound misreading of American political realities. On matters of foreign policy the public outlook is not at all volatile. In the post-World War II period it has enjoyed an orderliness, an inner logic and a grounding in principle that has been, if anything, more stable and consistent than American policy itself.

It is true that the opinions of the public do not arise spontaneously. The press and national leadership exercise a great influence on the public, but their voices are diverse, and often the public's response to events is not the same as the leadership's. On Iran, for example, the public was far more aggressive and oriented toward risky action than most press or leadership commentators.

In the conduct of foreign policy a President draws upon several great forces: America's military strength, its economic vitality, its geopolitical resources, and its public mandate. All are important, but the public mandate—the most intangible factor—may also be the most potent, as our policymakers discovered during the Vietnam War. Public opinion largely shapes the context within which policymakers work. There is wide latitude for discretion in policymaking because in a representative democracy the public mostly judges by results rather than insisting on specific policies and actions. Given considerable room for maneuver, a determined President can always oppose the public mandate, or else proceed by secrecy, stealth and indirection—though the latter is more difficult now than in the past.

About any public mandate, it is useful to ask two questions: how restrictive is it, and what kinds of actions does it encourage or inhibit? In an earlier article in *Foreign Affairs*, we argued that in recent years public mandates for the presidential conduct of foreign policy have grown more restrictive. In the pre-Vietnam period, the public assumed that a President had access to information available to no one else, and thus the President "knew best."[14] Since Vietnam, however, there has been a notable shrinkage in the automatic support a President receives in foreign affairs. The poor marks given President Carter's foreign policy make it unlikely that his Administration succeeded in restoring any of the former aura of prestige and blind trust for the presidential conduct of foreign affairs. The Reagan Administration will, therefore, have to learn to live with the new kind of post-Vietnam public mandate—skeptical, opinionated, critical, impatient, giving careful scrutiny to all initiatives, and quick to conclude that while the President may mean well he may not know what he is doing.

In this respect, the Reagan mandate is similar to that which brought Mr. Carter into office. But in all other respects the Reagan mandate—the pattern of actions encouraged or inhibited—is strikingly different from Mr. Carter's. Mr. Carter was elected in a spasm of post-Watergate, post-Vietnam anguish: it was an essential part of his job to restore to the presidency its ability to symbolize America's moral worth (as it had been Mr. Ford's before him). Carter's 1976 campaign promise to form a government "as good as the American people" held a profound appeal for the voters by reassuring them of their own high moral standards.

The Carter Administration, for all its other limitations, succeeded in completing the task the Ford Administration had begun: it fulfilled that part of its mandate which called for a restored sense of honesty and goodness of intent in the office of the presidency. Americans can tolerate a conception of themselves as good people who stumble on occasion; we cannot tolerate an image of ourselves as an immoral people motivated by bad faith.

Thanks to Presidents Ford and Carter, the task of restoring our image of ourselves as good and decent people had been accomplished before the 1980 campaign, and it therefore has little bearing on the Reagan mandate. The Reagan presidency is charged with a far different task—reasserting control over the disarray in our international relations and our economy.

Mr. Reagan started his presidency with a firm vote of citizen confidence that he would accomplish the first part of the task and make substantial gains toward the second. Post-election polls show that overwhelming majorities of the public believe the Reagan Administration will "increase respect for the United States abroad." On economic problems, the margins are narrower, but

[14] Daniel Yankelovich, "Farewell to President Knows Best," *Foreign Affairs*, "America and the World 1978," pp. 670–93.

pluralities think that Mr. Reagan will reduce unemployment, lessen inflation, and reduce the size and cost of the federal government. The public's expectation that Mr. Reagan will be able to make substantial gains on the foreign policy front is much higher than its confidence in his ability to restore control over the economy. This high level of expectation gives the Reagan Administration considerable room to maneuver, but it also imposes a heavy burden.

V

On our analysis of survey data, the American public holds strong and clear ideas about how the nation can regain control over its foreign policy and vindicate the country's honor. The actions encouraged by the new public mood include: a tougher stance in dealing with the Soviet Union; adding muscle to our defense capabilities; showing a willingness to aid our allies, with military force if necessary, in the event of Soviet aggression; brushing aside the moral squeamishness that diminished the usefulness of the CIA; employing trade as a legitimate weapon in support of our national interests; and in general acting more forcefully against our enemies and on behalf of our friends.

It is worth emphasizing that while the public response to the events of 1980 offers the most dramatic evidence of a "toughened" stance, many public opinion trends supporting a more assertive foreign policy began taking shape in the mid-1970s. In 1976, William Watts and Lloyd Free showed that the nation had begun to express "a diminished sense of progress in our dealings with the Soviet Union; a substantial increase in concern over the threat of war . . . and a more pessimistic view about the prospects for future relations with the Soviet Union."[15] Even before the seizure of American hostages in Iran or the Soviet invasion of Afghanistan, the post-Vietnam ambivalence about American assertiveness had started to dissipate. In the spring of 1978, a 53 percent majority agreed that the United States should "get tougher" in its dealings with the Soviet Union.[16] In the aftermath of the invasion of Afghanistan, an even larger 67 percent majority supported a tougher posture.

Given the growth over the past several years of "assertive" trends in public opinion, it would be imprudent to dismiss the

[15] William Watts and Lloyd A. Free, "Nationalism, Not Isolationism," *Foreign Policy*, Fall 1976, pp. 3–26.
[16] CBS/*New York Times*, June 1978.

public stance of 1980 as a temporary mood that will pass after a few months of less bellicose Soviet activity. Sensitive at having been "burned" in the détente relationship with the Soviet Union, Americans are likely to retain that sensitivity for some time to come. Although the public outlook is more cautious and selective than in the crusading period of the 1950s and early 1960s, and containment is no longer singled out as the preeminent foreign policy goal, a national resolve to get tough is likely to be an underlying theme in public attitudes toward U.S.-Soviet relations for some time to come.

One of the most visible vehicles for an enhanced posture of toughness is defense spending, and nowhere has the assertive trend in public attitudes been more conclusive or dramatic than in the growing support for increases in the U.S. military budget. In 1971, with the war in Vietnam still unresolved, only 11 percent of the public wanted to increase U.S. defense expenditures. As late as December 1978, majorities still opposed higher defense spending; but by the middle of 1979, months before the taking of American hostages in Iran, a 42 percent plurality thought defense spending should be increased. Since that time, growing majorities have endorsed higher defense spending, and the events in Afghanistan pushed support for an enlarged military budget up to 74 percent, the highest point since the early days of the Vietnam War.[17] Thus, in the space of a single decade, support for increased military spending soared from one in nine to three out of four!

When Mr. Carter argued in January 1980 that reactivating the mechanism of draft registration was a way of showing U.S. resolve in the face of the Soviet invasion of Afghanistan, a majority of the American people agreed with him. In this sensitive area, too, slowly growing sentiment over the past several years found in the events of 1980 a catalyst that brought forth a new willingness to demonstrate American strength. In early 1977, a 54 percent majority in a Gallup poll still opposed any return to conscription, with 36 percent supporting a revived draft. A year later, Gallup recorded a nearly even split on the subject, with 45 percent supporting a military draft and 46 percent opposing such a move. Afghanistan pushed public sentiment toward solidity, and since February 1980 support for a peacetime draft has received majority support.[18] An August 1980 ABC/Harris poll found a 78 percent level of endorsement for President Carter's call for draft registration.

[17] NBC/Associated Press, January 1980.
[18] Gallup Index No. 178, June 1980.

A related question is the willingness of Americans to use military force in a variety of international situations. After a post-Vietnam hesitancy to send U.S. troops into any situation that might embroil us in a wider conflict, Americans are now responding to a more threatening world with a cautious willingness to project armed force, especially in defense of our allies. Although events in Iran and Afghanistan fanned this new manifestation of assertiveness, trends supporting the use of U.S. military force had begun to develop before these events.

Looking at the key indicator of willingness to intervene in defense of Western Europe, in 1974 only a 39 percent minority of Americans supported direct military involvement in the event of a Soviet invasion. In 1978, the level of support for military involvement crossed into majority status, and after the invasion of Afghanistan crystallized public concern about Soviet aggression, a two-thirds majority (67 percent) favored the use of American forces to repel such an invasion.[19] This renewed willingness to defend allies, however, should not be construed as an indiscriminate rush to armed confrontation. Even in the cases of Iran and Afghanistan, after an initial venting of national ire, majorities favored either "holding off for now" or preferred the use of diplomatic and economic pressures.[20]

The CIA, after several years in the unflattering limelight of congressional and public attention, suddenly emerged in a new light following the Embassy seizure in Tehran. Scourged by a 49 percent to 32 percent negative rating from the public in 1975 after revelations of unsavory domestic and international operations, the CIA gradually rebuilt its support to a 59 percent positive level in 1978 (to strengthen U.S. interests overseas and "weaken those forces that work against" us).[21] A year later, as a result of events in Iran, the agency received a 79 percent endorsement for "overhauling and stepping up" its activities; in the flush of post-seizure anger, the CIA was the designated arm of the U.S. government that should work "to overthrow the Ayatollah Khomeini in Iran."[22]

A new, more assertive public stance also prevails on the question of international trade. Even when reminded that cutoffs of trading

[19] ABC/Harris, No. 25, February 26, 1980.
[20] CBS/*New York Times*, January 1980.
[21] Gallup for the Chicago Council on Foreign Relations. See John E. Rielly, ed., *American Public Opinion and U.S. Foreign Policy 1979*, Chicago: The Chicago Council on Foreign Relations, p. 16.
[22] ABC/Harris, December 3, 1979.

relations with an offending country can have a negative impact on the U.S. balance-of-payments and employment prospects, a 56 percent majority of the public favors the use of trade as a diplomatic weapon. Although a clear consensus exists for restricting export of weapons and armaments, including nuclear technology, a 50-percent majority also endorses the idea that grain and food products be "among the first" products cut off from an offending country.[23]

Together, then, these trends supporting geopolitical toughness, increased military spending and preparedness, less moral squeamishness in the realm of worldwide intelligence operations, and a new willingness to use trade leverage as a weapon in the interests of the nation, amount to a call for a new U.S. assertiveness in world affairs. The message to the Reagan Administration is at least partly telegraphed by the 77-percent majority of registered voters in a post-election CBS/*New York Times* poll who expect President Reagan to "see to it that the U.S. is respected by other nations."[24]

VI

There are three major ways in which the Reagan mandate differs from the Carter version. The first relates to the uses of military power. Americans have come a long way since 1976 in resolving their ambivalence about military power. Critics have often accused American intellectuals of believing that military power is inherently immoral, and therefore that increases in defense spending and weapons systems are automatically to be opposed. In a diluted form, echoes of this same outlook have also been detected among the general public. But as we have seen, moral reticence about the use of military power has now abated. Public hesitancy about military power was linked to its use in Vietnam: many Americans came to feel that the force we applied in Vietnam was inconsistent with our claim to be a good people. While this matter remains controversial, it has receded as an influence on the public mind, and, at least in moral terms, the vast majority of Americans now enthusiastically support stronger military power in the service of our national objectives.

At the beginning of the Carter presidency, there was a similar ambivalence about internationalism—the extent to which the United States should take strong initiatives abroad to bolster its

[23] YSW Survey, 1980.
[24] CBS/*New York Times*, November 16, 1980.

role as a world leader. The public's ambivalence about U.S. internationalism had a different source than its troubled feelings about military power. Here the concern was practical. Vietnam was America's first brush with our limits as a world power, and it left the nation both bruised and deeply concerned that we not extend our commitments beyond our capabilities.

The postwar low point for internationalism came in 1974 in the aftermath of the Arab oil embargo and the recession that followed. At that time, the dominant outlook was that the United States should mind its own business, recognize its limitations, and concentrate on domestic problems. This outlook has been well documented in studies conducted by William Watts and Lloyd Free, using an "internationalism/isolationism index." According to this measure, in 1974 only a 41 percent minority of Americans held a firm internationalist outlook, feeling that we should take the concerns of other countries into account, actively support our allies, and come to the military aid of our West European and Japanese allies if they were attacked by the Soviet Union. Two years later, at the time of the Carter election, internationalism, as measured by the Watts-Free index, stood at virtually the same low level: 44 percent. Since the Carter election, however, American internationalist sentiments have been rising steadily, and internationalist attitudes are now held by a solid 61 percent majority. This is a large increase in a short period of time. Moreover, internationalism correlates with education and affluence, thereby characterizing the most aware and active American citizens.

The third difference between the Reagan and Carter mandates is the least tangible though perhaps the most important. In the Reagan mandate there is a strong element—almost totally absent from the Carter mandate—of desire to vindicate American honor. Clearly the introspective brooding of the Ford-Carter period on the agonized question, "Are we a good people?" can hardly contrast more sharply with today's impatient question, "Why are we letting ourselves be pushed around?" Psychologically speaking, the first question has to be resolved before the second can be raised. As long as people are not sure they are on the ethical side of an issue, they will not interpret other people's actions as efforts to push them around. Instead, they will say things like: "Maybe they are right and we are wrong." "Maybe we *have* injured the North Vietnamese; maybe in supporting the Shah we *have* done a grave injustice to the Iranian people; perhaps we *have* betrayed the Chilean people." These kinds of moral judgments are credible to Americans only in moments of national doubt about our goodness as a people. But it is probably impossible for any nation to sustain these kinds of doubts for long; they soon grow intolerable and are transformed into other sentiments. Individuals may mire themselves in guilt over long periods of years, but nations quickly shrug off such self-doubts.

The moral self-doubt that characterized the Ford-Carter period has now been replaced by a powerful assertion of national pride. The conviction that we have in the past few years permitted ourselves to be manipulated, bullied, humiliated, and otherwise abused, has given rise to a powerful urge to vindicate the national honor. This is a strong part of the Reagan mandate, and in some ways, as noted earlier, it frees the new Administration to take actions needed to reassert control over our foreign affairs. But in other ways the public's convictions about how to restore the national honor collide with the geopolitical realities of the 1980s.

It will take several years before we can fully measure the effects of tension between the Reagan mandate and the constraints of modern geopolitics. But it may not be premature at this stage to illustrate both the opportunities and the inhibitions the new public mandate implies for a Reagan foreign policy.

Within its frame, the Reagan Administration will be able to take initiatives denied to previous administrations. For example, many foreign policy thinkers agree with Henry Kissinger that our failure to counter the Soviet's use of proxy Cuban troops in Angola in 1975 led directly to the Soviet invasion of Afghanistan and the present Soviet threat in the Persian Gulf. Strategists who hold this view see a direct link connecting Angola to Ethiopia to South Yemen to Afghanistan as part of a systematic Soviet pincer movement aimed at the oil resources of the Middle East, with one arm of the pincer through Africa and the other arm through Afghanistan.

In 1975 it was politically impossible to take a bold American initiative to counter Soviet influence in Angola. The situation there looked too much like Vietnam to gain support, either among the general public or in the Congress. Now, in light of the 1980 mandate, Mr. Reagan will meet little public opposition in seeking to counter future Angolas.

Consider, for example, the current situation in the Middle East. In his visit to India in December 1980, Leonid Brezhnev proposed a "nonaggression pact" in the Persian Gulf area, in part to forestall U.S. initiatives in establishing military bases in the region. Under the terms of the Camp David accords between Egypt and Israel, the Israelis are scheduled to withdraw from their bases in the

Sinai Peninsula at Etzion and Eitam in 1981. From the U.S. point of view, these desolate and unpopulated spots are ideal for military bases, from which to defend U.S. interests in the Gulf more effectively than from more remote locations. The calculations that might lead the Reagan Adminstration to assay such a move will depend on many factors. But one overriding political fact that did not exist in the Ford-Carter years is the strong potential for public support of such a move, were it to be made.

Other possible initiatives come to mind, such as giving massive support to Pakistan; supporting an effort by President Sadat to subdue the troublesome Colonel Qaddafi in Libya; getting tough with Cuba on the subject of the Russian brigade there and the 40,000 Cuban troops in various locations in Africa; pressing much harder for greater European and Japanese contributions to mutual defense; cracking down on pro-Khomeini Iranian student groups in the United States, and so forth. We are not recommending or even suggesting that such actions make sense; we are merely pointing out that they are the kinds of initiatives that would receive strong public support under the new mandate.

Some political risk remains, of course. If, responding to the public's assertive state of mind, the new Administration takes actions that backfire or prove imprudent, it will have to accept the political consequences. But unlike the climate of opinion that prevailed in the past few administrations, there now exists widespread support for initiatives that were virtually unthinkable only a few years ago.

Ironically, the present public mood would have fitted better with our position in the world of the 1950s and 1960s than it does in today's circumstances. At that time, our economic and military dominance was unchallenged—we accounted for a staggering half of the world's total industrial production. Then we could afford to adopt a more casual attitude toward the subtleties of balance-of-power politics, the will of other nations, and the limits of the American economy. But in the world of the 1980s, it may prove extraordinarily difficult to execute bold, simple initiatives that vindicate American pride.

The world is now full of countries disinclined to blindly follow America's lead. Much of the disarray of the Carter years came from the perception in other countries that the United States had lost its ability to support its friends, thwart its enemies, and execute its role as a responsible world leader. In the aftermath of Afghanistan, the Pakistanis began to wonder whether in today's world it was even safe to have America as an ally. Throughout the Carter years the Japanese and Germans often questioned aloud whether the United States knew what it was doing, and came to feel it more prudent to plan independent courses of action. There were also times when the Saudi Arabians wondered aloud whether we knew how to protect our own interests, let alone theirs. Some of this questioning of American competence came in the aftermath of our failure to support those elements in Iran that would have permitted an orderly transition from the Shah's regime to a government less inimical to the West than the rule of the Ayatollah Khomeini and the mullahs.

In the next several years, the United States will be obliged to execute many delicate and skillful geopolitical maneuvers that in skeptical eyes might show signs of expediency. How, for example, will the press and the general public react if we suddenly are obliged to rebuild Iran? At present the Soviet Union is seeking, in its posture toward the Iraq-Iran war, to preserve its position in both countries without committing itself strongly to either. But as the war goes on, or if it should die down, the Soviet leaders might be tempted to take actions designed to gain major influence in Iran or even to win it for the Soviet camp. It is probably in America's vital interest to prevent this from happening, and the competition for influence might entail strong U.S. support for Iran even under its present regime or one similar to it. But such an about-face would cause some of Mr. Reagan's supporters great discomfort. At the very least, the appearance of double-talk about Iran could easily confuse the public, unless the Reagan Administration shows exquisite skill and subtlety in explaining its policies and actions.

On another front, some of our most cherished European allies see détente with the Soviet Union from a different perspective than our own. For the Europeans, détente is no mere bilateral relationship between the United States and the Soviet Union. Rather, it is a complex fabric of ties between Western and Eastern Europe, ties that permit Western Europe to achieve autonomy, prosperity and unity. Thus there is a difference of interest which is easy to exploit. Even apart from the troubled issue of Poland, the Reagan Administration will have to work hard at negotiating differences in perceptions of the détente relationship with our European allies to find a common basis for action. It will have to undertake such negotiations with partners who increasingly demand equality, have ideas of their own, differ among themselves, and, from a U.S. perspective, are often perverse in their outlook. The kind of patience, skill, endurance and spirit of give-and-take required for such negotiations lies at the opposite end of the pole of emotions from those that thirst for bold, simple actions in the name of national honor.

It is possible that the balance of opportunities and constraints may turn out to be highly productive. Much depends on the skill of the new Administration in diplomacy and in communicating with the American people. The Reagan Administration has a good chance to live up to the public's high expectations. The stakes could hardly be greater: the rewards for success would be impressive, but the price of failure could also be high.

If a new national program forged at the conservative end of the American political spectrum, and responsive to deep public yearnings for an "assertive America," has a substantial measure of success, conservatives will have won a great victory at a crucial time. We will then probably see a new conservative consensus flow into the policy vacuum left by the disarray of the liberal consensus that has dominated our public life for the past 50 years.

However, if the Reagan Administration fails in its efforts to regain control, it does not follow that the liberal position will necessarily be the beneficiary. If Mr. Reagan is proven not able to forge a program appropriate to the world of the 1980s, and a constructive opposition program has not materialized, the country is less likely to swing back to liberalism than to move further toward the right—toward the strongly ideological right, with its villains, scapegoats and calls for righteous authoritarianism.

A failure by the Reagan Administration on the economic front could destabilize American society for years to come; the corrosive effects of runaway inflation, added to the other strains of American life, could unleash social havoc. And a serious failure on the foreign policy front could leave the United States not only weakened economically but so vulnerable in its national security that it might even be panicked into some frightful military adventure leading to a nuclear confrontation.

In short, the stakes in the new Administration's efforts to bring our domestic and foreign affairs back under control are enormous. The national mood of 1980 does not yet reflect the kind of clear consensus that existed on both domestic and foreign policy from the late 1940s to the mid-1960s. But it is not alarmist to suggest that if such a consensus cannot now be recreated—or if major issues are addressed in an excessively partisan or belligerent spirit—the very future of partisan politics in this country may be in question.

Robert E. Osgood

THE REVITALIZATION OF CONTAINMENT

The Reagan Administration is repeating the first beat of a familiar rhythm of America's international and political life. Each newly elected Administration of the alternative political party launches its foreign relations with themes that were developed during the national campaign in opposition to the policies of its predecessor. But then comes the down beat: unexpected domestic and international conditions contradict (or appear to contradict) the underlying premises of the "new" foreign policy. Then either the Administration abandons or modifies its themes (in substance, if not in rhetoric) or it takes uncontested credit for the transformation. This phenomenon began with the Eisenhower Administration. It has deep roots in the American political system and the American approach to the outside world.

Beneath this familiar rhythm the continuities of American foreign policy are always greater than the political claims to innovation would have one believe. The greatest discontinuities spring from responses to unanticipated events, not from changes of Administration. Moreover, the rhythm is itself one of the most notable continuities. It corresponds to the oft-noted oscillations in America's world role between assertion and retrenchment, between the affirmation and restraint of national power. And in the postwar period it has responded to the onset and aftermath of crises and wars. As the nation revises its estimate of the Soviet threat to its foreign security interests upward and downward there is an alternation between repeated efforts to close the chronic gap between ever-expanding interests and the available power to support them, and efforts to seek relief from the ardors of containment.

The Reagan Administration has assumed the task of once again augmenting and reaffirming American power, under the impetus of heightened fears of the Soviet threat. The Carter Administra-

The late Robert E. Osgood was the Christian A. Herter Professor of American Foreign Policy at the School of Advanced International Studies of The Johns Hopkins University. He was a member of the Senior Staff of the National Security Council in 1969–70 and served on the Reagan Administration's Policy Planning Council. He wrote, among other works, *Limited War: The Challenge to American Strategy*.

tion had already substantially reversed its initial policy of re-trenchment and self-restraint, but the themes of the new Admin-istration's efforts reflect a vigorous reaction to those that its predecessor brought into office in 1977. It launches this new effort, however, in the face of a set of troublesome domestic and inter-national conditions which have emerged largely in the last decade and which impose unprecedented constraints on the effective exercise of American power in its economic, diplomatic, and military dimensions. Most of the policy expedients to which previous administrations resorted in order to close the gap between interests and power—whether by enhancing U.S. power, accom-modating the Soviet threat, or blunting its impact—are, in prac-tice, either no longer available or seriously limited.

How well the Reagan Administration performs in bringing American power into a safe balance with American security interests and commitments under these novel constraints will not only determine the reputation of President Reagan's Administra-tion; it will establish an historic landmark in the nation's capacity to adjust the principal continuities of postwar foreign policy—most notably, the overriding objective of containment—to porten-tous developments that have deprived the United States of its primacy while extending its involvement in world politics.

II

A brief review of the previous oscillations of U.S. foreign policy since World War II indicates the magnitude and significance of the task of national revival that President Reagan has undertaken.

At the outset of the cold war, Soviet moves in Iran (Azerbaijan), Poland, Berlin, Greece and Czechoslovakia refuted hopeful expec-tations of a new international order based on U.S. collaboration with the U.S.S.R. and Great Britain; in 1947 Britain's abandon-ment of its strategic role in Greece began the still-expanding process, unforeseen at the time, of America's global role of con-tainment. Nevertheless, it took the shock of the Korean War to drive the United States to close the widening gap between its expanding commitments and the military power available to support them. The latter had been restricted by a rigid ceiling of about $13 billion on the defense budget and by a military strategy adapted only to the defense of Western Europe and a chain of Pacific islands running southward from Japan (thereby excluding the Korean peninsula from the U.S. "defensive perimeter").

In the aftermath of the frustrations and exertions of the Korean War and the accompanying four-fold defense build-up and expanded commitments to the defense of Europe, the Eisenhower Administration came into office with a dual mandate: economic retrenchment and avoidance of future Korean Wars, on the one hand; deterring Soviet aggression-by-proxy more effectively, on the other. Its formula of substituting nuclear deterrence and a network of alliances—a "political warning system," in Secretary of State John Foster Dulles's words—for conventional forces and local intervention worked well enough for a while. The 1955 summit meeting with the Russians seemingly confirmed the success of this formula in a widely perceived "thaw" in the cold war and the "spirit of Geneva." But then the Soviet orbiting of Sputnik, the fear of an imminent "missile gap," Khrushchev's instigation of a second Berlin crisis and his harsh antics in May 1960 following the shooting down over Russia of America's acknowledged U-2 spy plane, coupled with growing troubles with Castro, political turmoil in the Congo, and Nasser's turn toward Moscow for arms, put an end to the incipient détente.

President Kennedy came into office dedicated to campaign themes of restoring American power and prestige on the basis of a revived American economy. He translated these themes into policies intended to strengthen and diversify the nation's military power, counter the new threat of wars of national liberation, identify America with the forces of non-communist nationalism in Africa and elsewhere, and overcome the vulnerability of the less-developed countries to Communist penetration through economic development keyed to social and economic reform. By the mid-1960s the resulting military build-up, a surge of domestic economic growth, the successful surmounting of crises in Berlin, Cuba and the Congo, and new evidence of Soviet troubles in Eastern Europe and with China produced perhaps the greatest sense of security and well-being that Americans have enjoyed in the entire postwar period.

Kennedy's successor, Lyndon Johnson, took office determined to concentrate his and the nation's attention on domestic social and economic improvements. But fate and the inertia of settled axioms of containment, given new impetus by the heightened confidence in American power born in the Kennedy years, determined that Johnson's Administration would be preoccupied with a war in Vietnam which could not be won—perhaps not even at the price of a protracted and expanded war, which neither Johnson nor the nation was willing to pay.

Given the national trauma inflicted by the war in Vietnam, any succeeding Administration was bound to oscillate again toward retrenchment. The Nixon-Ford-Kissinger regime conceived its first task, after honorable extrication from the war, as bringing American power into balance with vital interests at a reduced level of national effort and a lessened risk of armed intervention. It sought to shore up containment at a level of involvement that would be acceptable to the American public and consistent with constraints on unilateral American power that had emerged during the last two decades. But to reconcile containment with retrenchment it could not resort to the expedients available to the Eisenhower Administration. Instead, it turned to a more selective projection of U.S. force in Third World crises; a greater reliance on less-developed countries to help themselves in countering internal threats; the orchestration of a global modus vivendi, or détente, with the Soviet Union (with SALT as the centerpiece); instrumental to détente, a rapprochement with the People's Republic of China; and reliance on Iran as a security-keeping surrogate in the Middle East.

On the whole, this strategy worked well, but over the years some of its underlying premises about the international environment began to run into conflict with intractable realities. The atmosphere of détente helped to reinforce post-Vietnam restrictions on U.S. defense expenditures (which declined in real dollars), although the U.S.S.R. continued an annual four to six percent increase in its defense outlays—beyond the requirements of parity, as Americans saw them. The underlying assumption of the Nixon-Kissinger strategy, that the turbulence of the Third World—contrary to Kennedy's dramatization of its significance as the decisive arena of the cold war—need not impinge on vital American security interests was refuted by the Yom Kippur War of 1973, with an ominous, though muted, threat of Soviet intervention to compel a cease-fire, and with the emergence of an Arab embargo on oil to the increasingly oil-dependent United States. Then the unanticipated collapse of the Portuguese empire in Africa in 1974 led directly to Soviet intervention, in collaboration with Cuban troops, in the Angolan civil war; the withdrawal of America's indirect and covert participation in that war under pressure from Congress portended, in Kissinger's view, a repetition in resource-rich southern Africa of the fateful 1930s scenario of unopposed piecemeal aggression, which underlay America's whole postwar effort to vindicate the interwar lessons through vigilant containment.

Even these developments, however, did not overcome the post-Vietnam mood of retrenchment. The apparent success of Kissinger in blending containment with détente blunted the force of retrenchment, but it also postponed a revival of containment. This enabled the Carter Administration to focus its criticism on the containment side of the Nixon-Ford-Kissinger strategy, in what became a less constrained, delayed accommodation to the psychological wounds of the Vietnam War. President Carter came into office with an avowed mandate to reverse what he and his aides portrayed as Kissinger's Machiavellian and anachronistic preoccupation with the containment of the Soviet Union through clever personal diplomacy and Realpolitik. Without really abandoning the overriding objective of containment, the new Administration set out to implement it in a manner congenial to American geopolitical retrenchment and moral resurgence—by downplaying the "inordinate fear of communism" that had led the country "to embrace any dictator who joined us in our fear" (as the President put it in his famous Notre Dame speech on May 22, 1977); aligning the United States with the forces of black majority rule in southern Africa; and concentrating on the transcendent "global questions" of justice, equity, and human rights through revising the international economic order to accommodate the needs of the "South," preventing nuclear proliferation, curbing the arms trade, and promoting the rights of the individual against cruelty and oppression.

In the face of a steady Soviet military build-up and of mounting turbulence and new opportunities for the expansion of Soviet influence in the Third World, the Carter Administration's emphasis on "world-order politics" and the "global agenda," in the fashionable academic phrases of the time, was bound to enlarge the interests-power gap that was already emerging under the cover of Kissinger's Realpolitik. Reacting against this trend on pragmatic and domestic political grounds, the Administration began after only a year to modify, abandon or reverse major components of its original grand design. As in previous oscillations of American policy, the driving factor was a shift in the prevailing estimate of the Soviet threat.

After Moscow's 1977 intervention (with East German and Cuban assistance) in behalf of Mengistu's self-styled Marxist-Leninist regime in Ethiopia, Zbigniew Brzezinski, the President's National Security Assistant, emerged as a militant critic of Soviet violations of "what was once called the code of conduct." By the spring of 1978 he was depicting an "arc of crisis" that came to include the Soviet alliance with Vietnam, the 1978 installation of a puppet regime in Afghanistan, the establishment of military dependencies in South Yemen and in Ethiopia (in the latter case with Soviet military personnel and proxy forces), and the invasion of the Katanga (Shaba) province in Zaïre from Angola. President Carter reversed the decade-long decline in the real defense budget (notably in his address at Wake Forest University in March 1978) and declared that détente must be based on reciprocal restraint, whereas the Soviet Union, he charged (at the U.S. Naval Academy in June), had exploited détente to cover "a continuing aggressive struggle for political advantage and increased influence in a variety of ways."

This rhetorical reaffirmation of containment was matched, not only by a reversal of the decline in real defense expenditures, but also by increased arms sales (especially to Middle Eastern countries), U.S. leadership in establishing a Long Term Defense Program under which the NATO allies pledged to increase annual defense expenditures by three percent in real terms, and support of a long-range theater nuclear force modernization program (first publicly advocated by Chancellor Schmidt) culminating in the NATO decision of December 1979 to install 572 Pershing II and cruise missiles on European soil.

Capping this shift, President Carter, in urgent response to the dual shock of the overthrow of the Shah of Iran (followed by the imprisonment of American hostages) and the Soviet invasion of Afghanistan, proclaimed the most far-reaching extension of American commitments since the redefinition of America's Pacific defensive perimeter after the Korean War. In his January 1980 State of the Union address, he declared, in what immediately became known as the Carter Doctrine: "An attempt by any outside force to gain control of the Persian Gulf region will be regarded as an assault on the vital interests of the United States of America, and such an assault will be repelled by any means necessary, including military force." Giving substance to this new sense of urgency, he promised to increase defense expenditures by five percent a year, ordered the creation of a Rapid Deployment Force (RDF), deployed naval forces and sent heavy arms to protect North Yemen from the Soviet client in South Yemen, imposed a partial grain embargo and other sanctions on the U.S.S.R., and removed some restrictions on militarily significant sales of technology to China. With the ratification of SALT II already doomed by Afghanistan, it was formally withdrawn from the Senate in Carter's last days in office.

This reassertion of American power in support of containment, however, did not save the Carter Administration. Beginning in the middle of the 1970s (according to the opinion polls), the tide of opinion which President Carter had ridden into office had been reversed; by 1980 it was flowing strongly in the opposite direction. Indeed, Carter's switch only reinforced the politically fatal image of an indecisive, somewhat schizoid President presiding over an erratic, incoherent policy.

In the 1980 presidential campaign Governor Ronald Reagan emerged as the rallying point for, and articulator of, the pent-up reaction to the "Vietnam syndrome." Like President Kennedy, he interpreted his political mandate as, above all, the restoration of the nation's power and prestige in response to a heightened and neglected Soviet threat. But he did so in the face of domestic and international constraints that Kennedy never imagined. Unlike Kennedy, Reagan approached this task with a clear priority in favor of economic restoration. Lacking Kennedy's familiarity or concern with foreign affairs, his pretensions to innovative policies, or the ebullience and missionary impetus that Kennedy had imparted to his program of American resurgence, the simplicity of Reagan's foreign policy themes stood in even sharper contrast to the complexity of his task.

III

President Reagan avowed that in foreign policy, as in other matters of public policy, simplicity has its virtues and should not be equated with simple-mindedness. He had a point. It would have been difficult, even in the luxury of one's analytical imagination, to invent a single strategic concept to embrace the full complexity of the international conditions of 1981. And the failure of previous concepts—really stratagems more than strategies—to fulfill the expectations they raised (for example, Eisenhower's massive retaliation, Kennedy's promotion of self-sustaining economic growth and nation-building among the LDCs, the Nixon Doctrine, and Carter's vision of world-order politics) suggest that the absence of a grand strategy may be prudent as well as pardonable.

Journalists and academics complained that the vaunted simplicity of Reagan's foreign policy was an excuse for incoherence. By normal standards, however, it was not the incoherence of the new Administration's policies that stood out—in fact, they were comparatively coherent in action as well as rhetoric—but rather their incompleteness, both in scope and detail, when measured against the realities of the international environment. One reason for this was the President's decision, as a choice of political strategy as well as substantive priority, to concentrate on domestic economic goals at the beginning of his Administration. But there were other reasons: the failure to organize an effective system for the conduct of policy that would enable the President to make reasoned choices of strategic implementation (a failure due, in large part, to the downgrading of the National Security Council staff); the President's unfamiliarity with foreign policy and his lack of interest in taking an active role in the implementation of policies; the resulting lack of a dominant locus of policymaking, whether in the State Department, the Defense Department, or the White House; and the associated lack in any of these quarters of articulate intellectuals with the role of rationalizing policy for domestic and foreign audiences.

Nevertheless, despite the slowness of the Administration to formulate and articulate the components of a national strategy, the outlines and much of the substance of a set of foreign policies, linked to the central goals of policy and fairly well integrated with each other, were emerging by the end of 1981. As in the case of previous new Administrations, the process of elaborating the outlines and filling in the substance would be the result of themes and positions developed in the victorious campaign for office rubbing up against the stubborn continuities of the past. At the end of its first year the Administration was altering the tone and content of its original policies in response to intractable domestic and international constraints at a faster pace than most of its predecessors. Perhaps this was partly because the elementary nature of its strategic design enabled it to adapt more readily to elusive realities; but it was also because some of its own priorities—particularly rejuvenating the economy and refurbishing alliances—were, at the outset, in conflict with other themes and programs developed in the campaign. Some of the President's own simple objectives, in practice, also conflicted with each other.

The dominant theme of President Reagan's foreign policy, to which all major policies were subordinated, was revitalizing the containment of Soviet expansion. Of course, declarations about the urgency of strengthening containment were accompanied by familiar affirmations of containment's twin: the achievement of a world hospitable to free societies, where the Soviet Union would observe the international code of decent conduct, and peaceful change would become the norm. But the attainment of this world-order goal was declared to depend centrally on containing the enemy—not, as in the Carter Administration's initial formulations, on addressing the transcendent problems of the global agenda or, as in the Kissinger era, on achieving a global modus vivendi with the competing superpower.

The centrality of containment, moreover, followed from a new emphasis on the danger of the Soviet global threat. In the incoming Administration's view, while Americans had been paralyzed by illusions of détente and the trauma of Vietnam, the Soviet Union had achieved an epochal reversal of global power. Transforming itself from a continental to an ascendant imperial power, it had pursued global preponderance through a steady build-up of military capabilities ever since the Cuban missile crisis. It made no practical difference whether one attributed Soviet ascendancy to ideologically driven expansionism or to the defensive paranoia of a geopolitically encircled power center—both interpretations were to be found in the new Administration. The result was the same: a cautiously but relentlessly expansionist state opportunistically capitalizing upon its two great assets, military ascendancy and the political turmoil and vulnerability of the Third World.

To counter this Soviet threat, the priority task for the United States was to reverse the trend toward Soviet ascendancy and regain a safe military balance. Military revival would require liberation of the American spirit from the paralyzing effects of an era of national self-doubt and timidity. It would require overcoming the "strategic passivity" that had subordinated urgent security concerns to unrealistic scruples about the moral and political purity of friendly countries. And the revival of American power and spirit, the President and his spokesmen repeatedly stressed, would depend, above all, on the rejuvenation of the American economy by liberating the creative impulses of free enterprise from the dead hand of government control.

In proclaiming this central theme, there was no pretension of an all-embracing grand design or even intimations of a Reagan Doctrine. The important point was to establish a central purpose and priority and to develop coherent policies consistent with each other.

The closest the Administration came to elaborating or refining this common-sense view in its first year were the oft-repeated but little noted "four pillars" set forth by Secretary of State Alexander Haig, who called them the President's "coherent strategic approach."[1] But the "pillars" were really goals: the restoration of American and Western economic and military strength, the rein-

---

[1] At the end of the year, these were succinctly presented in an article by the Secretary, "A Strategic American Foreign Policy," *NATO Review*, December 1981. The summary of the "four pillars" is taken directly from that article.

vigoration of alliances and bilateral relationships with friendly states, the promotion of progress, in an environment of peaceful change, among less industrialized countries, and the achievement of a relationship with the U.S.S.R. based on greater Soviet restraint and reciprocity. They fell far short of delineating a strategy, if strategy means a comprehensive plan for applying the instruments and resources of national power most effectively to support a hierarchy of interests in a range of specific contingencies and circumstances.

But their very generality made it easier to adjust campaign themes to the complexities of domestic and international realities. Furthermore, despite the fact that the Administration's organization for conducting foreign policy was woefully deficient in analyzing policy options at the NSC level and did not regularly engage the President in strategic choices, and despite an extraordinary amount of "turf-fighting" in the foreign policy structure, the existence of unusual ideological affinity among the key policymakers made for relative coherence in the major substantive areas as policies evolved. The greatest substantive differences were between unilateralists and multilateralists (to use oversimplifications current within the Administration). By the end of the year the latter clearly prevailed, but the balance was unstable.

IV

The overriding goal of the Administration's foreign policy was to make American and Western power commensurate to the support of greatly extended global security interests and commitments. There was no disposition to define interests more selectively and no expectation of anything but an intensified Soviet threat to these interests. Hence, the emphasis in closing the gap between interests and power would be placed on augmenting countervailing military strength—first of all unilaterally, but also collectively with allies and bilaterally with countries willing and able to defend themselves against Communist incursions and revolution.

In pursuit of this goal the Administration's determination to increase the U.S. defense budget was clearer than its strategy for applying military resources to foreign policy requirements. After initially projecting more than double the percentage increase of the Carter budgets for FY 1981 and FY 1982, the program leveled off to a seven percent annual increase instead of Carter's five percent for the next four years, and added up to $1,280.6 billion by the end of 1986, which was about a $200 billion increase beyond the projected Carter program. In terms of constant dollars, these amounts would be by far the largest peacetime military outlay in American history.

This ambitious target, however, was arrived at without the benefit of any comprehensive strategic review, and it depended on equally ambitious targets of growth in domestic economic production. The scattershot approach to defense spending, along with Secretary of Defense Caspar Weinberger's decentralization of the management of programs and resources into the hands of the separate armed services, meant that defense expenditures would be undisciplined by strategic guidance until budgetary and other constraints compelled choices among priorities.

Initial strategic pronouncements indicated little more than that the new Administration intended to restore American military power to meet an extraordinarily wide range of contingencies. First of all, it would close the "window of vulnerability" resulting from the presumed Soviet capacity to destroy most of American land-based missiles in a first strike and regain a "margin of safety" in the U.S. strategic nuclear posture. (Significantly, even before taking office the Administration had dropped the 1980 Republican platform's less credible pledge to "superiority," which implied the rejection of parity.) In Europe it would move ahead with the development of 108 Pershing II and 464 ground-launched cruise missiles (GLCMS), in accordance with the long-range theater nuclear weapons program (LRTNF). But it also stressed the necessity of strengthening conventional capabilities and reaffirmed that the NATO commitment to three percent annual real increases in the long-term defense program (LTDP) must be fulfilled.

Outside the NATO theater, too, the Adminstration's objectives were comprehensive. It would build up general purpose forces, not only to support the previously planned Rapid Deployment Force in the Gulf with a full-time regional presence and reinforcement capabilities, but also to prepare the United States to fight protracted conventional wars in more than one theater simultaneously. In this connection Secretary Weinberger explicitly rejected the artificial constraints implied by previous commitments to a 1½- or 2½-war strategy. If one took his repeated statements about the need to meet Soviet aggression in one location by responding at points of vulnerability elsewhere—a concept soon dubbed "horizontal escalation"—as a strategy with operational significance, this would put an even higher premium on a multi-theater capability. For no one could reasonably assume in the

1980s that the threat to respond at "places of our choosing" would—as John Foster Dulles seemed to hope when he used the same phrase in the 1950s—so enhance deterrence as to obviate the necessity of fighting local wars at all.

One indication of how the Administration's goals might be translated into strategy and forces was Secretary of the Navy John Lehman's exposition of a posture of "unquestioned naval superiority," based on a 600-ship fleet with 15 battleships clustered around large aircraft carriers, surface ships with cruise missiles, and enhanced amphibious forces. This formidable force would do far more than control the sea lanes and establish a presence in crises. It would be capable of coping singly or simultaneously with local conflicts in every theater, at least in terms of maintaining access to land against Soviet or Soviet-proxy forces and thus, if necessary, removing the need to depend on U.S. or other land-based forces. But it would also be able to fight a global war between U.S. and Soviet forces at sea and perform traditional naval tasks in general war, such as protecting the sea lanes.

If nothing else, these intimations of all-purpose strategic goals indicated the Administration's firm intention to change what a number of its officials had criticized as America's "Euro-centered" strategy and to prepare the armed forces, for once, to support the nation's global commitments with truly flexible, global capabilities. The far-reaching scope of this intention was confirmed by the demanding objective, as put forth by the Under Secretary of Defense for Policy, Fred Iklé, to expand the capacity of the industrial base of American defense production so that it could support not only rapid mobilization for a crisis but also a prolonged large-scale war.

But the extent to which the Administration would actually implement its expansive strategic goals, or maintain the goals if they could not be implemented, was another matter. The major factor likely to move the Reagan Administration toward a revision and refinement of its strategy over the long run was the state of the American economy. Ronald Reagan came to office pledged to balance the budget, lower taxes, and reduce inflation and unemployment, yet at the same time greatly increase defense spending. Only with at least an annual four percent growth in the economy, by the Administration's own accounting, might these goals be reconciled. But, as of the end of 1981, the prospect of tax reductions had failed to stimulate growth. Despite extensive reductions in other government expenditures, increased defense budgets ensured an expanded federal deficit. Higher interest rates and continuing inflation discouraged productive investment, while unemployment rose. The President, although acknowledging a recession and the prospect of bigger deficits, found it politically difficult to raise taxes by much.

This left reductions in the defense budget as the most obvious economic adjustment. Reagan's strong commitment to defense kept him from approving more than a $13 billion cut over fiscal years 1982–1984, but the economic trends were bound sooner or later to have a restricting effect on defense appropriations requests and grants. For FY 1982 the Administration had already cut several billion dollars from its projected budget. Congress would be extremely reluctant to permit further cuts in social programs without exacting comparable cuts in defense. Equally restrictive, and one of the most costly deficiencies to correct, was the shortage of trained military personnel to operate sophisticated weapons, flesh out the Rapid Deployment Force, and man the increased number of naval ships envisaged. To meet these manpower needs would be difficult even with a draft, which the Administration continued to oppose.

The caution of the Reagan Administration in confronting the dilemmas that afflicted its first "pillar" was demonstrated in the surprising decision, announced on October 2, not to go through with the "race-track" deployment of the projected MX missile in Utah and Nevada. Instead, the plan is to emplace a limited number of MX missiles in existing silos while continuing to explore other possibilities to reduce the vulnerability of land-based strategic missiles. This decision may have been motivated more by domestic political objections and technical military factors than by economic considerations. Nevertheless, in so conspicuously subordinating the highly advertised urgency of closing the window of vulnerability to other considerations, it showed how readily initial defense projections might yield to unanticipated constraints.

Moreover, the organization, program support and funding of the Rapid Deployment Force continued to proceed at a sluggish pace that belied its declared urgency—and the strategy for using it remained unresolved. The Administration's discovery of the political obstacles in the Middle East to local stockpiling of military supplies and equipment, let alone stationing military brigades, strengthened advocates of sea-based projection forces; but the utility of naval and Marine forces in implementing a trip-wire strategy against a hypothetical Soviet drive toward the Gulf was highly questionable.

Nevertheless, as its decisive vote to approve a defense budget of almost $200 billion in December showed, Congress remained prepared to support an unprecedented peacetime increase in defense appropriations. Whatever the details of actual programs, authorizations, and outlays in FY 1982 might turn out to be, the President could correctly declare that the U.S. government had definitely reversed the military decline of the 1970s. This tangible expression of national will might be the most important achievement of Reagan's defense policy, but in the long run it would be an empty achievement if increased expenditures were not translated into increased capabilities related to a coherent strategy.

v

Domestic economic difficulties, strategic incoherence, and a range of bureaucratic and external political obstacles to defense programs were not the only factors modifying and shaping foreign policies. Equally important were critical tensions abroad that impinged on vital interests of established priority. This was especially the case in Western Europe, where differences between the United States and several of its allies had created a more deep-seated challenge to the cohesion and security of the Atlantic Alliance than any of the half-dozen previous crises. What made this crisis more serious was that it turned upon fundamentally divergent approaches to East-West relations and that it occurred when the United States had lost the economic and military primacy—and therefore much of the confidence of its allies and its influence with them—that it had enjoyed before the 1970s.

At the root of the trans-Atlantic crisis was an insoluble but manageable predicament. On the one hand, there was the dependence of West European security upon American nuclear protection—more specifically on the efficacy of a nuclear first-use strategy as a deterrent to Soviet conventional aggression. On the other hand, there was the unavoidable reality that if the deterrent had to be used, it would lead to a nuclear war that included European soil. This geostrategic fact, plus the contrast between the global scope of American security interests and containment concerns and the more restricted national or regional concerns of the European allies, had from the beginning of the Alliance been the source of European anxieties about American policy. Depending on the occasion, Europeans were almost bound to fear that the United States might—or that it might not—counter Soviet aggression with nuclear weapons, that it might destroy an accommodation with the Soviets—or reach one unilaterally.

When Reagan took office this predicament was once again the

source of tension between the United States and its European allies—most importantly, with the Federal Republic of Germany. The demise by 1980 of the U.S.-Soviet détente threatened to jeopardize the European-Soviet détente, which to Germany especially had become a primary national interest during the 1970s. In addition, the suspension of SALT, coupled with the American rearmament effort, portended a new arms race that might undermine the general bargain that European governments had struck with domestic political constituencies dedicated to expanded social welfare programs: that European defense increases would be sustained at a politically tolerable level while arms control negotiations were conducted in parallel.

This bargain took on new importance when the allies' agreement in 1979 to deploy 572 intermediate-range missiles on European soil was followed by the resurgence of a European antinuclear movement with anti-American overtones. This deployment was now attacked not only as a provocation to an arms race, but also as the implementation of an American limited warfighting strategy that would confine a nuclear war to Europe. From the American standpoint the military program had been intended, in response to Chancellor Schmidt's 1977 proposal, to reassure the European allies that the defense of Europe would remain coupled to an American strategic response and that the rapid Soviet deployment of the SS-20 missile against European targets would be countered by visible European-based weapons that could reach Soviet targets. Thus the rising opposition seemed a frustrating demonstration of allied irresolution and irresponsibility.

If, in addition to this opposition, and following Europe's faint support for sanctions to punish and warn the Soviet Union with respect to its behavior in Southwest Asia and Poland, European governments began to renege on their long-term defense commitments, the American congressional reaction might go beyond frustration to the threat of withdrawal. Surely, if allied governments felt compelled to accept Soviet arms-control proposals that clearly upset the military balance, let alone to accede to suggestions of a European nuclear-free zone, America would have to reappraise the viability of a Continental strategy. Meanwhile, the interaction of European "pacifism" and American "unilateralism" might lead to real European neutralism.

Thus the Reagan Administration faced a serious prospect of the paralysis and unraveling of the North Atlantic Alliance. In the face of a heightened Soviet threat, the foremost European response was to urge renewed arms control negotiations, which President Reagan had condemned during the campaign and suspended upon taking office. The popular stereotype in Europe of Reagan as a bellicose cold warrior, some militant statements by his Cabinet and staff, and some artless remarks about neutron weapons and limited nuclear options added to the tension. Yet the Administration's general response to the existing and potential crisis was not to scold or threaten the allies or to retreat to unilateral globalism in reaction to European "appeasement" and "neutralism." Rather, it went out of its way to avoid the aggravation of U.S.-European divergences on defense policies, arms control, and East-West relations and set out to revive a trans-Atlantic consensus.

Secretary of State Haig and his Assistant Secretary, Lawrence Eagleburger, both familiar with the European political scene for over a decade, reassured allied governments with their comprehension of the European perspective. Administration spokesmen were firm in their support of the LTDP and the LRTNF and continued to argue for a more equitable sharing of defense burdens, particularly to support and replace the diversion of American resources to Southwest Asia, where European security was even more directly imperiled than American security. But they refrained in public from the exasperated tough-talk that was attributed to some other American officials in private conversations. In fact, there was less behind-the-scenes arm-twisting and more intensive consultation than in the Carter Administration and no rigid insistence on a percentage increase in defense expenditures.

The most dramatic evidence of the Reagan Administration's effort to restore the trans-Atlantic consensus was its eventual position on arms control negotiations. One of the President's first acts had been to suspend the SALT process indefinitely, pending reappraisal, although significantly he refrained from terminating U.S. adherence to the unratified terms of SALT II. A number of Reagan's supporters who had taken positions in the Departments of State and Defense were convinced that the utility of arms control had been oversold; that arms control had become an excuse for the West's "strategic passivity," pursued at the expense of defense programs essential to Western security. The Administration's first pronouncements on arms control reflected these skeptical reservations, restating the original 1960s rationale of arms control as a complement to defense policy, as only one element of national security policy, not the centerpiece of U.S.-Soviet relations. Without specifying any particular quid pro quo, Secretary Haig and others had reiterated the moderate concept of "linkage" which held, as "a fact of political life," that Soviet violations of the civilized code of international conduct would jeopardize arms control. Having maintained that the world had become less secure in the 1970s despite—indeed, because of—continued arms control efforts, President Reagan and his Cabinet logically emphasized that the precondition for successful negotiations was the restoration of the military balance as well as Soviet reciprocity in self-restraint.

But however warily the Administration approached arms control, it was also convinced that the priority of "revitalizing alliances" required adhering to NATO's "two-track" agreement of 1979—that discussions to limit intermediate-range missiles by treaty must be conducted in parallel with the program of deploying TNF. It insisted that the latter should be the condition of the former, but it knew that the compelling political reality was the reverse. The rise of the anti-nuclear movement and the resulting pressure on Chancellor Helmut Schmidt and other European leaders made acting on this judgment an urgent imperative. So even while it was publicly discounting the impact of the anti-nuclear movement, the Administration agreed with the Soviets to begin discussions on TNF limitation in November 1981 "within the context" of strategic arms negotiations.

On November 18, as the negotiations approached, the President announced in a public address that the United States was prepared to cancel its deployment of Pershing IIs and GLCMs if the Soviets would dismantle their SS-20s, SS-4s and SS-5s. This was the "zero option" urged by Schmidt and other anxious European leaders. It signified not only a concession to European views but, more fundamentally, to the arms control process. Coming after the discovery of economic constraints on the defense budget and before either a military build-up or any improvement in Soviet behavior, it was a particularly significant sign of the Reagan Administration's priorities and its flexibility in adjusting policies to the "four pillars" when some of the pillars clashed.

Not that this solved any of the formidable technical and political problems of improving military security through arms control. The unprecedented complexity of assessing, verifying, and equalizing the military balance by mutual agreement, and the difficulty of inducing the Soviets to accept what the United States could consider an equitable balance when that would require offsetting a perceived Soviet advantage, guaranteed prolonged negotiations full of political and technical obstacles and the risk of thwarted popular expectations. But for better or worse the process had begun. Unlike the mutual and balanced force negotiations (MBFR), these negotiations could not go on fruitlessly forever without evoking concern by anxious publics and governments. The zero-option initiative signalzed the revival of a temporarily blocked strand in U.S.-Soviet relations, which, if past experience were a guide, would have a life of its own, affecting defense and foreign policy in sometimes unexpected ways.

That arms control might exceed the restrained subsidiary role that Reagan's experts originally preferred was suggested by the President's adoption of the acronym START (strategic arms *reduction* talks), put forth by the forceful new Director of the Arms Control and Disarmament Agency, Eugene Rostow. Appealing to both the Left and Right and promising a bilateral solution to the economic burden of defense, START might turn out to be an object of enthusiasm no less beguiling than SALT. Or, considering the difficulty of achieving agreement on arms reductions that would scrap programs and change the ratio of power, as compared to agreement on ceilings to existing programs that would ratify an existing balance, START might dash unrealistic expectations once again.

VI

The revitalization of containment through a unilateral defense build-up and through the strengthening of allied cohesion and defense was squarely within the core of the American consensus on U.S. foreign policy. The way the Reagan Administration handled alliance relations, moreover, promised to keep U.S. policy in the mainstream of the trans-Atlantic consensus.

Similarly, the Administration's management of relations with the other two major counterpoises to Soviet power, Japan and China, was consistent with established continuities of containment, although in both cases it faced great potential trouble. The relatively discreet urging that Japan increase its contribution to defense, in terms of roles and missions within the ambiguous limits of "self-defense" permitted by Article IX of the Japanese Constitution, avoided public acrimony. By the end of the year it seemed likely to lead to a marginally more satisfactory division of regional security efforts with American naval forces. But the record $15 billion surplus in trade with the United States, combined with Japan's reluctance to assume a larger share of the burden for its defense, was provoking a congressional reaction that could spell serious trouble for U.S.-Japan relations if Japan did not continue to increase its defense expenditures.

The lifting of restrictions on arms sales to China was an important extension of the policy of selling "dual-purpose" technology, in line with a trend established by the previous Administration. Despite general references to further strategic collaboration against the Soviet Union on such issues as Cambodia and Afghanistan, this action did not portend any basic change in the U.S. relationship with "a friendly non-aligned country." The limited convergence of interests and the economic constraints on China's military modernization inhibited such a change. But the geopolitical logic of the entente with China that began with the Nixon-Kissinger rapprochement might nevertheless be overridden by the legacy of Reagan's commitment to the Republic of China on Taiwan, if the Administration met Taiwan's request to sell it the FX advanced fighter aircraft or even military spare parts. Calling such military sales a "litmus test" of the whole Washington-Peking relationship, Peking, at the end of December, charged that they constituted "hegemonic" interference in China's sovereign affairs and warned that they would compel a downgrading of diplomatic relations to the level of chargé d'affaires.

From the problems incurred in relations with Japan, China and the European allies it was evident that revitalizing relations with major allies and friends would be more difficult than anticipated. Revitalizing containment in the Third World was likely to be even more difficult and also considerably more controversial both at home and abroad—especially if campaign themes were literal standards of policy. The extension and implementation of containment among the less-industrialized countries had always raised the most agitated issues at home and the greatest opposition abroad. In the politically turbulent and largely non-democratic Third World, the application of the interwar lessons about the necessity of stopping piecemeal totalitarian aggression, although compelling in security terms, repeatedly confronted the American conscience with the awkward expedient of supporting authoritarian and inhumane regimes. In this vast post-colonial area, America's implementation of containment inevitably carried the opprobrium of imperial intervention, and the opprobrium was sharpened by foreign acceptance of America's own claim of unique righteousness as a standard of judgment. At the same time, in this area lay the greatest opportunities for the expansion of Soviet influence, whether directly or by proxy.

The Reagan Administration entered office committed to a major campaign theme that condemned the Carter Administration for neglecting too long the expansion of Soviet influence, subversion, and presence in the "arc of crisis" and for failing to respond to the threat of Marxist revolutions and Cuban subversion in America's own "backyard": Central America and the Caribbean. According to this theme the Carter Administration's misguided moralism and conscience-bound timidity had not only obscured the threat and paralyzed countervailing action; by applying unrealistic standards of moral censorship, particularly liberal Western standards of human rights, against friendly authoritarian governments, it had precipitated their replacement by unfriendly totalitarians. The latter claim was directed particularly, though with doubtful historical accuracy, to the fate of the Shah in Iran and of Somoza in Nicaragua.

In contrast, the Administration proclaimed, President Reagan would restore cooperative relations with countries primarily on the basis of their sharing America's concern to halt Soviet and Soviet-proxy expansionism. As an instrument of this expansionism, international terrorism was said to be the greatest threat to human rights, while Soviet-inspired revolutions and interventions were the greatest threat to world peace and security.

In the aftermath of the Carter Administration this forceful message was bracing to many Americans, but it was unnerving to many governments in the Third World and also to West European governments responding to the growing interest of social democrats in supporting "progressive" forces in the developing countries (especially in Latin America and Africa). Furthermore, insofar as the risk of American armed involvement in local revolutions was implied, a broad cross-section of the American public, still in thrall to the bitter memory of Vietnam, would oppose bold reaffirmations of containment. In the forefront of this opposition would be traditional liberals whose special concern for getting on the right (which, in practice, meant the "left-center") side of social and political change was reactivated by official talk of supplanting concern for human rights and reform with opposition to terrorism.

VII

The worst apprehensions that Reaganism meant a militaristic revival of the cold war in the Third World, with the intention of destabilizing leftist regimes and defeating incipient wars of national liberation, were seemingly confirmed by the new Administration's first major foreign initiative. In February, Secretary Haig charged that the shipment of arms to the guerrillas opposing the Duarte regime in El Salvador was a "textbook case" of Sovietinduced, Cuban-executed subversion. He issued warnings that the United States might "go to the source" if outside involvement did not cease. In an action reminiscent of the Cuban missile crisis, he dispatched emissaries to allied governments in Europe with a White Paper documenting Cuban arms shipments to explain the seriousness of the threat. More tangibly, the U.S. government lifted restrictions on lethal arms aid and sent 56 military advisers to help the junta.

The alarmed reaction in Latin America and Europe and the revival of the Vietnam analogy in the United States evidently convinced the Administration that it had made a tactical error. A campaign that the press widely interpreted as an effort to draw the line against Communist aggression quickly subsided. Haig emphasized that far more economic than arms aid was being sent to El Salvador. Without dropping the charges of Cuban complicity, he acknowledged the internal sources of political turbulence in Central America, as elsewhere in the Third World. He announced a multilateral program of economic aid for the Caribbean Basin, which in the nature of its members' political orientation could not be overtly directed against Cuba, and launched an effort to engage Mexico and Venezuela diplomatically as well as economically in some sort of regional security relationship.

Actually, the Administration had substantially followed its predecessor's policy—indeed, the preferred American policy in all revolutionary situations—of supporting a supposedly centrist regime and hoping that it would be sufficiently reformist to broaden its political base and prevail. It acted about as the Carter Administration would probably have acted, although with neither apology nor self-righteousness. But its analysis of Central American developments remained pessimistic and might well be confirmed by events.

The Duarte regime seemed to be losing control. Whether either an election or a negotiated settlement could restore order under a not-unfriendly coalition of factions was doubtful. Meanwhile, Nicaragua continued to build up with Cuban help one of the largest armies in Latin America, to an extent that could hardly be explained solely as a defensive reaction to the Reagan Administration's rhetoric. In the background there were signs that Moscow was looking covetously toward Central America as the next disturbed area in which the support of "national liberation" movements (that is, pro-Soviet regimes) might remove U.S. influence, establish Soviet proxies, and tie down U.S. forces.

Faced with this situation, the Reagan Administration was understandably disposed to back diplomacy with private and public contemplations of the use of force. The trouble was that wielding a big stick in the 1980s might so arouse the domestic and international apprehensions of friends as to undermine the impact of tough words on enemies. All the worse if the stick were weak or not suited to the task. Administration officials hinted darkly of naval blockades to stop the flow of arms, and they kept up verbal attacks against Cuban global interventionism. But against either Nicaragua or Cuba there were probably no effective small-scale military options, and a serious blockade would entail a significant naval draw-down elsewhere, not to mention an explosive reaction among European allies and Latin American friends.

Consequently, although Secretary Haig would not explicitly renounce the use of force, President Reagan said in November: "We have no plans for putting combat troops anywhere in the world." The Administration prudently resorted to making the most of active bilateral and regional diplomatic representations in order to isolate revolutionary forces and limit their damage to other countries, while standing ready to reward diplomatic cooperation with increased military and economic aid. As in Europe, the prior condition for revitalizing containment had become the enhancement of America's credibility as a promoter of multinational diplomatic solutions to regional security threats. Only on this basis could a revival of military strength effectively support diplomacy.

VIII

The area of the Third World in which diplomacy seemed most promising was southern Africa, where American policy was conducted with little or no reference to U.S. military power, arms aid or covert action. Again, it was the rhetoric, tone, and tactics rather than the substance of diplomacy that most distinguished the Reagan Administration from its predecessor. Its keynote was basing relations in the area more on common security concerns against Soviet or Cuban penetration and relatively less on the national and racial concerns of black Africa, including the condemnation of South Africa.

The major immediate objectives were the same: to strengthen pro-Western regimes, to get the Soviets and Cubans out of Angola, and to get the South Africans out of Namibia—and, integrally related to this objective, out of Angola, which was a haven for the revolutionary group SWAPO's attacks into Namibia—under conditions that might stabilize the area against revolutionary and anti-Western forces. The first objective was most importantly implemented by economic aid to the pragmatic Marxist Robert

Mugabe's constitutional regime in Zimbabwe. The other two objectives had been effectively blocked by South Africa's refusal to go through with the agreed plan for Namibian independence. The Carter Administration's strategy for removing this obstacle, including the threat of sanctions against South Africa, was demonstrably impotent. The Reagan Administration's strategy, largely developed and executed by Assistant Secretary of State Chester Crocker, charted a different course.

The strategy was to cease public censorship and pressure against South Africa and convince the government that cooperation with the conservatively oriented Reagan Administration offered the last best opportunity to secure its northern border with a stable independent buffer in Namibia and an Angolan regime (based perhaps on a coalition between the Soviet-backed government and Jonas Savimbi's principal insurgent group, UNITA) free of Cubans and no longer a base for SWAPO attacks. To back this strategy the Administration secured the diplomatic support and cooperation of the other members of the so-called "contact group": Britain, France, West Germany and Canada.

To put all these logically related pieces together to solve such a complicated diplomatic puzzle, in an international environment of conflicting interests in which the United States had only limited leverage, would be difficult. But there was no good alternative to achieve the same objectives, and all the key parties seemed to recognize this. SWAPO's acceptance in mid-November of Western proposals, backed by the contact group, for guaranteeing the rights of the white minority in an independent Namibia was an auspicious sign.

IX

Of all the critical areas of the Third World the problem of strengthening containment was most important and most difficult in Southwest Asia: most important because of its strategic position, the dependence of the United States and its major allies on Middle Eastern oil, and the proximity of the Soviet Union, with a great concentration of Soviet forces athwart the border from Afghanistan to Turkey; most difficult because of the many clashes of national, ethnic, ideological, and religious interests in the area; the absence of reliable military counterpoises; the destabilizing effects of modernization on traditional regimes; and the special American commitment to Israel in an area in which few governments or movements were prepared to accept its legitimacy. Moreover, this was the area most responsible, in the aftermath of the collapse of Iran and the invasion of Afghanistan, for accentuating the chronic gap between American security interests and commitments, on the one hand, and effective power to support them against the Soviet threat, on the other.

Ever since the withdrawal of the British from this area in the 1950s (completed in the early 1970s), the United States, in its role of global container, had been faced with a "power vacuum." The problem was that each successive effort to fill the vacuum seemed either to upset the intraregional balance of power, as the 1955 Baghdad Pact had led Egypt to become a Soviet military dependent, or upset the internal equilibrium of the local base of American power, as the unrestrained U.S. assistance to the Shah had contributed to his demise. In either case, the effect was to facilitate Soviet penetration and influence.

Moreover, the problem of finding a reliable political base for American military power in the area was compounded by the deep-seated conflict between Israel and the Arab states, which became more acute after the 1967 War. Israel was by far the strongest and most reliable counterpoise to Soviet expansion in the Middle East, but its hostile relationship with the Arab states made it unsuitable as a base or surrogate. This was particularly the case after the political activation of OPEC in the course of the 1973 Yom Kippur War, for this development gave the United States a new degree of interest in maintaining harmonious relations with the major oil suppliers. And this interest merged with containment because of the presumed threat that the Soviets might directly or indirectly deprive the West of access to the oil fields. It also put the United States in the awkward position of trying to reconcile a cooperative relationship with Arab states with the security of Israel.

Confronted with these obstacles to containment, the American strategy was, first, to promote a stable peace between Israel and its Arab neighbors. After the Carter Administration's abandonment of a comprehensive settlement and Sadat's astonishing transformation from Soviet dependent to peacemaker, this objective had come to focus on an Egyptian-Israeli settlement through the process envisioned in the 1978 Camp David Accords, which by the time of Reagan's victory had either entered their final stages or an impasse, with Israel's scheduled withdrawal from the Sinai and the question of Palestinian autonomy remaining to be resolved. At the same time, the American logic of containment called for development among the "moderate" (that is, anti-Soviet and not anti-American) states a sufficiently cooperative arrangement to facilitate the operation of the RDF in the Gulf. Toward this end, the key states would have to be Egypt and Saudi Arabia, which, especially after Sadat's assassination, would regard movement toward a Palestinian settlement as an essential condition for their cooperation.

The Reagan Administration's approach to the regional problem—contrary to campaign rhetoric that strongly favored Israel's position—was essentially an extension of the prevailing strategy. It continued to play the role of broker and lever toward the consummation of the Camp David agreements, with a combination of sticks and carrots intended to enhance Israel's receptivity to a minimal formula for Palestinian autonomy. At the same time, it concentrated on building the political and physical foundation for military collaboration in Egypt and Saudi Arabia as well as in the older outposts of the Northern Tier, Pakistan and Turkey.

Consistent with the Reagan Administration's emphasis on the revitalization of containment, Secretary Haig gave this latter policy the name of "strategic consensus." He did not suppose that a common concern for containing Soviet influence and preventing Soviet aggression in the area would overcome all regional conflicts, least of all the conflict over Palestine. Nor was he insensitive to the political obstacles to stationing American troops in the area. But he did hope that this common concern might sufficiently mute the Saudi-Israeli antipathy and consolidate the Saudi-Egyptian convergence of interests to permit arrangements for the use of pre-positioned supplies, technical facilities, and bases in collaboration with local forces strengthened by American arms sales and assistance.

In 1981 the badly bungled sale of AWACS aircraft to the Saudis again showed the difficulty of strengthening Saudi collaboration without undermining Israel's sense of security. The Administration's concession to Israel's security was sign a pact for military cooperation, but this concession fell far short of the collaboration Israel sought and did nothing to reconcile the Begin government to a Palestine solution that the moderate Arabs might accept. Some European allies thought that Saudi Arabia's implicit recognition of Israel in its eight-point peace plan might break the impasse over Palestine, but the Arab states' rejection of this démarche was almost as adamant as Israel's. Meanwhile, the steady extension of Israeli settlements in the West Bank and Gaza convinced many observers that Begin's intention was annexation, which would foreclose any Palestinian settlement. Israel's annexation of Syria's Golan Heights in December and Begin's bitter retort to U.S. criticism and suspension of the pact for military cooperation seemed to move the dream of an Arab-Israeli accommodation even further from reality.

Added to these obstacles was an underlying uncertainty about the long-run stability of the Saudi regime. President Reagan's apparent extension (in a news conference on October 1) of the Carter Doctrine—initially characterized by Secretary Weinberger as "clumsy and ill-advised"—to cover any internal upheaval in Saudi Arabia that might shut off vital oil supplies to the West was an effort to reduce this uncertainty, but clearly it entailed some added risk of extending American commitments beyond American power. Furthermore, since stationing even small numbers of specialized American forces on Saudi or Egyptian soil was unwelcome by the hosts and politically disturbing in any case, the utility of the RDF even in contingencies involving Soviet forces seemed highly questionable. Against local military or internal revolutionary conflicts that threatened Western access to oil supplies, the utility of American forces had always been viewed as limited.

x

In the Third World the tone and rhetoric of diplomacy, the tactics and emphasis of policy, most differentiated the Reagan Administration's policies from those of its predecessor. In most respects, the content, as opposed to the style, of policy was marked by continuity; but in some cases the change of style amounted to a change of substance. This was markedly true in the case of policies concerning the trans-national issues on the global agenda that so engaged Third World representatives and liberal Western spokesmen in the arena of world opinion.

The style of the Carter Administration in addressing these issues was initially to elevate them to the status of critical elements in an emerging new international order, in which North-South relations would impinge upon American vital interests at least as significantly as would East-West relations. The Reagan style, in contrast, was to approach the "so-called" Third World as a huge heterogeneous aggregation of countries with a variety of political and economic problems deserving of American sympathy and help on grounds of enlightened self-interest, but to do so on a practical case-by-case, issue-by-issue basis, not as a class of states demanding a massive transfer of wealth to redress the economic inequalities of an unjust international system. Rejecting what it considered the false dichotomy of North-South and East-West relations, the Administration also rejected the view that one set of relationships turned upon social and economic, the other on security concerns. Rather, these relationships and concerns were fused and interdependent.

One aspect of this fusion to which the Administration gave extraordinary emphasis, implemented by a variety of countermeasures as well as words, was the threat to the security—and, therefore, the development—of less industrialized countries arising from the aggressive interventionism of two Third World states sponsored by the Soviet Union: Cuba and Libya. Indeed, against these two disturbers of the peace the Administration directed such a vigorous verbal onslaught as to convey the impression that it welcomed the chance to discipline them as more vulnerable extensions of the Soviet Union. And yet its actions were, in fact, cautious—even in response to what it publicly charged was an effort by Libya's Qaddafi to assassinate leading members of the Administration.

Notwithstanding its emphasis on Communist threats, the Reagan Administration did not ignore the Third World's preoccupation with economic development. Even though it did not speak with the compassion of the two preceding Democratic Administrations, in substance its approach was about the same as that of the Carter Administration. Both accepted the generalities about the West's commercial and humanitarian interests in economic progress and stability among the less industrialized countries, but Western governments had long ceased to regard development aid as an effective means of achieving this end except under congenial internal conditions which were usually beyond their control. Nor was the response of the two Administrations to Third World demands for an internationally organized transfer of wealth essentially different: rejection of most of the items put forth by the Group of 77 for structural reform of the international system, coupled with a willingness to bargain about a few of the more practical demands for economic concessions within the framework of the existing system.

The principal difference was that the Reagan Administration was less susceptible to egalitarian appeals and was unapologetically committed to capitalist self-help. That the candid but not unresponsive Reagan style of neither "confrontation" nor "condescension" in dealing with the less industrialized countries might enjoy some diplomatic success was suggested by the President's performance at the meeting of developed and developing countries at Cancún, Mexico, in October.

This meeting followed Reagan's effective opposition at the July

Ottawa summit to Canadian Prime Minister Pierre Trudeau's proposal for "global negotiations" on increased aid to the Third World, and his warm endorsement in September of the International Monetary Fund (IMF) and the World Bank (IBRD) as instruments for stimulating development through the private sector. At Cancún he gracefully agreed to the dominant concern of the less-developed countries for continuing global negotiations, but deftly defined these negotiations as a dialogue in the United Nations (not subject to votes) and within U.N. and multilateral bodies such as the IMF and IBRD (where weighted voting would prevent futile haggling)—while emphasizing the superior benefits of private investment and free enterprise demonstrated in the striking economic progress of some newly industrialized countries.

In its approach to two other issues on the global agenda, the Reagan style expressed the Administration's more candid emphasis on the objective of security and cooperative relations with friends: the transfer of conventional arms and nuclear proliferation.

The Carter Administration entered office with a strong disposition to regard arms transfers as wasteful and provocative distractions from economic development which must therefore be restrained. In practice, it found that arms sales, for a variety of political and military purposes, were one of the most effective instruments of policy that the superpowers have. It proceeded to develop a set of restraints that more or less came to terms with U.S. diplomatic and military interests. The only substantial planned reduction of arms sales was to Latin America—always in domestic political terms the most appealing and, in terms of U.S. security, the least costly arena for applying sanctions of various kinds—but the result was simply to substitute foreign for American sales.

The Reagan Administration entered office with a bias in favor of arms sales as a means of narrowing the gap between security interests and unilateral power—by strengthening friendly countries, revitalizing mutual security relationships, and fostering regional and internal stability. It developed a set of guidelines designed to restrain arms sales, but for purposes of cost-effectiveness rather than political virtue. It avowed an interest in multilateral restraints on arms transfers; but, seeing little or no foreign (including Soviet) interest in such restraints, it was opposed to jeopardizing U.S. security interests through unilateral restraints. Putting its money where its policies were, the Administration greatly increased military assistance to Southwest Asian countries and relaxed the Carter restraints on co-production of arms, on the production of weapons specifically for export, and on assistance by American embassies to arms exporters.

This shift of emphasis compounded the usual difficulty of restraining energetic arms salesmen in the Pentagon—especially the salesmen of advanced aircraft—but Administration spokesmen insisted that the new emphasis was not a disguise for uncontrolled sales. They pointed to the new program adopted for Pakistan—$3.2 billion over six years in military and economic aid, divided about 4-to-1 in favor of loans for military purchases and including the sale of F-16 aircraft—as an effective use of military transfers for overriding security interests, in contrast to the Carter Administration's suspension of military assistance as a sanction against Pakistan's nuclear program (and Pakistan's rejection, on grounds of inadequacy, of Carter's post-Afghanistan effort to resume aid). The explicit purpose of the program was to strengthen Pakistan against a "serious threat" from Soviet troops in Afghanistan; but, as often, arms transfers also seemed to be intended for purposes served best by public silence: bolstering the Zia government against neutralism and Soviet inducements; preserving a base for the harassment of Soviet occupation forces in Afghanistan; and gaining bases and access rights for the RDF. As in other cases in Southwest Asia, arms aid to enhance the security of one country tended to threaten the security of its rival—in this case, India. But the Administration evidently calculated that it could manage this dilemma without upsetting the balance in the subcontinent. In any case, India's quasi-alignment with the Soviet Union inclined the Administration to discount the cost of displeasing India.

The Reagan Administration, partly moved by Israel's air raid against Iraq's nuclear facilities, endorsed the well-established American goal of curbing the spread of independent nuclear capabilities. But, as with arms transfers, it integrated nonproliferation policy more explicitly with U.S. security policy. It put new emphasis on the position that, in the final analysis, discouraging a nation's acquisition of nuclear weapons depends on helping to meet its security interests by other means, and it added the argument that reestablishing the United States as a reliable partner for peaceful nuclear cooperation under adequate safeguards was essential to gain the support of recipients for nonproliferation goals. At the end of 1981 it was too early to say precisely what this emphasis would mean in operational terms, beyond the general relaxation of restrictions on nuclear reactor fuel sales and on civil reprocessing and breeder reactor development abroad, which had often been political irritants but seldom effective nonproliferation devices. It was clear, however, that nonproliferation policy would have to come to terms with the revitalization of containment and that, where the two conflicted (as was widely considered to be the case in Pakistan), the burden of proof would now rest on those favoring restrictions. Again, arms aid to Pakistan provided some indication of how the new emphasis might work out in practice. While giving precedence to mutual security interests, the Administration made it clear, informally, that the aid would be terminated if Pakistan were to explode a nuclear device; and Congress added provisions to the appropriation bill to make this explicit.

On human rights policies the divergence between the Reagan and Carter Administrations was, as both saw it, the sharpest of all the divergences on global-agenda issues. Representatives of the Carter Administration, with some reason, considered these policies the most distinctive and enduring expression of their moral enhancement of America's global posture. Representatives of the Reagan Administration considered them the most quixotic, biased and counterproductive. The controversy excited during the campaign by the New Conservatives' charge that human rights policies had undermined friendly right-wing authoritarian countries while turning a blind eye to left-wing totalitarians reached a crescendo in the Senate Foreign Relations Committee's opposition that led Ernest W. Lefever, a long-time critic of misguided moralism, to withdraw his nomination as head of the Bureau of Human Rights and Humanitarian Affairs in the State Department.

Yet the new Administration did not renounce the application of human rights standards to the conduct of foreign relations. In November it reaffirmed them as "a principal goal" "at the core" of U.S. policy. It did not dismantle the often intrusive machinery in the State Department for implementing human rights standards nor, for the moment, challenge the legislation that required such implementation, including the extraordinarily undiplomatic reports on foreign countries' state of moral health.

The State Department memorandum on human rights policy, published on November 4, amounted to a forceful restatement of the Carter Administration's policy, but there was an underlying difference of emphasis and philosophy. President Carter and his spokesmen often gave the impression, though seldom confirmed in practice, that they regarded this policy as an ideal to be pursued altruistically, in contrast to the policy of supporting right-wing dictators for the sake of containment. The State Department's memorandum, on the other hand, frankly stated the instrumental justification for such official idealism. Human rights, it affirmed, must be an integral, not just rhetorical, part of American foreign policy in order to maintain public and congressional support of foreign policy initiatives, to stave off neutralism, and to mobilize ideological opposition to the Soviets. This justification of official morality on grounds of enlightened expediency might offend moral purists, but the end result could nevertheless be to exalt moral values to the greatest practical extent, if the Administration adhered to the memorandum's view that to be credible and effective human rights standards must be applied evenhandedly, even if they adversely affect relations with friends as well as enemies.

The eventual continuity of human rights policies was apparently confirmed by the rapid and overwhelming congressional approval of the Administration's nominee to replace Dr. Lefever, Elliott Abrams, who advocated the reinvigoration of the human rights bureau. But, of course, the actual content of human rights policies would depend, as before, on the kinds of judgments the U.S. government would make in reconciling (and often subordinating) human rights standards to equally compelling diplomatic and security interests and means-ends calculations in particular cases. Here one could be sure that the Reagan Administration would apply human rights policies less publicly, be more discreet with friendly countries and tougher with enemies, give greater emphasis to "civil" and "political" (as distinguished from "individual") rights, apply all three components of human rights with more deference to favorable trends, seek amendments to legislation singling out particular countries as targets for restrictions on military and economic assistance, and give greater weight to security considerations and the necessities of combatting terrorism.

XI

To assess the general course of foreign policy in the Reagan Administration it may help to speculate how it might look in retrospect five or ten years from now. It is always too early to conduct this kind of exercise of the imagination for the purpose of prediction, but a year is time enough for a contingent evaluation.

It will be argued that the contingencies implicit in the following evaluation are skewed toward unwarranted optimism. I would say they are skewed toward *plausible* optimism, which may be refuted by the Administration's deficiencies and by events beyond its control. I assume, for example, that the preponderant influence in U.S. foreign policy of the judicious and informed pragmatic multilateralism which is now concentrated in the State Department will prevail; that President Reagan's best qualities of leadership will become actively engaged in the making of foreign policy; that the Administration will avoid the hazards of talking toughly with a weak stick it does not even wield; and that it will eschew the inclinations of some of its members toward the kind of unilateralism that could lead to disastrous national self-isolation. The reason for such conditional optimism is partly to present an appropriate model for emulation and partly to provide an antidote to widespread derogatory stereotypes of the Administration (especially abroad) that are even less warranted than absolute confidence that performance will coincide with the model. As for the multiplicity of adverse events and developments in trouble-prone parts of the world that may occur no matter how wise or foolish the U.S. government may be, I can only concede that some of them will almost surely occur, yet hopefully assume that the worst possibilities will remain only sobering hypotheses.

Whatever the future holds, it is safe to say that in retrospect the continuities in the broad outlines of American foreign policy will seem more striking than in November 1980. Both the Administration's claims and its opponents' fears of innovation will seem less important; and so will the inept remarks, bureaucratic collisions and tactical pratfalls that the media magnify. But, of course, continuity of the outlines does not preclude significant changes in the substance of policy. The momentous changes in American postwar policy have resulted from the process of translating the enduring premises and purposes of containment into policies and actions, in response to unpredictable events and basic changes in the international and domestic environment.

Amid the predictable continuities and unpredictable changes, the success or failure of the Reagan Administration, in retrospect, should be judged by the extent to which it has achieved its central goal, the revitalization of containment. The achievement of this goal requires bringing American power, in all its dimensions, into safe balance with America's expanded security interests and commitments—at a level of effort and by means that engage the moral and material support of the nation. The principal obstacles to achieving this balance lie precisely in the areas of policy concern— the four pillars—that the Reagan Administration has identified as most critical to the achievement of its central goal.

The obstacles are particularly formidable with respect to the two most immediately pressing objectives: the rejuvenation of the American economy and the restoration of the military balance. Inextricably related to restoring the military balance are two other objectives to which the Administration has properly assigned top priority: the revitalization of the North Atlantic Alliance and the achievement of a stable military and political equilibrium in Southwest Asia. Tying all these objectives to the revitalization of containment is the Administration's goal of achieving a relationship of restraint and reciprocity with the Soviet Union.

This constellation of related objectives deserves the highest priority simply because it has the greatest impact, for better or worse, on American security and well-being as Americans broadly define their vital interests. To be sure, the record of the past shows that developments in the Third World, even outside Southwest Asia, can become as critical to American interests as what happens in these major areas of policy concern if the mistakes and excesses of American policy make them so, but intrinsically they do not impinge on U.S. security nor strain U.S. power to the same extent.

In 1981 the Reagan Administration's most serious weakness lay in the foundation of its first pillar: the restoration of the nation's economy and, closely related to this objective, its defense posture. In 1982 one should be able to tell whether the Administration will be able to overcome its economic problems; it may take longer to judge the real efficacy of its defense efforts. Let us assume, not unreasonably but without any pretense of prediction, that in the course of the next few years the resilience of the American economy and society; the abundance of American resources, technological prowess, and ingenuity; the national consensus for a defense buildup; and the President's mobilization of the country behind the reaffirmation of national power and prestige will succeed in establishing this first pillar. Then, in retrospect, one could say that this achievement had given the United States the opportunity to cope with the closely related security problems in Western Europe and Southwest Asia.

It is unlikely that this Administration or any other will come very close to *solving* the complex of problems in these two areas, because these problems are, at their roots, insoluble dilemmas under any conditions that one can reasonably foresee. It is not unlikely, however, that the United States, as in the past, will at least *cope* with the dilemmas of the Atlantic Alliance by once again providing the key to preserving the essential security and cohesion of the Alliance, based on a solid core of common interests. The Reagan Administration has auspiciously entered the rocky two-track road to validate this judgment—but in the shadows of the Polish crisis, which could invalidate it.

It is less likely but not impossible that the Administration will be able to cope with the dilemmas of the Middle East. Whatever it does, there will be a lively danger of local wars and revolutions. The Arab-Israeli impasse over Palestine seems likely to continue, and it is not inconceivable that some kind of Israeli fait accompli may totally preempt movement toward a settlement. In either case, the situation will almost surely strain Arab as well as Arab-Israeli relations to an extent that will preclude a reliable regional "strategic consensus" for the projection of American military power. And even if the Palestinian question were settled, there is not likely to emerge among the Arab countries the kind of internal and inter-state stability that will provide a congenial environment for an RDF capable of containing a Soviet military incursion locally and short of the Gulf. Consequently, it will be a considerable tribute to the Reagan Administration if one can say in retrospect that it avoided the most serious hazards of excessive commitment to any of its several conflicting objectives in the area at the expense of the others, but retained a sufficiently credible political and material base for the projection of its power to reinforce Soviet caution against the military exploitation of regional turbulence.

If these minimal, yet challenging, objectives were achieved, would the Reagan Administration have succeeded in closing the chronic gap between American security interests and American power? Would it, thereby, finally have established the basis for sustaining containment over the long run without the disturbing oscillations between the assertion and retrenchment of American power? Not necessarily.

At the end of 1981 there were no signs, and no reason to think, that the extent and scope of American security interests and of American involvements in their behalf would cease to expand. Quite the contrary. At the same time, the disparity between security interests and the means of supporting them against internal, regional, and global threats seemed greater than at any time since the Korean War, partly because a military conflict in Southwest Asia would be more likely to spread than previous local wars in East Asia. Hypothetically, there were several ways to narrow the gap between interests and power to a safe margin; but in reality only a few of them were likely to be tried or to have much effect on the interests-power gap if they were.

In the abstract, the simplest way to narrow the gap would be simply to define security interests—especially those that might require the use of force to support them—more selectively. In practice, however, there seems to be no safe formula for doing this that would be consistent with containment. To plan to exclude some interests from the ambit of containment while trying to revitalize containment would be particularly disadvantageous and hardly something that the Reagan Administration would contemplate.

There is a beguiling geopolitical logic to the possibility that the Western European allies and Japan might fill in the expanded interests-power gap by contributing more to defense in their region and in the Middle East, where, after all, their security is more directly imperiled than American security. Some redistribution of security roles and contributions is, indeed, politically essential and feasible; but the political constraints against the scale of devolution that would be necessary to compensate for the shortfall in U.S. capabilities are too obvious to make it a practical target in the 1980s.

As for arms control, we must know by now that it cannot end the arms race, nor substitute for maintaining the military balance. At best, it is a complement to defense programs. It can make a military balance less volatile and provocative, more predictable and safer. It may also save money if it does not become an excuse for letting the military balance deteriorate. But it cannot, by itself, do much to close the gap between interests and power.

There remains one crucial key to narrowing the gap to a safe margin—one essential complement to redressing the military balance. This is diminishing the threat to American security interests by diplomatic accommodation. In the Third World this means putting the full weight of American power and prestige behind the resolution of regional conflicts and tensions through patient and discreet diplomatic intervention.

Even more important, in East-West relations this means maintaining a restraining balance of will and strength against Soviet expansion, while establishing over a number of years a set of formal and informal reciprocal restraints. If the Administration's other three pillars were firmly erected, it would have a good opportunity to construct and sustain such an equilibrium. Intractable internal and external problems could be important incentives to the Soviets, providing that they know that they cannot exploit U.S.-European divergences. The volatility of the Middle East, the persistence of the interests-power gap, and the imperatives of allied cohesion provide compelling incentives to the United States.

Needless to say, the opportunity for a new East-West equilibrium would be destroyed for a long time by Soviet military suppression of Poland. It would be enhanced if the Poles are able to settle their own affairs through peaceful compromise and the Soviets abstain from military intervention. General Jaruzelski's repression of the independent Polish labor movement in December cast an ominous cloud over East-West relations, and tested the Reagan Administration's ability to reconcile the management of

East-West tension with the cohesion of the Atlantic Alliance. The Administration's cautious and measured actions manifested its determination to preserve two of its pillars of policy under difficult circumstances.

Against the Polish government the Administration applied economic sanctions of graduated severity, while trying to distinguish between sanctions against the state and humanitarian concern—especially in the form of privately distributed food aid—for the people. Against the Soviet Union, which the Administration publicly held responsible for Jaruzelski's crackdown, it also applied phased sanctions, contingent upon the continuation of repressions; and it repeated previous warnings of unspecified reprisals in the event of overt Soviet military intervention. The President also pledged that if the Polish government reached an accommodation consistent with basic human rights, the United States would do its part to restore the Polish economy, as it had helped the countries of Europe after World War II.

These measures fell far short of the full-scale political and economic sanctions advocated by some labor leaders and Congressmen, but even these were not matched by the European allies. Failing to secure parallel sanctions by its allies, the Administration nevertheless felt compelled to impose them unilaterally; but it refrained from publicly pressuring the allies to follow suit. Indeed, on the diplomatic level the Administration conspicuously eschewed a tougher stance and continued normal relations, not only with allies but with Moscow as well. Thus, it explicitly delinked the Geneva negotiations on TNF from the Polish situation on the grounds of their "unique character and significance," and it guardedly looked forward to a summit meeting between Presidents Reagan and Brezhnev.

To some critical observers, these actions merely confirmed a pattern of talking loudly while carrying an inadequate stick. But underlying the Administration's actions were substantial considerations of Realpolitik. The threat of military intervention to deter Soviet intervention was, of course, excluded. Massive multilateral economic aid, with political strings, to prevent repression by the Polish government was of doubtful economic or political efficacy and was politically unfeasible to organize with the Allies anyway. That left rhetoric and sanctions as a protest and deterrent, and the promise of economic aid as an incentive toward a peaceful accommodation and a rescue operation if accommodation were achieved.

The Administration had not yet devised a comprehensive strategy for East-West trade, but it was skeptical of the utility of economic sanctions as an instrument to affect Soviet actions or weaken Soviet power to carry out its actions—a view amply supported by the whole history of sanctions. (In April President Reagan's lifting of the partial grain embargo that President Carter had imposed on the Soviets in response to the invasion of Afghanistan reflected this skepticism as well as the payment of a political promise to American farmers.) On the other hand, no Administration, and least of all one as vehemently anti-communist as President Reagan's, could fail to express its condemnation of Polish repression by the most widely accepted tangible means available to major trading countries in modern international politics: punitive or demonstrative economic sanctions.

In imposing such sanctions, however, the Administration was mindful that, for sanctions to be effective economically or symbolically, the European allies and especially Germany would have to take parallel action or at least not rush in to supplant American exports. Partly because they were major trading partners with the Soviet bloc they were reluctant to curb exports, either for the purpose of putting pressure on the Polish government or to hold Moscow responsible for repression. Therefore, the Administration was anxious that sanctions at least not divide the United States from its allies, as they had tended to do after the Soviet invasion of Afghanistan. It was also anxious that sanctions not foreclose the opportunity for East-West accommodations—especially in arms negotiations, where suspension of the TNF talks would be far more damaging to the United States in its relations with the allies than to the Soviet Union, which would seize upon the suspension to exploit U.S.-allied differences. In the end, sanctions could hardly improve conditions in Poland, but they could easily worsen relations with the allies and the Soviet Union. More constructive might be multinational implementation of the President's proposal of a program for economic restoration if the Poles were to achieve a stable and liberal resolution of their internal affairs.

Whether the Reagan Administration would succeed in translating these several considerations and objectives into successful policies would depend, in the final analysis, on developments in Poland that are fundamentally beyond American influence. But if it were to emerge from the Polish crisis with a realistic prospect of more constructive relations with its allies and with Moscow, it would not only have earned valuable credit for statesmanship. It would also have demonstrated a familiar fact of American political life: it is easier for a conservative Republican than for a liberal

Democratic administration to exercise restraint and secure reciprocity in dealing with recalcitrant allies and with the principal adversary.

If the Reagan Administration could capitalize on this political advantage, it might eventually be known best for an achievement it seemed least to seek when it came into office. Having put the Vietnam syndrome to rest and consolidated the restoration of the American economy and defense, it might be known best for constructing a safer and more secure relationship with the Soviet Union. Such a relationship could be more substantial than the atmospheric détente of the late 1950s or the ephemeral détente of the 1970s precisely because it was neither a superficial escape valve for public anxieties nor the core of a grand design for a global modus vivendi, but the consequence of an integrated set of policies that brought American power into balance with vital interests on an enduring basis.

Coral Bell

FROM CARTER TO REAGAN

Analysts of President Reagan's reelection landslide have made much of the point that it was not necessarily a mandate for tougher policies: the voters' endorsement should be seen as primarily an enthusiastic expression of hope for continuance of the state of economic well-being and patriotic euphoria in which Americans, by and large, found themselves in late 1984. Be that as it may, it does seem quite clear by contrast that four years earlier Jimmy Carter lost votes on foreign policy issues. If Washington's relations with the outside world are going well, they may not be a decisive vote-getter, but the sense that they have gone badly can be a decisive vote-loser. Nothing fails like failure.

In my view, however, the two successive foreign policies have differed more in the images they have created at home and abroad than in their substance. Furthermore, in Mr. Reagan's case, ironically and surprisingly, words have proved an effective substitute for deeds in much of international politics, and maybe even of defense policy.

There is, of course, a difference between "operational" and "declaratory" policies and the signals both send to the outside world. The distinction was well traced in the pages of *Foreign Affairs* by Ambassador Paul Nitze in January 1956. Between what a government actually does and what it says or implies are its objectives and intentions lies some degree of divergence, sometimes a small gap, sometimes more of a chasm. These divergences do not mean that declaratory policy can be simply dismissed as bluff or hypocrisy. Nor are such differences always to be deplored, since they make possible a degree of flexibility. The French have a saying, "The soup is never eaten as hot as it is cooked." We might say that the hot soup of declaratory policy, as it emerges from the kitchen of the ideological cooks who prepare it, is always cooled a little by pragmatism before it is served up in the real world, which seldom matches the world of the ideologists' wishes.

While operational signals first require actual decisions by the

Coral Bell is Senior Research Fellow at Australian National University. She is the author of the forthcoming book *President Reagan and Foreign Policy: The Perils of Rhetoric,* to be published in 1988, and editor of the series *Canberra Studies in World Affairs.*

Administration (in major cases by the President himself), declaratory signals emanate from a variety of sources, some entirely non-official. Presidential rhetoric provides one source of declaratory signaling, of course—during Ronald Reagan's years an important one. But another source is the spoken and written words of people who come into office with the President, as distinct from the permanent bureaucracy.

The outside world makes its assessments of the international stance of any given administration from the mix of signals it receives from all U.S. sources, weighing operational against declaratory. In Moscow there is an entire learned institute to interpret these signals, and every foreign office has an "American desk" trying to do much the same thing in smaller ways. Some of Washington's troubles with Western allies during recent years, incidentally, have arisen from the diversity of sources of signals. London, Paris and Bonn are not disconcerted by changes of America's chief decision-maker; they change their own prime ministers and presidents and chancellors with reasonable regularity. But there is no precise equivalent in those capitals to the arrival of the new presidential entourage of policymakers; their own policymakers are well-entrenched permanent officials. Moreover, the Reagan circle tended to seem more "Reaganite" than the President himself, just as the Carter men had seemed more "Carterite" than that President. This is not surprising, since those who have been in electoral politics for many years (as tends to be the case for the persons who actually secure the nominations) have usually had the sharpest edges of their ideological stances blunted by the rough and tumble of political life.

The obvious differences in political philosophy between Presidents Carter and Reagan camouflage some basic points of distinct similarity. Each perceived and presented the conflicts of international politics in largely moral terms. Both implied that the moral assumptions of American foreign policy are not only important in themselves, but provide useful weapons in the American diplomatic armory. And both adhered to the notion of American "exceptionalism": U.S. society as the "shining city on a hill," its values a beacon for all the world.

In all that, both Presidents are heirs to a long-standing American tradition. Moralism and legalism have been central strands in American diplomacy from the earliest years of America's emerging consciousness of the United States as a power in a world of powers. To some analysts those strands have seemed the source of the disasters of U.S. policymaking; to others the source of its major accomplishments. To the outsider both points of view have evidence to back them up. Some major disasters (like the involvement in Vietnam) and some major successes (like the process of European recovery stemming from the Marshall Plan, or the Japan Peace Treaty) were rooted in both strategic calculation and moral feeling among the policymakers of the time.

Though it may seem a little cynical to say so, the real differences do not seem to have been in either quantity or content of the moral assumptions. The basic point, at least on the evidence of the turnabout of American sentiments, seems to be that moral feeling is unlikely to "stay the course" when the strategic calculations that go with it prove unsound. The process of disenchantment, once it starts (as with Vietnam in 1967–68), sweeps away the original moral assumptions that went into policy. Thus the moral components that go into policymaking have to be judged not only on their own merits but on whether they conduce to realism in the strategic assessments that go with them.

II

Declaratory signals may sometimes look, at first glance, as if they were operational. The Reagan defense budget, for example, may be considered a strong declaratory signal—a statement of intent about the *future* balance of forces—rather than a transformation of the existing balance of the 1980s. The almost universal popular impression is that President Reagan has achieved—not merely proposed—an unprecedented rate of increase in U.S. military muscle. But I would argue that since the image of U.S. military weakness was created chiefly by words (mostly from the Reagan camp from the Republican nomination fight of 1976 onwards) it is logical that more words from the same sources should have been effective in readjusting that somewhat distorted image to reflect the reality of effective (though asymmetrical) superpower parity.

President Carter also made potent use of words, but it would be quite unfair to attribute all the troubles of U.S. foreign policy in the four Carter years to his own declaratory signals. Even without such signals, an adversary assessment in Moscow or elsewhere could reasonably have perceived a window of low-risk, low-cost opportunities. The general signals from American society as a whole, and from the liberal foreign policy establishment in particular, had been conveying a message of dwindling opposition to other countries' adventurism ever since 1975. National battle-fatigue, progressively increasing from 1968 and overwhelming by 1975, made the foreign policy mood of the early Carter years inevitable, and impossible to conceal from adversary policymakers. Even before Carter, in fact, Congress had sent the world a very loud declaratory signal in the Angolan resolutions of 1975–76 that the American political mood would be enough to block any operational policy of a tough-minded sort for the immediate future, even though the Administration may have wanted it. In that political mood of 1976, part of Jimmy Carter's appeal was the moral reassurance he provided during a time when American values and traditions were still under heavy attack at home and abroad. He encapsulated in his political image traces of an earlier, more innocent America and of small-town values.

To stand for virtue reasserted is probably always an asset in domestic politics. In international politics, however, a reputation for conspicuous virtue is likely to be construed as meaning that the new man is naïve. The saying "nice guys finish last" originated in U.S. sporting circles, but a rather similar estimate is implicit in the conventional wisdom of diplomats. And that was an image that Carter could hardly escape, given his status as a Christian fundamentalist, a Sunday school teacher, and particularly his espousal of Wilsonian values in world affairs.

Woodrow Wilson is still, no doubt, a hero to many Americans. But that is not really so in the outside world, except among a few remaining left-liberal and Third World optimists. In the Soviet Union, Wilson is remembered for the interventions of 1918 and as the standard-bearer of a theory of international politics competitive with Lenin's. In the chancelleries of Europe his name tends to be associated with high-minded ineffectiveness, failure to get the United States to take on the responsibilities of membership in the League of Nations, and unrealistic insistence on introducing notions of national self-determination in areas where they were bound to disrupt the chances of viable settlements. The hearts of European policymakers tend to sink at the thought of Wilsonian preachings from the White House. President Carter's version of moral rectitude in international politics was centered on human rights rather than national self-determination, but the human rights concept was even more disruptive to some of America's allies in the late 1970s (such as Iran) than the notion of self-determination had been for some of America's European allies in Wilson's time.

In fact, the case of Iran seems to indicate that well-amplified U.S. declaratory signals can begin to erode a fragile personal autocracy even before their author is in power. According to various observers, including Sir Anthony Parsons, who was British ambassador in Teheran at the time, the Shah's self-confidence began to crumble from the time of the Carter election campaign, and this damage does not appear to have been retrieved even by the considerable support in actual operational terms he received during the early Carter years.

III

The first four Reagan years bore an almost eerie similarity to the years 1949 to 1954, when the concept of "negotiation from strength" had a previous airing.[1] In 1949, as in 1979, serious and respectable analysts were seeing a phase of major danger about five years ahead, with a "window of vulnerability" developing, because of a perceived major change in the underlying strategic balance. In 1949 the change was a true strategic milestone: the first Soviet atomic test. Along with the additional jolt of the Korean War, the West embarked on a major countervailing reaction: an ambitious NATO arms buildup, with U.S. defense expenditures reaching more than 14 percent of GNP by 1953 (twice the rate of the Reagan years). Then, as now, a technological "quick fix" to restore the original Western advantage glimmered in the minds of policymakers. Then it was the replacement of fission weapons by fusion; now it is the Strategic Defensive Initiative (SDI) or "Star Wars" image.

A powerful sense of déjà vu hung over the early 1980s for anyone who was once preoccupied with the early 1950s. Andrei A. Gromyko (the only major policymaker at a more or less similar level of influence in both patches of history) ought to be particularly haunted by it, because then, as now, there was a long drawn-out Soviet succession crisis which affected his personal fortunes. Then the succession was to Stalin, now the succession is still really to Brezhnev. Secretary of State John Foster Dulles then, like President Reagan until mid-1984, was given to combative but not always convincing declaratory sig-

[1] For a fuller account of the period, see the author's *Negotiation from Strength*, New York: Alfred A. Knopf, 1963.

nals, for instance, the doctrine of "massive and instant retaliation" in 1954.

Robert Murphy, one of Dulles' chief aides in that earlier phase of "negotiation from strength," once said that some of his master's signals had to be taken with "a whole warehouse full of salt." The question remains whether that level of skepticism can be retrospectively justified for the Reagan years. But we must start with a point whose importance is seldom conceded in European analyses, or liberal Democratic ones. Despite the general souring of relations between Washington and Moscow during the Reagan first term, there was not in fact a serious adversary crisis between the superpowers in that period.

A serious crisis between the United States and the Soviet Union has to be defined as one that produces not merely an exchange of insults but a measurably increased risk of actual hostilities. By that criterion, no such crisis can be discerned. The nearest approach, perhaps, was the shooting down of the Korean airliner in September 1983. Commentators who should have known better invoked the memory of Sarajevo, but the very evocation of that flashpoint makes it clear how remote the two great adversaries of the contemporary world were from that brink of an earlier era. This is reassuring, for it means that the crisis-management techniques and other factors which have built some stability into the central balance of power over the past 40 years have remained workable, even after several years of robust and continuing asperities between the superpowers.

To say this is not, of course, to deny that relations between Moscow and Washington by 1983 were at their lowest point since the death of Stalin 30 years earlier. One may fully assent to that proposition, and agree also that the situation had disastrous consequences for some areas of international life (especially the effort toward arms control), and yet still hold that the basic mechanisms for preserving the peace, such as they are, do not appear to have been much impaired. In fact, perhaps the contrary.

The many crises which were already on stream before January 1981 have not been visibly mitigated, and some have probably been marginally worsened. Poland, Afghanistan, the Persian Gulf war, the Middle East, Central America and the Caribbean, southern Africa, Vietnam and Kampuchea—all bear their normal tides of human misery along the accustomed pathways. I am not proposing an unduly rosy view of international politics during these past four years, merely pointing out that all was actually quiet, *save on the rhetorical front*, in the central confrontation between the superpower adversaries.

A potential explanation for this state of affairs can be found on the Soviet side of the confrontation. President Reagan's first term spanned the final decline of Leonid Brezhnev, the quasi interregnum as his death approached, the brief rule of Yuri Andropov, and the early months of another ailing veteran of the Politburo, Konstantin Chernenko. The decisions made in Moscow during those four years were those of men who (like their elderly though sprightly counterpart in Washington) all had good reasons to be conscious of their own mortality. Elderly, ailing men (ayatollahs may perhaps be excepted) are not usually given to bold adventures in foreign policy.

Not only were the decision-makers in Moscow declining in health during the Reagan first term; the Soviet policy machine had too many problems on its hands to take the sort of initiatives which might create more. Afghanistan and Poland, the needs of useful allies in Cuba, Vietnam, South Yemen, Syria and Ethiopia appear to have left few resources even for marginal and faltering allies in Angola and Mozambique, much less for taking on major new commitments. One might also argue that the domestic difficulties in the Soviet sphere of power, largely the results of economic failures, impose their own constraints. Or, less optimistically, one could say that there appears in Soviet policy an alternation, accidental or deliberate, of periods of "forward policy" (as 1976–79) and of relative pause while the gains of the forward policy are consolidated or digested. On that interpretation, the comparative quiet of the first Reagan term could be seen as a natural consequence of Soviet activism in the Carter years. President Reagan, in other words, enjoyed the good fortune of President Carter's bad fortune. If so, the relative immobilism of Soviet policy would have to be seen as a short-term phenomenon, not likely to persist for four more years.

Other possible explanations focus on the American side, and involve the distinction between operational and declaratory signals. The contrast between the Reagan and Carter years seems particularly illuminating. It owed more to contrasts in what the two Presidents and their respective entourages *said* than to any vast differences in what the two Administrations actually *did*.

Indeed, it is difficult to think of any major operational

differences at all, save the sharper and more combative stance during the Reagan years in the Caribbean and Central America and a greater skepticism on arms control (though I would be inclined to put arms control proposals into the sphere of declaratory policy anyway). If one looks at the basic substance of the major operational policies—continuance of support for NATO; continuance of a wary cultivation of China; continuance of support for Israel, along with as much or as little cultivation of moderate Arab governments as is compatible with the Israeli connection; a continuing consciousness that the security importance of Japan outweighs any economic rivalries; continuing orientation to the Association of South East Asian Nations and to the Pacific, including ANZUS pact countries Australia and New Zealand; a continuing restraint of the basic hostility to Vietnam and Iran—on all these it is difficult to see more than marginal change.

Observing these continuities in operational policy and contrasting them with the differences in media images, and the differences also in the overall international fortunes of the two Administrations, it becomes difficult to resist the inference that President Reagan's declaratory signals have been, on balance, useful to his purpose, not only electorally but internationally, and that the opposite was true for President Carter. Perhaps this outcome is as yet more clearly visible in Carter's case, when we remember that the mildness of his initial declaratory signals left him derisively (and unfairly) still seen at the end as a "terminal case of meekness," despite actual operational policies in some respects tougher than any so far in the Reagan period.

IV

To substantiate this assessment, let us look at a small cross-section of policy issues during the Reagan years and compare the declaratory and the operational signals that have been associated with them: China, Lebanon, the Persian Gulf, Poland, the Korean airliner, and the trans-European gas pipeline.

On China policy, the difference between the early declaratory signals that seemed to establish President Reagan as a dedicated friend of Taiwan and his actual operational policy, following precisely the path taken by Presidents Nixon and Carter to the Great Wall, is so obvious as hardly to need demonstrating.

Lebanon offers a more subtle and complex pattern, but one, to my judgment, of much the same meaning. Initially the

Reagan Administration approach seemed to promise a discarding of earlier U.S. mediatory efforts in favor of something both more ambitious and more in line with stated neoconservative positions. In March 1981 Secretary of State Alexander Haig told the Senate Foreign Relations Committee that the objective was to "establish a consensus in the strategic regional sense among the states in the area," all the way from Pakistan to Israel and Egypt. But during the episode of Syrian antiaircraft missiles in April 1981, the Israeli bombing of the Baghdad reactor in June 1981, and the initial phases of the Israeli invasion of Lebanon in June 1982, the true operational message seemed to be that Washington was leaving the direction of events in the hands of the local actors.

Then there were the commitment of the marines in August 1982 and the Reagan Plan initiative in September: both ambitious declaratory signals of what was desired and desirable. But that did not really entail a new operational commitment, save in the diplomatic time and energy of U.S. envoy Philip Habib and other policymakers, mostly somewhat below the topmost level. Even the commitment of marines was at a token level. When President Eisenhower put marines into Lebanon in 1958, he used about 14,000 and left them there until the political objectives of the U.S. government had been secured, for the time, and for good or ill. The small detachment that President Reagan put in did not have a military purpose but a diplomatic and political one; it was a declaratory signal. When the marines suffered the casualties of October 1983, the President declared that the United States had "vital interests" in Lebanon. And Secretary of State George Shultz said, "We are in Lebanon because the outcome will affect our whole position in the Middle East. To ask why Lebanon is important is to ask why the Middle East is important." Again, strong declaratory signals.

A few months later, in February 1984, the marines were simply taken out. Congressional opposition, 259 deaths and the opening of election year were enough to make declared vital interests subject to reassessment. By late 1984 Lebanon had in effect been divided into Israeli and Syrian spheres of influence. The Maronite Christians, whose position of dominance in Lebanese internal politics had so long been sustained by the West (first the French and then the Americans), seemed to be losing ascendency to the Muslims. I offer no criticism of that outcome in itself; indeed, I think it may conduce to the chances of long-term stability. My point is merely the disparity between the declaratory signal: "This is interpreted by us as a vital interest," and the operational message that the United States can ultimately sail away. The Eisenhower Doctrine, by late 1984, appeared no longer operative in Lebanon. And to a chorus of surprise, Richard Murphy, the U.S. assistant secretary of state for Near East and South Asian affairs, could proclaim the Syrians to be no longer "Soviet puppets" as had been assumed so confidently earlier by Reagan spokesmen. On the contrary, the Syrians could be quite "helpful," Murphy told a congressional committee in July 1984, apparently endorsing their role in security and stability. In other words, the declaratory signal by then matched the operational signal: the Reagan Administration, far from being more ambitious in the area than its predecessors, was less ambitious and more prepared to leave local events in local hands.

In the Persian Gulf, one might argue similarly that the Carter Doctrine proved to be non-operative in President Reagan's time. Again the initial declaratory signals were strong: the transformation of the Rapid Deployment Force into the Central Command, and its fleshing-out with assigned forces such as carrier battle-groups and airborne divisions and fighter wings to a total of almost 300,000 men. But though a major war was in progress in the Gulf throughout the four years of the Reagan first term, there was hardly more than a hint of American intervention, even when tankers were subject to missile attacks. And when mines were laid along the tanker routes, the Western powers merely swept them up, with a bit of Soviet cooperation. On the evidence one would say that there has indeed been a tacit understanding between Washington and Moscow that each would limit its intervention in the area, on the assumption that the other continued to do so.

Again, no one in his or her right mind would complain. The point is just that there was in this case also a chasm, rather than a mere gap, between what the expectations had been back in 1980 of what the Reagan policy would be in the event of local hostilities threatening the Gulf oil routes to the West, and what actually happened. Or, more precisely, did *not* happen. For the world has in fact proved able to shrug off a major war, now into its fifth year, in which both sides have threatened or damaged oil installations or oil tankers in and around the Gulf. The oil glut persisted despite those events. OPEC has not only been unable to raise oil prices; it had by late 1984 seen the real price of oil fall, as cuts in production had to be made to keep the nominal price hovering somewhere near $29 per barrel. Present U.S. policy in the Gulf looks uncommonly like a tacit acquiescence in the Nixon Doctrine—that local powers must learn to fend for themselves in local crises.

In the Polish crisis, already under way when President Reagan came into office but reaching its decision-point only with the declaration of martial law in December 1981, the pattern hardly varied from earlier East European crises. The rhetoric was vehement, and the debate expressed U.S. outrage, but the actual sanctions against the Soviet Union were exceedingly mild. In particular, grain sales under existing agreements were not restricted; the United States continued to participate in the Helsinki review talks and the Geneva negotiations on arms control; a scheduled meeting between Haig and Gromyko was allowed to proceed. In fact, aside from the suspension of Aeroflot services and some restrictions on high technology purchases, it is difficult to see anything in U.S. operational policy that could have caused much wincing in Moscow. The unfortunate Poles themselves were rather more the true victims of any clampdown, suffering suspension of food aid and other economic blows for a time. Overall, American policy seemed a clear continuation of the tradition of well-signaled U.S. restraint in East European crises, which again dates right back to Dulles in 1953.

Washington's reactions to the shooting down of the Korean airliner in September 1983 were almost a carbon copy of the reactions to the declaration of martial law in Poland less than two years earlier. Again the level of rhetorical denunciation reached a new crescendo, again there were symbolic gestures of outrage—declaratory signals—like the denial of landing rights for Gromyko's plane when he sought to make his customary visit to the U.N. General Assembly. But again operational policies were not exactly severe. The grain deal was not rescinded. The Madrid meeting (essentially a continuance of the Helsinki Conference on Security and Cooperation in Europe which Reagan had so often denounced) was not only allowed to proceed but was chosen as a venue for a low-key meeting between Shultz and Gromyko. Shortly after the incident the arms control talks were suspended, but that was a Soviet declaratory signal against the Pershing II and cruise deployments, not Washington's choice.

The Soviet gas pipeline provides an example of a different

sort of crisis, an intramural crisis of the NATO alliance. The declaratory signals were as usual fierce: talk of sanctions against America's closest and most necessary allies. And Washington did have a case; dependence by the West Europeans on Soviet sources for even a small segment of their energy supplies does not seem a good idea, nor does the provision of a new source of hard currency to the Soviet Union. But the Europeans also had a point: their vulnerability to Middle East oil producers is so great that their total level of risk is not more than marginally increased, if at all, by some shift of energy dependence to the Soviet Union. And the Russians need to be able to sell commodities to the West if they are to buy Western goods in return. The advantages of détente, economically but also in human terms, are too great for the European powers to be willing to relinquish them, especially not at the instance of an American Administration as little credited with understanding Europe as that of President Reagan. So the Europeans dug their toes in and ignored the Washington rhetoric. The gas now flows westward, and hard currency eastward; U.S. sanctions have not exactly been overwhelming. Again the contrast was between a tough initial declaratory policy and an ultimate operational policy of shrugging the whole thing off.

Arms control (or the lack of it) provides the most complex example of declaratory signals. Formal proposals were made, such as those presented in the Strategic Arms Reduction Talks and intermediate-range nuclear forces negotiations, but there were informal but perfectly clear indications, evident even before he came to office, that Mr. Reagan was unlikely to be an enthusiast for arms control treaties, judging by all he had said about Strategic Arms Limitation Talks (SALT I and SALT II). And then there were his defense proposals, clearly likely to amount to a major rearmament effort, mostly in advanced nuclear weapons.

It is not totally impossible to combine a belief that the United States by 1981 needed to upgrade its nuclear capacity in some fields vis-à-vis the Soviet Union with a belief that arms control treaties have merit in promoting the stability of the general strategic relationship with the Soviet Union. But to formulate policies giving weight to both objectives takes more specialized knowledge of the field than even his aides would claim for the President. Given the necessities of the arms buildup, the nature of some of the arms control appointments made, and the actual process of the negotiations, no one reasonably conversant with the issues could have been surprised at the outcome, or lack of outcome, of the formal initiatives in the first Reagan term. An air of "doing it for the record" (ingenious though the proposals were) hung over them from the first. Nevertheless, and despite Reagan's earlier denunciations of SALT II, that unratified treaty seems to have remained operational. And despite heavy hints that the Anti-Ballistic Missile Treaty might be discarded, it has so far been preserved.

v

These instances seem to add up to reasonably solid evidence that on the whole the diplomatic bark of the Reagan Administration has been considerably fiercer than its bite; that is, the pattern has been one of declaratory signals a good deal sharper than the operational ones. There is one obvious area where policy may be seen as an exception to that rule: Central America and the Caribbean. In Nicaragua, the Administration has tried to see what some very heavy-handed declaratory signaling could accomplish. Possibly that will prove a mere prelude to actual combat operations. But perhaps the general Reagan pattern will be maintained, that of declaratory signals fiercer than operational policies, at least as compared with Eisenhower's 1954 covert intervention in Guatemala, Kennedy's Bay of Pigs fiasco and Johnson's 1965 use of marines in the Dominican Republic.

The point of real interest, however, is not in which areas the Administration's bark has proved fiercer, but whether it can be argued with any plausibility that the fierceness of the signaling has precluded the necessity for action. Could it be that the rhetoric has raised assessments in Moscow of a higher level of risk in any kind of Soviet forward policy, making the "correlation of forces," the central concept in a Leninist analysis, look less favorable? Factors against adventurism stemming from the Soviet side were, in any case, strong. Even a slight extra weight of assessed risk, created by U.S. declaratory signals, might have proved substantial enough to tip the scales.

If we compare that putative payoff from one kind of declaratory policy with the misfortunes of the Carter period when an alternative kind of declaratory policy was in force (though the operational policies were not all that different), it seems to suggest a revised view about the general relationship between declaratory and operational signals—a view possibly applicable beyond this eight-year stretch of American experience.

Both sets of signals contribute to the expectations which the superpowers have of each other. Those expectations in turn are incorporated into the assessments of costs and risks which determine actual policy decisions on both sides of the central balance. But there is an important distinction between declaratory signals and operational signals that is particularly relevant to the present and the most recent past (the last two decades, more or less). The powers have for these 20 years or so had independent means of seeing for themselves, with the aid of satellites and such, what the capabilities of the other side are. So the ambiguities from which have traditionally arisen the miscalculations that precipitate crises, and sometimes wars, are no longer in the field of relative capabilities. They are almost exclusively now in the field of will; sometimes the will of a society as a whole, sometimes the will of its dominant political elite, but more often the will of the chief decision-maker and the small group of policymakers who immediately surround him.

And of that small group's will, in a situation of crisis, no satellite can provide direct observation. Operational policy does provide some signals bearing on will, of course, but in this particular field declaratory policy—speeches and such—provides the most direct guide to *mood*, and thus cannot safely be discounted by an adversary as a signal of *will*. In other words, declaratory signals may be a rather more important component of the total mix of signals now than they were before the age of surveillance (i.e., before about 1965) because the remaining ambiguities of the power balance are in the area of will rather than capacity, and declaratory signals tend to determine the image of will which each group of adversary decision-makers forms of the other.

In summary, a general war in the nuclear age is more likely to come from miscalculation than from deliberate challenge, and miscalculation, in the age of surveillance, is more likely to derive from uncertainties about the will of the chief decision-maker in the adversary camp than about the strategic capacities of the two systems. Khrushchev's apparent miscalculation about Kennedy offers a parallel: he is reported to have come away from their Vienna meeting in 1961 convinced that the young new President was "too liberal to fight." The genesis of the Cuban missile crisis, undoubtedly the most dangerous war-threatening crisis of the entire nuclear period, may in part be seen in that assessment. Carter was perhaps, because of his initial declaratory signals, in some danger of accidentally engendering that same kind of calculation or miscalculation; Reagan is clearly not. The preservation of peace rests, unfortunately, on nothing more substantial than the system of expectations in Moscow and Washington as to how the decision-makers in the other capital will react in the event of policies unacceptable to them. So one would not wish any kind of dangerous illusion to creep into those sets of expectations, such as the illusion that the other side had "no option but détente." Disillusion is no doubt very embittering. Illusion, however, is a great deal more dangerous in international politics. If either adversary has no option but détente, why should the other pay any price to preserve the détente? Soviet policy in the late 1970s might be taken as partial evidence of that mood, so Soviet reassessments, after the Reagan inauguration, were therefore useful rather than damaging to the basic mechanism that keeps the peace, in the sense of helping disperse any such illusion, and thus reducing the chance of some lethal miscalculation.

VI

It probably would be too optimistic to believe that noisy declaratory signals—i.e., hostile rhetoric—can become a substitute for more destructive international behavior. That would mean that the two superpowers had been sensible enough to adopt the technique of gorillas deep in their respective patches of jungle, loudly beating their respective chests—not as a prelude to fighting but because they want to avoid doing so—these declaratory signals being an established ritual for ensuring that their respective interests are not unacceptably encroached upon. Still, at least in the Western world and especially in the hands of a professional "communicator" like Ronald Reagan, rhetoric and gesture do seem to have been adequate substitutes for operational toughness with most of his supporters.

At this point, one final feature of the Reagan foreign policy, the popularity of the Grenada invasion, becomes illuminating. The wresting of that tiny island from the group of erratic left-wing thugs who had murdered the prime minister and half his cabinet seems to have been justifiably popular on the island itself, and I have no quarrel with the view that the upshot will enhance the Grenadians' chances for life, liberty and the pursuit of happiness. But in terms of geopolitical realities it was no big deal. The nationalist enthusiasm for the success of U.S. forces does seem rather on a par with proudly lauding a steamroller for its success in cracking a walnut.

What might, however, be said in approval of the Grenada operation was that as a declaratory signal of a dramatic sort it worked very well indeed. It focused the attention of the entire world, at least for a week or two, on that tiny patch of land, and on Washington's *will* (no one doubted the capability) to do something about developments it did not like in the Caribbean. The President even picked up a bonus when Suriname, having seen what happened in Grenada, sent its own Cubans packing. So, in effect, Mr. Reagan secured some inhibition on the growth of Cuban influence in two areas for the price of one, as well as a great deal of popularity with the U.S. electorate. He is an intuitive politician, and his intuitions were clearly on target in the decision to launch the Grenada operation at the time of the marine casualties in Lebanon.

Any such apparent payoffs from the Reagan policies must of course be balanced against costs. The chief debit, undoubtedly, in the eyes of most observers was the "opportunity cost" of the failure of arms control efforts. I would not myself rate this so high as many commentators, because I doubt that the early 1980s could have been a good period for arms control even if Jimmy Carter had been returned to power. The rows over the Pershing II and cruise missiles would have been the same; the ambivalence of the Europeans would have been the same; the felt need for NATO to stick to its 1979 resolution would have been the same. The rate of increase in military spending might perhaps have been somewhat less than President Reagan has secured, but in fact the Carter proposals on the MX (the most controversial item) were a great deal more extravagant both on numbers and basing than the program that the Reagan policymakers have apparently settled for, bowing to the recalcitrance of Congress: no vastly expensive mobile basing system, and probably less than half the numbers. Even attitudes on the nuclear freeze and the arms control "build-down" ideas might not have been all that different, since the freeze in particular is the sort of notion easier to go along with in opposition than in government.

Ought one then to say that the chief costs have been in the level of irritation at various Reagan declaratory signals among the policymakers of his major allies? But whether NATO has been seriously damaged—beyond what it might have been if

Jimmy Carter had stayed in power—seems to me again quite doubtful. NATO conduces so solidly to the respective national interests of its European members, and is so well understood to do so by the foreign policy elites currently in power in those capitals (and even by their domestic political opposite numbers), that it will take a great deal more than harsh words about gas turbines to really shake the alliance. And though European policymakers and analysts sharpen their considerable wits on both varieties of American foreign policy moralism, on the whole they probably see the more real danger in President Carter's kind of Wilsonianism, especially in respect to the West's fragile relationship with the Third World. (The reverse is true, of course, of left-liberal critics and also of many Third World elites. They tend to respond sympathetically to the Wilsonian value-system, at least until they work out what national self-determination might imply in the cases of their own national minorities, and what any serious observance of human rights might do to their own authority structures.)

One might make a better case for true damage to U.S. credibility in the Middle East, with certainly a reduction of assumed U.S. capacity to control events, whether one is thinking of Lebanon or the Gulf. The Saudis have been irritated by the neglect of the Fahd Plan and by the U.S. debates over the supply of aircraft and missiles. Kuwait and Jordan have been irritated enough to purchase Soviet missiles. Morocco has contracted its improbable marriage of convenience with Libya, a government ranking almost equal with the Soviet Union in the demonology of American neoconservatives. Syria has undoubtedly advanced its status and sphere of influence, not only vis-à-vis Lebanon but also the United States, and even apparently Israel. And the Soviet Union, which had been successfully excluded from real (as against titular) power in Middle Eastern crises might be deemed to be back now, as the shadow behind Syria. All the Arab countries, even Egypt, have obviously been irritated by the strategic cooperation agreement with Israel.

Yet even assuming some loss of U.S. influence in the Middle East, I am not sure one ought to go on to assume reduced prospects of reasonable stability there. Actual settlements may be out of reach in the foreseeable future, but paradoxically, a more viable balance of conflicts seems to be emerging from the increased Syrian ascendancy, a rearrangement of alliances in the Arab world, and the Israelis' recognition of the limits of their capacity to operate in Lebanon. Again paradoxically, the strategic cooperation agreement would thus prove a prelude to some Israeli retreat, not an increase in dominance.

VII

Finally, we must look at what will probably seem an insuperable objection to any policy that allows a substantial gap between declaratory and operational signals: that the gap is bound to be noticed after a while and thus the credibility of future declaratory signals will be diminished, not only among allies and in the Middle East and Central America, but much more importantly, in Moscow. True, but what that means chiefly is that the Administration will need a new policy for the new term. In a wildly optimistic moment, one might hope that some such thought, along with the simple cynical electoral calculation, was among the reasons for the universally noticed Reagan change of rhetorical style in the last year of his first term. The true nature of that change, in the terms we have been using, was that the declaratory signals were softened to match the continuing mildness of the operational signals. Obviously, in the second term the original gap could easily be restored by a new sharpening of the declaratory signals, or the two could be kept in tandem, so to speak, by a sharpening of both.

It is, however, difficult to see what exactly would be the advantage of such a course, either for the President personally, or for his Republican Party backers, who will want to continue keeping Democrats out of the White House, and who will presumably continue to remember that the war issue was the one on which their man came closest to being vulnerable. Moreover, though Mr. Reagan was able to campaign in 1980 and during his first two or three years in office on the alleged deficiencies in his predecessor's defense policies, that will hardly do for his fifth and subsequent years in power. From 1985 any further talk of American strategic weakness will imply a reflection on his own past policies.

Thus it has become logical for the Administration instead to imply (as was done in the September 1984 U.N. speech) that the "strength-building" part of the negotiation-from-strength concept is already adequately under way. Therefore the phase of negotiation may be approaching. If the President can successfully make this transition, he might even manage to avoid the difficulty which defeated the policymakers who propounded the same strategy in the early 1950s: the difficulty of choosing the moment when the optimal chance of diplomatic progress has been reached. During that earlier historic phase, the best situation for the West in terms of potential negotiating leverage seems in retrospect to have been late 1953, with the Soviet decision-makers still in the phase of post-Stalin disarray, and while the impetus of the first NATO rearmament effort still looked strong. But that moment was lost, and by 1956 a new and rather incautious Soviet decision-maker, Nikita Khrushchev, was in control, and a new upswing in Soviet strategic capacity was under way.

That cycle does not have to be repeated, though all the conditions that make it likely already exist. The parallel with the early 1950s could be bleakly completed with a new rise in the level of danger as the Strategic Defense Initiative research begins bearing fruit, and perhaps an early 1990s crisis to parallel 1962.

That could happen, but sufficient intelligence applied to U.S. policy could prevent it. There is a case for assuming that on both sides of the balance a new phase of détente and arms control looks possible and desirable. On the Soviet side, the only interpretation which makes sense of Mr. Gromyko's decision to come calling *before* the election is that the decision-makers in Moscow had by September 1984 concluded that they were stuck with Mr. Reagan, little as they liked him, for another four years, and must pursue a damage-limiting strategy by trying to re-create enough détente to take the impetus out of the SDI research, if possible. Otherwise they would have to try and match it: a very expensive decision for their faltering economy. Once they had decided on that strategy, it became tactically logical to make the bid *before* the election, when the Administration's incentive to appear conciliatory was at its strongest.

It may be objected that while the Russians had nothing to lose by such an approach, President Reagan will be in severe danger of losing the ideological support of neoconservative "true believers" if he continues the softened declaratory signals of election year into the new term, and particularly if his operational signals indicate an actual move toward negotiation and détente. There are indications already of some loss of faith in the President among the sharper-tongued gurus of this group.

But in his second term President Reagan obviously has to worry about how he will stand with history rather than about the support of groups once tactically useful, but now certainly no longer necessary. There is reason to be skeptical that he is a typical neoconservative: he seems to lack the urbane sharpness, the pessimism and disillusion, and the worries about theoretical consistency that distinguish the more notable members of the intellectual clique who developed that doctrine. Many of them are people for whom Soviet policy, especially in the Middle East and Eastern Europe, has been a source of true emotional trauma, especially if they were liberals or radicals to begin with. That gives them some piercing insights, but it does not give them much in common with an easygoing, relaxed Californian of Irish Protestant background, with a sunny optimism of temperament and a rather short attention span. So there appears psychological scope for a parting of the ways.

If the President does lose the neoconservatives, or they him, it will make relations with his European allies a good deal easier. The thoroughly conservative foreign policy establishments of the European powers tend to regard American neoconservatives with a jaundiced eye, because the neoconservatives tend to picture the Europeans as hovering perpetually on the brink of Finlandization. That is seen as a very real insult by the European policymakers concerned, since it implies stupidity as well as cowardice.

Of course only the second term will determine which way the choices will go, but the auguries for renewed dialogue and perhaps even eventual gains in the field of arms control appeared promising as 1985 began. Soviet alarm over the potentialities in the Strategic Defense Initiative has already been heavily signaled, and appeared a major incentive for Moscow to try further shifts in tactical positions. The need to bring the deficit, and therefore the arms budget, under control had almost the same effect for Washington. The pressure of grassroots feeling about nuclear dangers and the discontents of their respective allies bore on both superpowers, though asymmetrically. A reason for arms control still better than any of those is, or should be, present in the minds of decision-makers on both sides: the pressing need for reinforced crisis stability at a time when the balance between offensive and defensive weaponry may be liable to sudden change. There are not many arms control objectives of equal urgency and importance for both sides, but crisis stability is one, and it could provide the guiding thread through the labyrinth their arms control negotiators are about to enter.

As a final paradox, one might note that despite the fact that

Presidents Carter and Reagan were both foreign policy moralists in their respective ways, their contrasted experiences appear splendidly to exemplify Machiavelli's reflections on the roles of *fortuna* and *virtu* in political life. Fortune has certainly been with Mr. Reagan so far, in comparison to his recent predecessors. Unlike those who came to office in 1969, he had no disastrous war to wind up. Unlike Mr. Carter, he was not borne into office on a wave of liberal guilt and loss of U.S. self-confidence. On the contrary, he has benefited domestically and internationally by the swing of the pendulum back to nationalist buoyancy. As a patch of historical experience, it tends to reduce an analyst to reflections about the luck of the Irish. But from the point of view of the theory of foreign policy, the greater importance of declaratory over operational signals in an age of surveillance may be the idea to be noted.

Henry Grunwald

FOREIGN POLICY
UNDER REAGAN II

The second Reagan Administration has a rare opportunity to reshape American foreign policy. The opportunity obviously springs from President Reagan's overwhelming election victory, which, if he remains in office for four more years, will make him the first full two-term president since Eisenhower. This victory has further strengthened his already impressive capacity for political leadership, reinforcing his authority to deal with the factions of his own party, with the feuding wings of the bureaucracy, and with foreign countries. The question is whether he will seize that authority and will know how to use it. Which Reagan, and which group of Reagan advisers, will dominate the second term? Will it be the stubbornly hard-line or the flexible President, the "ideologues" or the "pragmatists" among his counselors?

That distinction is, of course, somewhat oversimplified; the divisions within, and around, the President are not quite so clear-cut. There are apocalyptic and rational ideologues; there are very tough and semi-tough pragmatists. Still, the familiar labels do describe a genuine conflict, and in the first term, the evolution of that conflict was quite evident: from ideology to pragmatism.

The Administration started out by confronting the world with a hard-line, aggressive and Manichean set of policies, or pronouncements, that in nearly every instance gave way to compromise and at least outward accommodation. This was true of attitudes toward the Soviet Union, arms control, Central America, the European allies, and support of the International Monetary Fund, among others. The retreat and reversal on the Soviet-European gas pipeline issue was typical of this trend. These accommodations happened only after bitter bureaucratic infighting, and in response to various outside pressures: public opinion, politics, allied complaints, the risk of diplomatic debacles.

The need to compromise was symbolized by the resort to more or less bipartisan commissions: the Scowcroft panel on

Henry Grunwald is Editor-in-Chief, Time Incorporated.

the MX missile, the Kissinger group on Central America. These commissions did extremely useful work and produced sound, generally centrist recommendations, which by no reasonable standard could be described as weak. What remains to be seen is whether, in the second term, these and similar policies will prevail, demonstrating in effect a learning experience by the Administration, or whether the right-wing "true believers" will succeed in dismissing them as mere temporary, tactical adjustments and will try to reassert the ideological super-hard line. A great deal depends on the answer, including the possibility of reaching at least the rudiments of a new national consensus on foreign and defense policy.

II

In fairness, it should be said that, up to a point, the hard line was a useful corrective for weak and confused policies of the past and was welcomed in many quarters as a sign of a new American assertiveness. Administration critics almost automatically preface "ideology" with "right-wing." But there is liberal or left-wing ideology too, and its reading of Soviet intentions and of the causes of Third World instability often has been just as simplistic as right-wing interpretations, if not more so.

Besides, the Reagan Administration, often reckless in rhetoric but cautious in action, did have its successes. One of them was the championing of American military power. The arms buildup may have been excessive, and ill-advised in some particulars; very little was done to reform the armed services. But the buildup was plainly necessary and, despite much bickering, it was essentially supported by Congress and the public. It constitutes the most important single "foreign policy" action by Reagan so far.

Another clear achievement, of course, was the deployment of the Euromissiles for NATO, in the teeth of all-out Soviet opposition. In dealing with China, despite some early ideological rumbles and despite the baggage accumulated during decades of a deep Republican commitment to Taiwan, the Reagan Administration acted prudently and professionally. The same may be said, at the risk of considerable disagreement, about the Reagan policy toward South Africa. In other instances, policy was muddled through lack of skill and understanding, as in the Middle East.

On balance, the Reagan Administration often proved itself quite capable of realistic and largely nonideological policies, but they did not fit into any unified concept. Thus "more pragmatism" is not a sufficient foreign policy prescription for Reagan II. A pragmatism that merely and artificially splits the difference between sharply opposing views, or cobbles together a compromise for political and public relations effect, is hardly what we need. What is required is pragmatism within a framework of principle; firm assertion of American goals combined with a recognition that there are different ways of attaining them, and that some may be unattainable in the near future; a realization that, especially in foreign affairs, passion without skill can be worse than skill without passion. Reagan II, one would hope, will recognize that toughness, while indispensable, can take many forms. On the whole, the Administration has been deficient in seeing that strength has political and diplomatic components, that charging head-on at an objective is not necessarily the best way to reach it, and that guile and the ability to maneuver are every bit as important as muscle.

III

In perspective, the Reagan Administration's difficulties in dealing with the Soviet Union are familiar, almost traditional, even though pushed to extremes. From the outset, the Administration had difficulty coping with what can only be called the yes-but formula, which has been advanced for the last three decades by just about every specialist in the field: Yes, we must be strong, but at the same time flexible. Yes, we must understand that the Russians are relentless foes, but at the same time we must seek ways of coexisting. And so forth. As a general proposition, this formula is so obvious that it is no longer worth debating; the question is how it is to be applied specifically. Yet almost every new Administration comes into office paying lip service to the yes-but principle, while actually believing that a fresh start, a new approach—either softer or harder—will permit escape from the painful and laborious double track.

The Reagan Administration was particularly determined to reject the yes-but formula, which requires the ability to hold two opposite ideas at the same time (the mark of a first-rate intelligence, according to F. Scott Fitzgerald). This runs against the American tendency to see the world as good or evil, a mind-set not invented by Reagan, and to believe in solutions; the yes-but formula implies that U.S.-Soviet strains are not a problem to which there is a solution, but a more or less permanent condition that can only be alleviated, not cured.

In fact, each Administration sooner or later has been disappointed in its hope that these constraints can be escaped, the only exception being the Nixon Administration which knew better from the start. The fact is that the Reagan Administration is being pushed toward something that, by any other name, is still détente. Indeed, détente is constantly being reinvented, redefined or relabelled (as in Richard Nixon's afterthought, "hardheaded détente"). As long as it can be protected from the utopian left, which sees it as institutionalized brotherhood, and from the triumphalist right, which sees it as institutionalized surrender, and defined as no more or less than controlled conflict, it remains the inescapable intellectual framework for American policy.

It has been eloquently argued that arms control has been made to bear too much of the burden of U.S.-Soviet relations, and that there can be no hope for significant progress on arms control unless a degree of trust can be restored or created between the superpowers.[1] The notion brings to mind the observation by Salvador de Madariaga, writing about the 1930s in his memoirs, that "nations don't distrust each other because they are armed; they are armed because they distrust each other. And therefore to want disarmament before a minimum of common agreement on fundamentals is as absurd as to want people to go undressed in winter." It is hard to quarrel with this insight, and yet it is equally hard to see how the United States and the Soviet Union can retrieve even a few clothes of confidence unless there is at least a possibility of moving, however slowly, toward an accord on nuclear arms.

In short, the argument is circular and irresistibly leads back to the imperative of arms control. Its achievements in the past have been modest at best. Progress has been glacial, and exaggerated expectations have been aroused by the process. But there is simply no convincing alternative to it.

IV

The Reagan Administration has often acted as if any arms control proposal that might be acceptable to the Soviets must be automatically flawed, when in fact the Soviet Union, like the United States, will naturally accept only proposals it considers to be in its own self-interest. This negative attitude, plus the open contempt for arms control expressed by some members of the Reagan circle, plus the unrealistic proposals for cuts offered at the outset of the Strategic Arms Reduction Talks

[1] See Robert W. Tucker, "The Nuclear Debate," *Foreign Affairs*, Fall 1984.

(START), has obscured a central fact: the major source of the problem lies in the Soviets' own aggressive nuclear buildup and their excessive view of what they require for their own security. It is therefore entirely possible that even a "reformed" Reagan Administration with a more tolerant approach to arms control may not get anywhere with the Soviets. There are certain concessions beyond which no administration can or should go in order to win an agreement. At the same time, President Reagan seems to have disavowed the possibility that America can permanently restore any significant nuclear superiority over the Russians. What is at issue is an acceptable but more realistic definition of parity.

It has become fashionable to say that arms control is virtually dead. This view is held not merely because of the acrimonious breakdown of both the intermediate-range nuclear forces (INF) and START negotiations, but, more importantly, because it is argued that technology keeps outpacing the negotiators. While advancing technology immensely complicates arms control efforts, it is not beyond the reach of negotiated agreements.

Politically, of course, one of the vast problems about arms control and nuclear strategy is their complexity and the inability of the public—or of most politicians—to grasp the issues in any detail. Much of the arms control debate seems like a scholastic exercise about how many warheads can dance on the head of a missile. This frightful air of unreality has much to do with the desire both on the left and on the right, in a curious mirror image, to escape these dilemmas and to find simple and understandable solutions.

On the left, the desire to escape takes the form of a utopian belief in good will or in unilateral actions. (The widely proposed "mutual and verifiable" freeze would not assure balance and would take extensive negotiations.) On the right, it takes the form of a search for "superiority," in the belief that we can outspend the Soviets and outdo them more or less indefinitely in technology. The Administration's Strategic Defense Initiative ("Star Wars") is an elaboration of this view.

The Star Wars program has a certain appealing plausibility: defense is better than offense, safety behind a shield in the sky is better than the "balance of terror." Professional analysts of course do not commit such oversimplifications, or at least not obviously. Lieutenant General James A. Abrahamson, head of the Strategic Defense Initiative research program, admits that no system the United States deploys will ever be entirely foolproof. But he argues that a less than total but highly efficient defense, which might mean anywhere from 50-percent to 99-percent effectiveness, depending on the scale of the system deployed, would make it impossible for the Soviets to plan a first strike with any high degree of confidence. That circumstance will enhance deterrence. Furthermore, even a partially effective defense would be bound to save lives in the unlikely event of an attack.

For the moment, the Administration has committed itself only to a research and development program which the Department of Defense says will require about $26 billion over the next five years. Even the more optimistic scenarios see continued need for new offensive weapons, which would only gradually be reduced. And even the most sophisticated and cautious advocates of space-based defense seem to harbor the hankering for a short-cut to safety. They too seek somehow to transfer the task of peacekeeping from the precarious calculus of threat and counterthreat, from the area of human will, to a more or less automatic regime of laser beams and mirrors in orbit.

Technological feasibility aside, the opponents of Star Wars seem to have the better case. The prospect of one side more or less safe while the other side is open to attack is untenable in the nuclear age. Moreover, in the absence of a new bargain with the Soviets, such a situation is bound to be relatively short-lived. We have seen in the past that sooner or later the Soviets can catch up with American technology, the most notable example being multiple independently targetable reentry vehicles (MIRVs). All of this would mean great instability during a development period that might run for 20 years and, eventually, instability at a much higher and more complicated level of weaponry.

But this does not mean that development of a defensive system should be banned independently of what is done about nuclear weapons in general. The Soviets seem genuinely afraid of a technological race with the United States in space defense. This fear should be used as a major bargaining chip for an overall arms control agreement.

After an initial test of its low-altitude anti-satellite system (ASAT), which is not part of Star Wars but which the Soviets want to include in any talks about space weapons, the United States should offer a temporary suspension of further tests. This should be followed by negotiations that would tie any arrangements for space weapons to the rest of arms control. If it is too late for a total ban on space-based weapons, a possible outcome could be to permit relatively small defense systems for both sides, tied to an arms control agreement (reductions) in offensive weapons.

V

Despite the breakdown of arms control talks, the elements of an agreement for offensive weapons exist. They are summed up in the phrase, "off-setting asymmetries"—in other words, the recognition that the Soviets will not make any significant cuts in their principal arsenal of ground-based missiles unless the United States makes certain concessions in an area where it is particularly strong, namely bombers, cruise missiles and, increasingly, submarine-launched ballistic missiles. This principle is recognized in various schemes, including the so-called framework approach advanced by the State Department in August 1983 but never adopted by the Administration and in the so-called double build-down scheme. This last was put forward in the summer of 1983 by a somewhat shakily bipartisan group of Senators and Representatives which in effect forced it on the Administration. Advanced at the START talks without full conviction or complete details, the double build-down was quickly rejected by the Soviets as a mere repackaging of old, unacceptable American proposals.

The concept underlying these schemes, no doubt subject to a great deal of tinkering with the numbers, should become the basis for the Administration's arms control negotiating position. Despite its great complexity and uncertain beginnings, it remains a promising approach.

All this, of course, assumes that the Russians will allow themselves to return to the bargaining table, despite their earlier vow that they would not do so unless the United States halts deployment of Euromissiles. There is strong evidence that the Russians regret having backed themselves into that particular corner and want to come out of it. (It is interesting to recall that in 1979 the Soviets said they would not even negotiate on INF if NATO adopted the "two-track" approach, but they did in fact come to the table by 1981.) The conditions for improved relations reiterated in October 1984 by Konstantin Chernenko, in his interview with *The Washington Post*, did not include any reference to INF, and seem to offer enough room

for maneuver to resume talks without undue advance concessions by the United States.

The verification problem, of course, presents an extremely
difficult obstacle. But given determined research, it is hard to
believe that "national technical means" could not be steadily
improved. The Russians have made some forthcoming noises
about on-site inspection, but it is doubtful that this could
provide a significant overall solution. At any rate, those who
believe that verification problems vitiate arms control fail to
say how the situation would improve *without* arms control; both
sides would still be dependent on the fullest possible information about the armaments of the other side but without the
(admittedly incomplete) help on verification that arms control
agreements do and can provide.

Movement, if any, is likely to be excruciatingly slow. No big
breakthroughs should be expected. At all events, what is
needed is a merger or at least a link of INF and START negotiations plus space-defense negotiations. The talks need not be
fully integrated right away; they could begin separately and be
linked gradually. The drawbacks of such a procedure are all
too familiar: complexity and, through INF, the problem of how
to bring the allies into the picture without either compromising
their sovereignty and independence or else allowing them a
role in the START area where they do not belong.[2] Despite such
difficulties, it is impossible to see how anything can be accomplished without ultimately treating the issues of nuclear arms
and arms control in their entirety. There is simply not enough
room for bargaining and trade-offs if things are to be fought
out separately in different arenas.

The foregoing would represent a fairly drastic change in the
Administration's position on arms control—at least in its earlier
phase. But it would be necessary if the President really hopes
to make progress in the area during his second term, and there
is much evidence that he does. His sincerity would not be the
issue. The question is one of intellectual capacity and will. To
achieve anything he will have to become personally involved in
the process, understanding it far better than he has so far, or
else put policy and execution into the hands of a really trusted,
high-level associate with the power to enforce his views.

The President will have to crack down hard on the guerrilla
war between various parts of the Administration, an action that

[2] See James A. Thomson, "After Two Tracks: Integrating START and INF," *The Washington Quarterly*, Spring 1984.

would go very much against his grain. Some bureaucratic infighting and genuine competition between ideas cannot and should not be prevented. But thanks to certain single-minded and obsessive positions on the civilian side of the Pentagon and elsewhere, throughout the first Reagan term, "negotiability" with the Russians was not the issue, but rather negotiability within the Administration.[3] This situation can only be ended by a firm and decisive President and very likely by a change in some of the principal cast of characters.

VI

While arms control is thus at the center of U.S.-Soviet dealings, it must not be allowed to distract us from the world of politics and psychology surrounding the enclaves of missiles and warheads. In that larger context, Reagan II would do well to take certain precepts to heart. One is that we have only very limited means of influencing events inside the Soviet Union. As has been amply observed, fierce rhetoric certainly will not do it. (During the past year, and especially during the last few weeks of the election campaign, the Administration's harsh language gave way to a much softer style, downright reminiscent of Beethoven's introduction to Schiller's *Ode to Joy*—"Not these tones, my friends, but let us raise more agreeable ones. . . .")

Criticism, of course, must not cease, but the United States must also be very cautious in linking condemnation to practical policy, or in suggesting, as has been done by members of the Administration, that peace requires drastic changes in the Soviet regime. A lesson from pre-Reagan days, but still applicable, involves one of the most destructive actions of U.S. foreign policy, which was championed by the usually very wise late Senator Henry M. Jackson: the attempt to force liberalization of Jewish emigration from the U.S.S.R. by denying Russia most-favored-nation treatment. Focusing on Jewish emigration as distinct from any other, possibly worse abuses in the Soviet system was not only arbitrary, it was clearly counterproductive.

The Reagan Administration also needs to get better at matching means and ends, as is suggested, for instance, by its reaction to the imposition of martial law in Poland. The means were at hand for a much faster and more forceful reaction,

<hr>

[3] See Strobe Talbott, *Deadly Gambits*, New York: Alfred A. Knopf, 1984.

notably suspension of the then still running INF talks and calling in the Polish debt to the international banks. But if for whatever reason it was decided not to react in that way, the mere denunciations and attempts at economic sanctions were futile. In fact, it can be argued that imposition of martial law was the minimal reaction that could have been expected from the Soviets and that no Communist state could ever permit an organization like Solidarity to subsist.

But aligning means with ends does not imply ceding anything to the Soviets that need not be ceded—and certainly not without exacting a price. True, the Soviet Union is a superpower with global interests that cannot be totally denied. Those who urge a last-ditch stand against Soviet influence in every corner of the globe, a sort of Churchillian resistance sometimes suggested by apocalyptic right-wingers, overestimate both our will and our resources. America must differentiate, without of course publicly drawing a map, between areas and situations of the first or second or fifth importance. Pressure on the Soviets and their surrogates should be applied everywhere, constantly, but in varying degrees. Above all, pressure should not cease without a quid pro quo, very likely in some other area.

Certain basics are beyond compromise. But many policies can and should be stopped or moderated in exchange for something else. American aid to resistance fighters in Afghanistan, for example, should continue. The embarrassment and material and human losses suffered by the Soviet Union in Afghanistan are of course beneficial to the West. But eventually there may come a point when the Soviets might be willing to curb certain actions elsewhere in the world in exchange for Western accommodation over Afghanistan. In such situations, there is always the risk that we will be outmaneuvered by the Soviets. But, despite such dangers, the willingness to deal at the right moment is essential.

This very much applies to an especially neuralgic area, Eastern Europe, currently in a state of considerable political restlessness. Any blunt, open political intervention there would be extremely, perhaps intolerably, provocative to the Soviets. But there should always be unpublicized, indirect probes, to be eased or stepped up in reaction to restrained or aggressive Soviet behavior elsewhere.

VII

Certain other areas require specific consideration because they will continue to test the Administration in special if quite disparate ways. They are the North Atlantic Alliance, the Middle East and Central America.

Obviously, NATO is by far the most important to America's position in the world and to its permanent contest with the Soviets. The Administration started out on the wrong foot with the allies. Somewhat paranoid in the best of times, West European leaders and intellectuals were panicked by Reagan's rhetoric and image, by some of the rather casual if actually routine references to nuclear war, and especially by the attempt to veto the Soviet pipeline, which seemed to impose economic sacrifices on the West Europeans when the United States was lifting its grain embargo. Since those days of anger and suspicion, the atmosphere between the United States and the allies has improved considerably.

Today, NATO is widely proclaimed to be in crisis. The litany is familiar. Militarily, NATO strategy is seen in disarray: inadequate conventional forces to resist a possible Soviet attack, and a less than credible nuclear deterrent. Politically, Britain, Holland and West Germany harbor strong, more or less neutralist-pacifist forces which want to opt out of the East-West conflict—and, some would say, out of history. These forces are in the minority, but majority governments (which may not be in the majority forever) cannot afford to ignore them. West European countries tend to press for American accommodation with the Soviet Union, sometimes, it seems, at any price, refuse to support or understand American responsibilities in the Third World, and still take for granted the American defense of their territory.

Either in sorrow or in anger, various remedies or retaliations are being advocated and pressed on the Administration. These include what Richard Burt, Assistant Secretary of State for European Affairs, calls "global unilateralism" (i.e., reducing forces in Europe so as to enhance U.S. flexibility to act in other regions) and "Atlantic reconstruction" (threatening withdrawal from NATO to provoke the allies into doing more for their own defense). The leading reconstructionist, Senator Sam Nunn (D-Ga.), has called for American troop reductions in Europe unless the allies meet a detailed and sophisticated list of requirements to improve NATO's military footing. But the threat of troop withdrawal in the near future is likely to be counterproductive. The NATO commander, General Bernard W. Rogers, evangelizes tirelessly for larger European conventional forces to be equipped with dazzling new high-tech weapons. But the price tag is estimated to add a one-percent increase in defense spending to the three-percent pledge the allies have already made but few have kept.

Various military thinkers are advancing new strategies, including mobility and counterattack, to avoid what *The Economist* has called a Maginot Line mentality without a Maginot Line. But such schemes make the Europeans highly nervous. Henry A. Kissinger has advanced an imaginative plan for restructuring the Alliance, with an American secretary general and a European commander, to emphasize the need for greater responsibility by the Europeans for their own defense.[4] The plan was welcomed as highly thought-provoking, which presumably was its purpose, but few leaders in NATO countries are likely to do anything about it any time soon.

The Administration attitude toward much of this agitation about NATO was summed up by Burt, who conceded the need for improvements while adding: "There must also be limits to our departures" (his own version of *"Surtout, pas trop de zèle"*).[5] That may not be a bad prescription for American policy toward the Alliance in the second term. A top priority must be to undercut and contain the potentially disastrous left-wing neutralist movements. This is best done through a stable, realistic policy toward the Soviets, including arms control. The Administration should continue to press for greater European defense contributions in various forms, even though this contribution is considerably more significant than popularly understood in the United States.[6] The Administration should encourage any proposals for greater military cooperation among European countries, including that ever-elusive goal, standardization of equipment.

Reagan II should also continue to press for greater cooperation to prevent the transfer of military technology to the Soviet Union, for greater solidarity in major East-West crises, and for more of a role by European countries in "out-of-area" contingencies. As always, these efforts will be frustrating and often futile. We will have to accept the fact that the European view of the world, and of the Soviet Union, is different from ours. We will continue to be lectured on proper global conduct by nations which achieved their present peaceable outlook not through wisdom or virtue, but through exhaustion, after

---

[4] *Time*, March 5, 1984.

[5] Address to the *Time* Conference on the Atlantic Alliance, April 1983, *Department of State Bulletin*, August 1983.

[6] See Secretary of Defense Caspar W. Weinberger, *Report on Allied Contributions to the Common Defense*, Department of Defense, March 1984.

hundreds of years of waging their own wars. But we will have to continue, even at great cost, to help hold the indispensable Alliance together. With much patience, some diplomatic skill, the quieter kind of public relations—and the almost always dependable help from the Soviet Union in the form of political overkill—the task is not beyond us.

A major problem between the United States and Western Europe lies in the economic area. There are major joint concerns about growth in an increasingly interdependent industrialized world, including policies toward the developing countries. The Europeans keep complaining about high American interest rates resulting from the deficits. While these complaints are justified, they are also excessive and tend to overshadow the Europeans' own responsibility for outmoded and ineffective trade and industrial policies. Fortunately there is a growing realization in Western Europe that central economic control and welfare statism are no longer working very well. It is not yet clear, however, what is to take their place.

As far as the developing countries are concerned, the debt crisis has been at least temporarily alleviated by the International Monetary Fund, backed by a somewhat reluctant United States and other Western industrialized states. Longer-range solutions remain elusive. There is a healthy realization among many Third World countries that prospects are very dim for achieving a "new international economic order" and the pieties of the Brandt Commission, all pointing to massive wealth transfers from the industrialized developing countries. The Reagan Administration's Third World prescription of capitalism, entrepreneurship and market incentives is theoretically sound, as has been acknowledged, indirectly, even by China. But in many developing societies, these prescriptions standing alone will not mean much or will be politically destructive. They will have to be part of a mixed economic system. Without going into details here, it is obvious that the Reagan Administration has a major opportunity in the economic area, including the international exchange system. It would also be useful if Reagan II could quietly abandon such dubious missionary efforts as trying to impose certain views about population control and abortion on other societies.

VIII

In the Middle East, the Administration has swung from overactive and ill-conceived involvement (former Secretary of State Alexander M. Haig's whirlwind attempt to rally the area for an anti-Soviet "strategic consensus") to extreme caution bordering on inactivity. The attitude in the second term should be somewhere in between.

The Administration can base itself on one solid conceptual piece of work, the Reagan peace initiative of September 1982, essentially a distillation of many earlier comprehensive peace plans. But the Administration never followed through with further diplomatic action. Instead it got lost in maneuvers to bring about a settlement in Lebanon, having failed to keep the Israelis from invading, if not actually having condoned the move. Today there are some new factors in the area which offer some modest opportunities.

Israel has a new coalition government, however shaky, whose prime minister and Labor Party members hold somewhat more moderate views on West Bank policy and other issues than the Likud governments of Menachem Begin and Yitzhak Shamir. Virtually all factions now want the Israeli army out of Lebanon, provided some kind of halfway reassuring security arrangements for South Lebanon can be achieved. Syria, enjoying the new prominence which it snatched from the jaws of defeat thanks to Soviet resupply and inept American diplomacy, is in no hurry to let the Israelis go. But it is finding its role as peacekeeper in Lebanon somewhat sticky. The ever-cautious King Hussein of Jordan has taken the very bold step—for him—of resuming diplomatic relations with Egypt while continuing his public refusal to have anything to do with the peace process. It is conceivable that Iraq may eventually follow Hussein in his move toward Cairo.

The United States should encourage what has already, if prematurely, been called the Egyptian-Jordanian axis. At the same time it must deal with Syria, treating it less as a Soviet dependency than as a regional mini-power with local interests and fears of its own. A tacit arrangement between Syria and Israel to stabilize the situation in Lebanon seems quite possible. That is a long way from a point at which Syria might stop vetoing any significant peace move, but under the circumstances in the Middle East one must be grateful for small mercies.

Some analysts argue that, ever since the Lebanese invasion, the Palestinians are no longer the key to the Middle East. The suggestion is that the Palestinian problem can be ignored with impunity.[7] It is obvious that the Palestine Liberation Organi-

[7] Robert W. Tucker, "Our Obsolete Middle East Policy," *Commentary*, May 1983.

zation has been shattered, with one part merely a Syrian puppet organization and another part, under Yassir Arafat, a cause in search of a home. It is also true that among Arab states both the sympathy (always conditional) for, and the fear of, the PLO has been greatly overshadowed by a new concern with Islamic fundamentalism. Nevertheless, the Palestinian issue cannot be put aside permanently. The Administration should pressure the Israeli government to improve conditions on the West Bank and to place a freeze on new settlements. Prime Minister Shimon Peres may be receptive to this.

In U.N. Security Council votes and in other ways, the Administration should also attempt to restore at least some image of evenhandedness toward Israel and the Arab states. The Reagan peace initiative should be pursued behind the scenes, avoiding big public efforts that are too likely to end in disappointment. Meanwhile the Administration should look for every opportunity to take small bilateral steps to improve the situation and ease the atmosphere. In a postmortem on Lebanon, Richard W. Murphy, Assistant Secretary of State for Near Eastern Affairs, put it well: "We must work on the margins to protect our interests." He continued on this sobering note: "Lebanon reminded us that we cannot remake society, that we can work for peace but we cannot impose it. It also reminded us that the commitments we undertake must be ones that we as a government and as a people can sustain over time. We did not do well in that regard. Hence the need for both pragmatism and fortitude."[8]

IX

Nothing is more futile or arid than the debate between those who argue that the chief cause of Third World insurgencies is economic and social injustice, and those who argue that it is interference by the Soviets or their surrogates. Obviously both forces are at work, reinforcing each other, and both must be coped with. The Reagan Administration has balanced the two approaches—the stress on force and the stress on development—more successfully than it is generally given credit for.

The Reagan team undoubtedly started with an excessively apocalyptic view of the situation. But it was essentially right in believing that a successful communist revolution in El Salvador, or neighboring countries, no matter how seriously driven by

[8] Richard W. Murphy, "The Response from the United States to Current Political Developments in the Middle East," *American-Arab Affairs*, Spring 1984.

the thirst for social justice, would be an American defeat. It can be argued reasonably that such revolutions are not preventable at acceptable costs, but it cannot be maintained that, in the Central American context, they are not against American interests.

The Reagan Administration often gave the impression that it was unconcerned about human rights in the area, and that it regarded dealing with this problem as a sort of moralistic luxury that could not be indulged in the midst of a civil war. U.N. Ambassador Jeane Kirkpatrick's now celebrated analysis distinguishing between irreversible totalitarian regimes and reversible or improvable authoritarian ones is impeccable in theory. In practice it does not answer the question, crucial in many parts of the Third World, about just when an authoritarian regime, no matter how strong its anti-communist credentials, becomes so corrupt and unpopular that it loses all legitimacy and, in fact, opens the door to totalitarianism. This almost always involves excruciatingly difficult decisions. Under Carter these decisions were made too naïvely, and human rights policy was too simplistic and patronizing. But such phenomena as the death squads in El Salvador had to be coped with for the most practical of reasons.

For some time now the Reagan Administration seems to have understood this and has in fact used a great deal of influence to curb the squads' worst abuses. Without such progress, the election of President José Napoleón Duarte would have been impossible. This election was something of a turning point—and incidentally one that would not have occurred had the Administration followed the counsel of those congressmen who, since 1981, have sought to condition continued military aid to the Salvadoran government on the commencement of indiscriminate negotiations between the government and the guerrillas, which would have led to "power-sharing." The election had significant impact on foreign countries. In 1981, France and Mexico had issued a joint statement calling the Salvadoran rebels "a representative political force," which implicitly equated their legitimacy with that of the government; such a statement would hardly be issued today. Last July, on the occasion of Duarte's visit, the Bonn government resumed aid to El Salvador. An extremely useful move would be the repeal of the Helms Amendment, which bans U.S. aid to land reform in El Salvador.

It is painfully obvious that Duarte's position remains highly fragile. The slight improvement in the performance of the Salvadoran army may not last. The far right may yet succeed in sabotaging Duarte's regime, especially if he pursues his dialogue with the guerrilla leaders. Moreover it is far from clear what can come of this dialogue since, from the beginning, the guerrilla leadership has not been interested in the success of a moderate, reformist regime like Duarte's, but in revolution. There are signs that the guerrillas are flagging militarily, and that they are more than ever split into hostile factions. It is premature to hope that they will put down their arms, trusting in the government's security guarantees, and take part in elections. But that is in effect what happened in Venezuela in the late 1960s, as well as what is beginning to happen in Colombia today, and the prospect of a similar outcome in El Salvador is at least somewhat more plausible than it seemed a year ago.

The situation in Nicaragua is more complicated and less hopeful. In considering that situation one should, at the outset, discard a great deal of cant about nonintervention. President Anastasio Somoza was overthrown, at least in part, thanks to American intervention. The Sandinista regime is clearly supported from the outside with arms as well as thousands of Cuban, Soviet, East German and other East Bloc advisers who constitute a significant influence in a country of 2.9 million. The claim that the Sandinistas were forced into kicking out their democratic political partners and lining up with Cuba because of American hostility is plainly wrong. By January 1981, the Carter Administration had allotted to the Sandinista government $117 million in aid, the largest amount from any single country. In its first two years, the new government in Managua received five times more U.S. aid than Somoza received in his final two years. But it is now evident that the Sandinistas planned to build an enormous army (by Central American standards) long before the United States turned hostile.

Still, with all this conceded, it is not clear what the United States hopes to or can accomplish in Nicaragua. The choices for Washington are painfully limited. Much can be said in defense of aid to the counterrevolutionaries, or "contras." They are not simply mercenaries or holdovers from the Somoza National Guard, but a genuine anti-communist movement, and it is not absurd to call them freedom fighters. Yet there is no serious prospect that by themselves they could overthrow the

Sandinista regime, much as that would be in the American
national interest. But they have proved important as an instrument to make the regime more malleable; there is little evidence to support the opposite view, namely that they solidified
the regime. By cutting off aid to the contras, Congress irre-
sponsibly deprived the United States of an important bargaining counter.

Contadora can be useful, depending on how it is handled.
The provisions of the original proposal are potentially far-
reaching. As applied to Nicaragua they could, in effect, amount
to interference in the country's internal affairs, in order to
change and democratize the regime; and could, if pushed to
their maximum, provide for the removal of Cuban and other
foreign forces, prevent foreign bases, and eliminate arms assistance to other revolutionary forces elsewhere in the area.

But the problems are several. First, some of the language in
the treaty drafts seen so far is slippery. Second, it is far from
clear how effectively the provisions could be enforced. Third,
barring special unilateral arrangements, the Contadora provisions could mean a cutoff of American military help to the
Duarte regime and other democratic forces in Central America. A deal has been suggested whereby the Sandinistas promise
to stop aiding the guerrillas in El Salvador in return for
cessation of American support for the contras. In view of the
congressional cutoff of funding for the contras, that may be
academic; but at any rate it does not seem like a very advantageous deal for the United States. In general, the United States
should continue working with Contadora, but press for foolproof enforcement and maximum interpretation of its provisions (including the rejection of the November Nicaraguan
elections as legitimate). This may mean a lengthy delay, but
America should not let itself be pressured into accepting a
premature and incomplete agreement. Standing on principle
and playing for time may not be the worst policy here. Obviously, the appearance in Nicaragua of sophisticated offensive
weaponry could change the equation.

X

Ultimately, the most important foreign policy goal for
Reagan II lies in domestic politics: to achieve at least some
measure of consensus on foreign and defense issues, especially
regarding the Soviet Union.

Unfortunately, the more or less bipartisan approach to foreign policy that prevailed from World War II till Korea—some would say till Vietnam—was neither typical nor natural. In a functioning democracy the major issues of how a country deals with other countries, how it copes with questions of war and peace, cannot for long be excluded from the political process. For these matters are close to a nation's sense of self, its perception of its values and its meaning. In most elections, including the last one, it is simply unrealistic to ask both sides to throw away a major weapon, namely the argument that the opposing side is wrongheaded about the world—naïve or villainous, weak or reckless. And this is not a matter of cynicism, or at least not primarily. The more sincere the disputants, the more implacable. Yet there are special moments—this may be one—when the normal partisan quarrel over foreign affairs can be muted if not suspended.

It will be very difficult, putting it mildly, to persuade the fervent ideologues in the Republican Party of this. They are riding high, and they see the election as a clear mandate for the hard-line Reagan and for their more extreme goals. Nor will the right wing necessarily hesitate to attack the President if it considers him too weak.[9] While victorious, President Reagan will also increasingly be a lame duck. Nevertheless, he remains a hero to a majority of Americans, and thus a huge asset to the party; the right-wingers will have to be careful not to go against him too blatantly. Besides, he benefits from what might be called the Nixon-China syndrome: his anti-communist credentials are so strong that the country at large would have a hard time accepting the notion that he had gone soft.

The experience of the first term has shown that extreme hard-line positions not only fail to work with the Russians, but fail to work in domestic politics as well. An analysis of preelection polls and the election returns themselves makes clear that voters liked Reagan's patriotism, his emphasis on American strength and even rearmament. Especially blue-collar workers liked his macho image. But at the same time, voters wanted far more serious effort in arms control and peaceful diplomacy. The fact that President Reagan moved in that direction in recent months neutralized the peace issue, which was one of Walter Mondale's big potential assets, and helped increase the Reagan landslide.

The race for 1988 has already begun. If the President wants

[9] See Norman Podhoretz, "Appeasement by Any Other Name," *Commentary*, July 1983.

to play to history, leaving a legacy of better relations with the Soviets, as well as gain a serious chance of another Republican victory in 1988, everything indicates that he must follow more or less centrist policies. The best hope for the Democrats would be a Republican candidate and a set of policies to revive the "warmonger" fear of the earlier Reagan days. Moreover, despite his huge victory, Reagan will have to deal with a Democratic majority in the House of Representatives, where the Republicans made only modest gains. And even if North Carolina's Senator Jesse Helms were to assume the chairmanship of the Senate Foreign Relations Committee, President Reagan would not have clear sailing for his policies in the Senate (in fact, he might occasionally need Democrats to protect him from Helms' more outrageous positions). Thus, for political reasons as well as for idealistic ones, Reagan has every incentive to reach out to the Democrats in search of consensus.

Would the Democrats have any incentive to meet him even halfway? There is a strong case that they do. They have learned that the peace issue is highly complicated. Just as Reagan had to move to the center, they did too. Although there was much emotional support for a nuclear freeze and for the notion of banning nuclear weapons from outer space, voters did not favor positions they suspected might mean unilateral U.S. concessions. And if Reagan II is at all successful in restarting arms control talks and in otherwise improving U.S.-Soviet relations, the Democrats will have very little to gain from the issue. They would either have to come in on the left of the Republicans or else follow a me-too line, both politically highly unattractive. Thus they would have considerable reason to ease the peace issue out of politics, concentrate their 1988 strategy on the economy, and earn at least some of the credit that would derive from bipartisanship.

The Democrats would have to disown the quasi-isolationist and quasi-pacifist positions of many liberals (which Walter Mondale did only partly toward the end of the campaign). Similarly, Reagan would have to continue distancing himself from the far right. As the preceding pages suggest, there is a lot of room for him to do that without in any real sense "going soft." He can argue with reason that he is now able to negotiate from strength. A tough but realistic position on arms control may well win bipartisan approval. (A formally constituted, bipartisan body to deal with Soviet policy, which has been proposed, sounds excessively bureaucratic, but if it is necessary to get Congress involved, it should be tried.)

Agreement might be harder on issues like Central America and the military budget. But among the things Reagan could safely concede would be some further reductions in the defense budget combined with overall reform of the armed forces. Defense expenditures growing at a somewhat slower but sustainable rate backed by bipartisan consensus would be far more impressive to the Soviets than higher defense expenditures, which are probably not sustainable and at the mercy of congressional or partisan politics. One of the greatest boons to the Soviets over the years has been American inconsistency and the chance of playing Democrats off against Republicans. To avoid this and to achieve at least partial consensus would be worth a great deal.

George P. Shultz

NEW REALITIES AND
NEW WAYS OF THINKING

Albert Einstein once observed that the advent of nuclear weapons had changed everything except our modes of thinking. If even so dramatic a development as the nuclear revolution has taken a long time to be fully understood, how much longer has it usually taken to understand the implications of the more subtle, intangible historical changes taking place around us.

The international order at the end of this century is certain to be far different from the pattern of world politics when the century began. The distribution of power and the dynamics of international relations have undergone a continuous transformation, driven by many factors—technology, economic and social changes, and the often-underestimated force of ideas. This process goes on; history never stops. As we head toward the 21st century, Einstein's observation takes on new relevance: our ways of thinking must adapt to new realities; it is imperative that we grasp the new trends and understand their implications.

The United States of America is not just an onlooker, however. We are participants and we are engaged. America is again in a position to have a major influence over the direction of events—and the traditional goals and values of the American people have *not* changed. We have a duty to help shape the trends, as they evolve, in accordance with our ideals and interests, to help construct a new pattern of international stability that will ensure peace, prosperity and freedom for coming generations.

What are the forces of change? What new "modes of thinking" are required? And what are the possible elements of a new and more secure international system?

II

The U.S.-Soviet relationship, for better or worse, remains a crucial determinant of the prospects for world peace, even

---

George P. Shultz is Secretary of State.

though the political predominance of the two superpowers is less than it was a few decades ago. How to manage this relationship as conditions change remains a major conceptual challenge for the United States.

So long as the Soviet system is driven by ideology and national ambition to seek to aggrandize its power and undermine the interests of the democracies, true friendship and cooperation will remain out of reach. The West must resist this Soviet power-drive vigorously if there is to be any hope for lasting stability. At the same time, in the thermonuclear age both sides have a common interest in survival; therefore both sides have an incentive to moderate the rivalry and to seek ways to control nuclear weapons and reduce the risks of war. We cannot know whether such a steady Western policy will, over time, lead to a mellowing of the Soviet system. Perhaps not. But the West has the same responsibility in either case: to resist Soviet encroachments firmly while holding the door open to more constructive possibilities.

Today, with the accession of Mr. Gorbachev, there may be a fresh opportunity to explore these more constructive possibilities. President Reagan is approaching this prospect in a positive spirit, as well as with a realistic appreciation that the difficulties between our countries are grounded in objective problems that we must work hard to resolve.

The democracies, unlike the Soviets, have long had difficulty maintaining consistency, coherence, discipline and a sense of strategy. Free societies are often impatient. Western attitudes have fluctuated between extremes of gloom and pessimism, on the one hand, and susceptibility to a Soviet smile on the other. Our ways of thinking have tended too often to focus either on increasing our strength or on pursuing negotiations; we have found it hard to do both simultaneously—which is clearly the most sensible course and probably the only way we can sustain either our defense programs or our ability to negotiate.

In the last four years, nevertheless, the underlying conditions that affect U.S.-Soviet relations have changed dramatically. Ten to fifteen years ago, when the United States was beset by economic difficulties, neglecting its defenses, and hesitant about its role in the world, the Soviets exploited these conditions. They relentlessly continued to build up militarily; they and their clients moved more boldly in the geopolitical arena, intervening in such places as Angola, Cambodia, Ethiopia and Afghanistan, believing that the West was incapable of resisting.

They had reason for confidence that what they call the global "correlation of forces" was shifting in their favor.

Today, our key alliances are more united than ever before. The United States is restoring its military strength and economic vigor and has regained its self-assurance; we have a President with a fresh mandate from the people for an active role of leadership. The Soviets, in contrast, face profound structural economic difficulties and restless allies; their diplomacy and their clients are on the defensive in many parts of the world. We have reason to be confident that the "correlation of forces" is shifting back in our favor.

Nevertheless, history will not do our work for us. Experience suggests that the Soviets will periodically do something, somewhere, that is abhorrent or inimical to our interests, dampening hopes for an improvement in East-West relations. Witness the examples of Czechoslovakia, Afghanistan, the Korean Air Lines shootdown and Soviet human rights practices. The question is how the West should respond to such outrages. Clearly our objective should be to act in a way that could help discipline Soviet behavior; at the same time, our posture should not leave our own strategy vulnerable to periodic disruption by such shocks.

We must never let ourselves be so wedded to improving relations with the Soviets that we turn a blind eye to actions that undermine the very foundation of stable relations; symbolic responses to outrageous Soviet actions have their place, and so do penalties and sanctions. Experience also shows, however, that as a practical matter we can best deter or undo Soviet geopolitical encroachments by helping, in one way or another, those who are resisting directly on the ground. And many negotiations and endeavors we undertake with the Soviets serve mutual interests—indeed, they all should.

Thus we are left with tough choices. Whether important negotiations ought to be interrupted after some Soviet outrage will always be a complex calculation. When the Soviets shot down the Korean airliner in 1983, President Reagan made sure the world knew the full unvarnished truth about the atrocity; nevertheless, he also sent our arms control negotiators back to Geneva because he believed that a reduction in nuclear weapons was a critical priority.

In short, our "mode of thinking" must seek a sustainable strategy geared to *American* goals and interests, in the light of Soviet behavior but not just in reaction to it. Such a strategy requires a continuing willingness to solve problems through negotiation where this serves our interests (and presumably mutual interests). Our leverage will come from creating objective realities that give the Soviets a growing stake in better relations with us across the board: by continuing to modernize our defenses, assist our friends and confront Soviet challenges. We must learn to pursue a strategy geared to long-term thinking and based on both negotiation and strength simultaneously, if we are to build a stable U.S.-Soviet relationship for the next century.

III

The intellectual challenge of a new era faces us in a related dimension, namely arms control. The continuing revolution in technology means that the strategic balance—and the requirements of deterrence—are never static. Unfortunately, conventional modes of thinking about many of these questions continue to lag behind reality.

Standard strategic doctrine in the West has ultimately relied, for decades, on the balance of terror—the confrontation of offensive arsenals by which the two sides threaten each other with mass extermination. Deterrence has worked under these conditions, and we must not let go of what has worked until we know that something better is genuinely available. Nevertheless, for political, strategic and even moral reasons, we owe it to our people to explore the possibility that we can do better than the conventional wisdom that our defense strategy *must* rely on offensive threats and *must* leave our people unprotected against attack. The Soviets, for their part, have always attached enormous doctrinal and practical importance to strategic defense, including not only air defense and civil defense but a deployed and modernized anti-ballistic missile system around Moscow—and intensive research into new defensive technologies.

Adjusting our strategic thinking to the constant advance of technology is never an easy process. The vehemence of some of the criticism of the President's Strategic Defense Initiative (SDI), in my view, comes less from the debate over technical feasibility—which future research will settle one way or another in an objective manner—than from the passionate defense of orthodox doctrine in the face of changing strategic realities. We are proceeding with SDI research because we see a positive, and indeed revolutionary, potential: defensive measures may become available that could badly disrupt any attack on us or our allies and thereby render obsolete the threat of an offensive first strike. A new strategic equilibrium based on defensive technologies and sharply reduced offensive deployments is likely to be the most stable and secure arrangement of all.

Our concept can be described as follows: during the next ten years, the U.S. objective is a radical reduction in the power of existing and planned offensive nuclear arms, as well as the stabilization of the relationship between offensive and defensive nuclear arms, whether on earth or in space. We are even now looking forward to a period of transition to a more stable world, with greatly reduced levels of nuclear arms and an enhanced ability to deter war based upon an increasing contribution of non-nuclear defenses against offensive nuclear arms. This period of transition could lead to the eventual elimination of all nuclear arms, both offensive and defensive. A world free of nuclear arms is an ultimate objective to which we, the Soviet Union, and all other nations can agree.

IV

As the political dominance of the superpowers began to erode in the last few decades, some saw a five-power world emerging—with the United States, the Soviet Union, Western Europe, China and Japan as the major players. After the energy crisis of the early 1970s, others emphasized the increasing importance of the North-South relationship. Some saw the U.S.-Soviet relationship as still central.

There are elements of truth in all these perceptions. Nevertheless, in the mid-1980s, in my view, the most striking trend in world politics is something else: the growing dynamism, cohesion and cooperation of like-minded nations that share an important set of positive goals.

American foreign policy is driven by positive goals—peace, democracy, liberty and human rights; racial justice; economic and social progress; the strengthening of cooperation and the rule of law. They are goals that inspire peoples and nations around the world, and they may well turn out to be the organizing principles of an international order that embraces the great majority of mankind. Already we see them reflected in new trends in many regions of the world and in many dimensions of foreign policy.

America's closest and most lasting international relationships, of course, are its alliances with its fellow democracies. This is no accident. Our ties with our democratic friends abroad have an enduring quality precisely because they rest on a moral base, not only a base of strategic interest. When George Washington advised his countrymen to steer clear of permanent alliances, his attitude was colored by the fact that there were hardly any other fellow democracies in those days. We were among the first, and we had good reason to be wary of entanglements with countries that did not share our democratic principles. In any case, we now *define* our strategic interests in terms that embrace the safety and well-being of the democratic world.

Today's conditions define the tasks of the Atlantic alliance. There is a new awareness, for example, of the importance of strengthening conventional defenses, as a way of bolstering Europe's security while reducing NATO's reliance on nuclear weapons. A strong Western deterrent posture is the most solid basis for engaging the East in constructive negotiations. For the short run, the allies are taking steps to improve NATO readiness and infrastructure. For the longer run, the alliance is looking to correct other critical deficiencies, as well as addressing the fundamental challenge of improving the efficiency of allied defense procurement.

The United States has always supported Western European unity, knowing that a strong Europe, while it would be a competitor in some ways, was in the overall interest of the free world. We wish the European Community well; we encourage our European friends to make further progress in developing a true Europe-wide market and in breaking down structural rigidities that impede both economic expansion and effective economic cooperation with us.

We also see, in Europe, new and creative thinking about the continuing pursuit of political unity, and about strengthening West European cooperation in the defense field. We support both these goals. The West can only benefit from a major European role in world affairs. And the peoples of Western Europe should see defense as an endeavor they undertake for their own future, not as a favor to the United States. With statesmanship on both sides of the Atlantic, this evolution will strengthen the common defense and heighten the sense of common political purpose among the democracies.

As we think about Europe's evolution, we cannot forget Eastern Europe. Since the days of the Marshall Plan, when the

West invited the East to join, we have always wanted the success of Western Europe to be a beacon to *all* of Europe. The present political division of the continent is wholly artificial; it exists only because it has been imposed by brute Soviet power; the United States has never recognized it as legitimate or permanent. In certain countries, there are efforts at liberalization. But *all* the peoples of Eastern Europe are capable of, deserve and yearn for something better. In recent years we have seen the powerful aspiration for free trade unions, for economic reform, for political and religious freedom, for true peace and security, for human rights as promised by the Helsinki accords. We hope to see the day when the Soviet Union changes its mode of thinking to consider its own security in terms compatible with the freedom, security and independence of its neighbors.

In East Asia and the Pacific, another new reality is changing our perception of the world. The economic dynamism of this region is taking on increasing importance, as a factor in America's foreign trade, as an economic model for the developing world, and as a unique and attractive vision of the future. We see the countries of free East Asia growing at seven percent a year over the past decade; for the past five years, our trade with East Asia and the Pacific has been greater than our trade with any other region and its relative importance continues to grow. In 1984, U.S. trade with the region reached $165 billion—about 30 percent of total U.S. trade. The Association of Southeast Asian Nations has become an impressive example of economic development and regional political cooperation. The Republic of Korea is a spectacular economic success story. Japan is playing a larger role—responsibly, positively and cooperatively—commensurate with its growing strength. In the People's Republic of China, the hopes for economic modernization have been invested—wisely—in a bold program of reform. China's long march to the market is a truly historic event—a great nation throwing off outmoded economic doctrines and liberating the energies of its talented people.

There are, of course, problems that pose dangers to this bright economic future: the Soviet military buildup in the region; aggression by the Soviet Union and its clients in Afghanistan and Cambodia; unresolved tensions on the Korean peninsula; internal problems in various countries. East Asia has a rich heritage of civilization—and also a turbulent history of bitter conflict. The symbolism of Angkor Wat—the damage done by modern violence to a great ancient monument—is both a paradox and a warning.

Nevertheless, the most striking trend in the region today is the positive trend, especially the new movement toward wider collaboration. A sense of Pacific community is emerging among many nations with an extraordinary diversity of cultures, races and political systems. There is an expanding practice of regional consultation and a developing sense of common interest in regional security. In this sense, a decade after Vietnam, the United States has more than restored its position in Asia. We can be proud of the vitality of our alliances, friendships and productive ties in this promising region. If nations act with wisdom and statesmanship, we may well be at the threshold of a new era in international relations in the Pacific basin.

In Latin America, another kind of trend is apparent—the steady advance of democracy. Democracy is hardly a new idea, but this new development *is* revising some earlier assumptions in some quarters about the world's political future. Pessimists in some quarters used to maintain that the industrial democracies were doomed to permanent minority status in the world community. Today, there is mounting evidence that the ideal of liberty is alive and well. In the Western hemisphere, over 90 percent of the population of Latin America and the Caribbean today live under governments that are democratic—in contrast to only one-third in 1979. In less than six years, popularly elected democrats have replaced dictators in Argentina, Bolivia, Ecuador, El Salvador, Honduras, Panama, Peru, Grenada, Brazil and Uruguay. Guatemala is in transition to democracy. After a long twilight of dictatorship, this hemispheric trend toward free elections and representative government is something to be applauded and supported.

The United States has always been a champion of democracy. Democratic institutions are the best guarantor of human rights, and also the best long-term guarantor of stability. On every continent, we see a trend toward democracy or else a yearning for democracy; both are vivid demonstrations that the idea of liberty is far from a culture-bound aspiration or monopoly of the industrialized West.

Today we see a significant new phenomenon. After years of guerrilla insurgencies led by communists against pro-Western governments, we now see dramatic and heartening examples of popular insurgencies *against* communist regimes. Today, in a variety of different circumstances—in Nicaragua, in Afghanistan, in Cambodia, in Africa—Marxist-Leninist rulers have clearly failed to suppress the aspiration for representative government. And communist systems have proved, uniformly, to be economic disasters. The American people have a long and noble tradition of supporting the struggle of other peoples for freedom, democracy and independence. In the nineteenth century we supported Simon Bolívar, Polish patriots and others seeking freedom—reciprocating, in a way, the aid given to us in our own revolution by other nations like France. If we turned our backs on this tradition, we would be conceding the Soviet notion that communist revolutions are irreversible while everything else is up for grabs; we would be, in effect, enacting the Brezhnev Doctrine into American law. So long as communist dictatorships feel free to aid and abet insurgencies in the name of "socialist internationalism," why must the democracies—the target of this threat—be inhibited from defending their own interests and the cause of democracy itself?

The future of democracy is precisely what is at stake in Central America. With Soviet and Cuban support, the Sandinistas are seeking to consolidate a totalitarian system in Nicaragua and to promote subversion throughout the region. Our policy is to promote democracy, reform and human rights; to support economic development; to help provide a security shield against those who seek to spread tyranny by force; and to support dialogue and negotiation both within and among the countries of the region. We are backing democratic governments and democratic political forces against extremists of both the left and the right. If we abandon those seeking democracy, the extremists will gain and the forces of moderation and decency will be the victims. This is why the Administration has worked so hard, and will continue to work hard, for effective negotiations, for economic and security assistance, and for the bipartisan plan that emerged from the Kissinger commission. Our nation's vital interests *and* moral responsibility require us to stand by our friends in their struggle for freedom and against those who glorify violent revolution and repression.

In other parts of the world, as well, the United States is actively engaged in the search for peaceful solutions to regional conflicts. Such mediation is, of course, a traditional American role, but new conditions always call for new ways of thinking—on the part of all parties—about how to make progress.

In the Middle East, for example, we have seen signs of a new realism and a new commitment on the part of key regional actors. If pursued, this could create the conditions for progress, which will come when both sides agree to sit down together at the negotiating table. The United States remains convinced that President Reagan's initiative of September 1, 1982, is the most promising route to a solution. We are intensively engaged this year in encouraging our Israeli and Arab friends to take further steps toward peace. We will continue to support and encourage those who seek peace against those who promote violence and try to block all progress.

In southern Africa, as well, the United States has a key role to play. We must pursue the dual objectives of racial justice and regional security. These twin challenges call for serious analysis and sober thinking, not emotional responses. We have already accomplished much, but our influence is not infinite. Today there is less cross-border violence in southern Africa than at any time in more than a decade. Progress is being made toward a Namibia settlement. We have strengthened ties with Mozambique and other regional states. And South Africa itself has developed cooperative relations with many of its neighbors.

Within South Africa, a dynamic of evolution is already at work. More positive change is occurring now than in the 1970s or 1960s or 1950s. The positive influence of the American presence—our diplomacy, our companies, our assistance programs for black South Africans—is helping to build the basis for further change. Apartheid must go. But the only course consistent with American values is to engage ourselves as a force for constructive, peaceful change while there is still a chance. It cannot be our choice to cheer on, from the sidelines, the forces of polarization that could erupt in a race war; it is not our job to exacerbate hardship, which could lead to the same result.

v

In the global economy, an important shift of another kind is taking place—an intellectual shift. Reality is intruding on some long-held notions about economic policy. Lord Keynes' point about practical men being slaves to some defunct economist may be less true now than in the past. Or perhaps the views expressed by Adam Smith over two centuries ago on the creation of the "wealth of nations" are once again showing their practical validity. At any rate, recent experience has fueled a broad and long-overdue skepticism about statist solutions, central planning and government direction.

This intellectual shift is partly the product of the extraordinary vigor of the American recovery. The United States has revised its tax system to provide real incentives to work, to save, to invest, to take risks, to be efficient. We have reduced government regulation, intervention and control. We have opened opportunities for freer competition in transportation, finance, communication, manufacturing and distribution. Last year's real growth in the gross national product was the sharpest increase since 1951; inflation (as measured by the GNP deflator) was the lowest since 1967. The overall result has been the extraordinary creation of over seven million new jobs in two years.

Success inspires emulation. Not only in East Asia, but on every continent—Europe, Latin America, Africa and elsewhere in Asia—we see movement to decentralize, to deregulate, to denationalize, to reduce rigidity and to enlarge the scope for individual producers and consumers to cooperate freely through markets. In Africa, the American response to the food crisis includes not only a tremendous relief effort but a longer-term aid program supporting African efforts of economic reform, particularly in agriculture.

Serious challenges to the global economy remain, but the future holds promise. A worldwide revolution in economic thought and economic policy is under way.

And it is coming just in time, because it coincides with yet another revolution—a revolution in the technological base of the global economy. This is what Walter Wriston has called "the onrushing age of information technology." The combination of microchip computers, advanced telecommunications—and a continuing process of innovation—is not only transforming communication and other aspects of daily life, but is also challenging the very concepts of national sovereignty and the role of government in society.

The very existence of these new technologies is yet another testimony to the crucial importance of entrepreneurship—and government policies that give free rein to entrepreneurship—as the wellspring of technological creativity and economic growth. The closed societies of the East are likely to fall far behind in these areas—and Western societies that maintain too many restrictions on economic activity run the same risk. Moreover, any government that attempts heavy-handedly to control or regulate or tax the flow of electronic information will find itself stifling the growth of the world economy as well as its own progress. This is one of the reasons why the United States is pressing for a new round of trade negotiations in these service fields of data processing and transfer of information. The entire free world has a stake in building a more open system, because together we can progress faster and farther than any of us can alone.

This points to another advantage the West enjoys. The free flow of information is inherently compatible with our political system and values. The communist states, in contrast, fear this information revolution perhaps even more than they fear Western military strength. We all remember the power of the Ayatollah's message disseminated on tape cassettes in Iran; what could have a more profound impact in the Soviet bloc than similar cassettes, outside radio broadcasting, direct broadcast satellites, or photocopying machines? Totalitarian societies face a dilemma: either they try to stifle these technologies and thereby fall further behind in the new industrial revolution, or else they permit these technologies and see their totalitarian control inevitably eroded. In fact, they do not have a choice, because they will never be able entirely to block the tide of technological advance.

The revolution in global communication thus forces all nations to reconsider traditional ways of thinking about national sovereignty. We are reminded anew of the world's interdependence, and we are reminded as well that only a world of spreading freedom is compatible with human and technological progress.

VI

These broad trends I have described are mostly positive trends. However, we can also see social dislocation arising from economic change; we see urban alienation, political turbulence, and the many potential sources and forms of disorder I have mentioned. The future evolution of the international system will follow the positive trends only if we—the United States and the free world—meet our responsibility to defend our interests and shape events in accordance with our own ideals and goals.

In at least one respect, the modern world, with its spreading technology and prosperity and democratic aspirations, is ironically becoming also more and more vulnerable. I am thinking, of course, about terrorism. Even as the world becomes more secure from the danger of major war, paradoxically the democratic world now faces an increasing threat from this new form of warfare.

Terrorism these days is becoming less an isolated phenomenon of local fanatics, and increasingly part of a new international strategy resorted to by the enemies of freedom. It is a vicious weapon used deliberately against democracies; against the interests, policies and friends of the democracies; and against completely innocent people. There are disturbing links, as well, to international drug trafficking. Terrorism is a problem that, more than many others, is forcing us into new ways of thinking about how to safeguard our future. During the year ahead we must be prepared for serious terrorist threats in Western Europe, in the Middle East and in Latin America, much of it supported or encouraged by a handful of ruthless governments. ·

A counterstrategy for combatting terrorism, in my view, must encompass many things. We and our allies must work still harder to improve security, share information, coordinate police efforts and collaborate in other ways. We in this country must also think hard about the moral stakes involved. If we truly believe in our democratic values and our way of life, we must be willing to defend them. Passive measures are unlikely to suffice; means of more active defense and deterrence must be considered and given the necessary political support.

Finally, while working tirelessly to deny terrorists their opportunities and their means, we can—and must—be absolutely firm in denying them their goals. They seek to blackmail us into changing our foreign policies or to drive us out of countries and regions where we have important interests. This we cannot permit; we cannot yield position or abandon friends or responsibilities under this kind of pressure. If we allow terrorists even one such victory, we embolden them further; we demoralize all who rely on us, and we make the world an even more dangerous place.

There is, of course, a broader issue here. This is the basic question of the use of American power in the defense of our interests and the relevance of our power as the backstop to our diplomacy. It is reflected, for example, in what are often called "gray-area challenges"—the kind of regional or local conflicts and crises that are likely to persist in a turbulent world, below the threshold of major war but nonetheless affecting important

Western interests. Most of the major conflicts since 1945, indeed, have originated in such conflicts in the developing world. The end of the colonial order has not brought universal peace and justice; much of the developing world is torn by the continuing struggle between the forces of moderation and the forces of radicalism—a struggle actively exploited and exacerbated by the Soviet Union.

It is absurd to think that America can walk away from such challenges. This is a world of great potential instability and many potential dangers. It is commonly observed that we live on a shrinking planet and in a world of increasing interdependence. It follows that the United States, as the world's strongest democracy, must meet its responsibility as a defender of freedom, democratic values and international peace, and as a nation upon whom many others rely for their security. Americans have always deeply believed in a world in which disputes were settled peacefully—a world of law, international harmony and human rights. But we have learned through hard experience that such a world cannot be created by good will and idealism alone. We have learned that to maintain peace and preserve freedom we have to be strong, and, more than that, we have to be willing to use our strength. We would not seek confrontation, but we learned the lesson of the 1930s—that appeasement of an aggressor only invites aggression and increases the danger of war.

Americans have sometimes tended to think that power and diplomacy are two distinct alternatives. The truth is, power and diplomacy must always go together, or we will accomplish very little in this world. Power must always be guided by purpose. At the same time, the hard reality is that diplomacy not backed by strength will always be ineffectual at best, dangerous at worst. Americans will always be reluctant to use our military strength; this is the mark of our decency. And clearly, the use of force must always be a last resort, when other means of influence have proven inadequate. But a great power cannot free itself so easily from the burden of choice. It must bear responsibility for the consequences of its inaction as well as for the consequences of its action. In either case, its decision will affect the fate of many other human beings in many parts of the world.

We must be wise and prudent in deciding how and where to use our power; the United States will always seek political solutions to problems. Such solutions will never succeed, however, unless aggression is resisted and diplomacy is backed by strength. We are reasonably well prepared to deter all-out Soviet nuclear aggression—provided we continue with our strategic modernization—but we must be sure we are as well prepared, physically and psychologically, for the intermediate range of challenges that we will inevitably confront.

VII

I have touched on a wide variety of topics, but two very important, and very basic, conclusions can be drawn from them.

First, the agenda for the immediate future seems to me to be an agenda on which the American people are essentially united. These are goals that are widely shared and tasks that are likely to reinforce another important trend: namely, the reemergence of a national consensus on the main elements of our foreign policy. This, indeed, may be the most important positive trend of all, because so many of our difficulties in recent decades have been very much the product of our own domestic divisions.

Second, all the diverse topics I have touched upon are, in the end, closely interrelated. The United States seeks peace and security; we seek economic progress; we seek to promote freedom, democracy and human rights. The conventional mode of thinking is to treat these as discrete categories of activity. In fact, as we have seen, it is now more and more widely recognized that there is a crucial connection among them.

As I have already discussed, it is more and more understood that economic progress is related to a political environment of openness and freedom. It used to be thought in some quarters that socialism was the appropriate model for developing countries because central planning was better able to mobilize and allocate resources in conditions of scarcity. The historical experience of Western Europe and North America, which industrialized in an era of limited government, was not thought to be relevant. Yet the more recent experience of the Third World shows that a dominant government role in developing economies has often stifled the natural forces of production and productivity and distorted the efficient allocation of resources. The real engine of growth, in developing as well as industrialized countries, turns out to be the natural dynamism of societies that minimize central planning, open themselves to trade with the world, and give free rein to the talents and efforts and risk-taking and investment decisions of individuals.

Similarly, there is almost certainly also a relationship among economic progress, freedom and world peace. Andrei Sakharov declared in his Nobel lecture:

> I am convinced that international trust, mutual understanding, disarmament, and international security are inconceivable without an open society with freedom of information, freedom of conscience, the right to publish, and the right to travel and choose the country in which one wishes to live. I am also convinced that freedom of conscience, together with other civic rights, provides both the basis for scientific progress and a guarantee against its misuse to harm mankind.

The implication of all this is profound: it is that the Western values of liberty and democracy, which some have been quick to write off as culture-bound or irrelevant or passé, are not to be so easily dismissed. These values are the source of our strength, economic as well as moral, and they turn out to be more central to the world's future than many may have realized. After more than a century of fashionable Marxist mythology about economic determinism and the "crisis of capitalism," the key to human progress turns out to be those very Western concepts of political and economic freedom that Marxists claimed were obsolete. They were wrong. Today—in a supreme irony—it is the communist system that looks bankrupt, morally as well as economically. The West is resilient and resurgent.

And so, in the end, the most important new way of thinking that is called for in this decade is our way of thinking about ourselves. Civilizations thrive when they believe in themselves; they decline when they lose this faith. All civilizations confront massive problems, but a society is more likely to master its challenges, rather than be overwhelmed by them, if it retains this bedrock self-confidence that its values are worth defending. This is the essence of the Reagan revolution and of the leadership the President has sought to provide in America.

The West has been through a difficult period in the last decade or more. But now we see a new turn. The next phase of the industrial revolution—like all previous phases—comes from the democratic world, where innovation and creativity are allowed to spring from the unfettered human spirit. And on every continent—from Nicaragua to Cambodia, from Poland to South Africa to Afghanistan—we see that the yearning for freedom is the most powerful political force all across the planet.

So, as we head toward the 21st century, it is time for the democracies to celebrate their system, their beliefs and their success. We face challenges, but we are well poised to master them. Opinions are being revised about which system is the wave of the future. The free nations, if they maintain their unity and their faith in themselves, have the advantage—economically, technologically, morally.

History is on freedom's side.

Richard Nixon

SUPERPOWER SUMMITRY

Forty years ago, U.S. nuclear power was indispensable in ending World War II. In the postwar era, American nuclear superiority was indispensable in deterring Soviet probes that might have led to World War III. But that era is over, and we live in the age of nuclear parity, when each superpower has the means to destroy the other and the rest of the world.

In these strategic circumstances, summit meetings between leaders of the United States and the Soviet Union have become essential if peace is to be preserved. Such meetings will contribute to the cause of peace, however, only if both leaders recognize that tensions between the two nations are due not to the fact that we do *not* understand each other but to the fact that we *do* understand that we have diametrically opposed ideological and geopolitical interests. Most of our differences will never be resolved. But the United States and the Soviet Union have one major goal in common: survival. Each has the key to the other's survival. The purpose of summit meetings is to develop rules of engagement that could prevent our profound differences from bringing us into armed conflict that could destroy us both.

With this limited but crucially important goal in mind, we must disabuse ourselves from the start of the much too prevalent view that if only the two leaders, as they get to know each other, could develop a new "tone" or a new "spirit" in their relationship, our problems would be solved and tensions reduced. If history is any guide, evaluating a summit meeting in terms of the "spirit" it produces is evidence of failure rather than success. The spirits of Geneva in 1955, of Camp David in 1959, of Vienna in 1961 and of Glassboro in 1967 each produced a brief improvement in the atmosphere, but no significant progress on resolving major issues. Spirit and tone matter only when two leaders of nations with similar interests have a misunderstanding that can be resolved by their getting to know each other. Such factors are irrelevant when nations have irreconcilable differences, which is the case as far as the United States and the Soviet Union are concerned.

116

The obsession with style over substance among some observers is ludicrous. The fact that General Secretary Mikhail Gorbachev has a firm handshake, excellent eye contact, a good sense of humor and dresses fashionably is no more relevant to his policies than the fact that Khrushchev wore ill-fitting clothes, drank too much and spoke a crude Russian. Anyone who reaches the top in the Soviet hierarchy is bound to be a dedicated communist and a strong, ruthless leader who supports the Soviet foreign policy of extending Soviet domination into the non-communist world. We can "do business" with Gorbachev, but only if we recognize that the business we have to deal with involves intractable differences between competitive states.

President Reagan will be urged to prove to Mr. Gorbachev that he is sincerely dedicated to peace and that, despite his tough rhetoric, he is really a very nice man. President Reagan does not have to prove that he is for peace. Mr. Gorbachev knows that. What is vitally important is that he also understand that President Reagan is a strong leader, one who is fair and reasonable, but who will, without question, take action to protect American interests when they are threatened.

Debates about ideology will serve no useful purpose. Mr. Gorbachev is as dedicated to his ideology as President Reagan is to his. Neither is going to convert the other.

In the postwar era, no two leaders come to a summit with more political support at home or more endowed with charm and charisma. But for one to try to charm the other would bring not affection but contempt; this would certainly be Mr. Gorbachev's reaction. An essential element of a new relationship is not sentimental expressions of friendship but hardheaded mutual respect. In 1959, before I met Khrushchev, British Prime Minister Harold Macmillan told me that he sensed in his meetings with the Soviet leaders that, above all, they "wanted to be admitted as members of the club." This is a small price to pay for laying the foundations for a new structure of peace in the world.

II

Can two powers with diametrically opposed geopolitical interests avoid war and develop a peaceful relationship? It is important to recognize clearly the major dangers which could lead to nuclear war. In descending order of likelihood they are:

1) War by accident, where one side launches a nuclear attack because a mechanical malfunction creates the mistaken impression that the other side has launched an attack;

2) Nuclear proliferation, which could put nuclear weapons in the hands of a leader of a minor revolutionary or terrorist power who would be less restrained from using nuclear weapons than the major powers have been;

3) Escalation of small wars in areas where the interests of the superpowers are both involved, such as the Middle East and the Persian Gulf;

4) War by miscalculation, where a leader of one superpower underestimates the will of the leader of the other to take ultimate risks to defend his interests.

In all four of these scenarios, the United States and the Soviet Union have a mutual interest in reducing the danger and risks which could lead to a nuclear war. They are, therefore, areas where tough-minded diplomacy culminating in agreements at the summit level can play a constructive role.

The next most likely danger is a Soviet preemptive strike to liquidate the Chinese nuclear arsenal. This is not a danger at the present time because China lacks the industrial base and military capacity to be a serious threat to the Soviet Union. But as China begins to develop such a capacity in the future, a Soviet leader could decide that it is better to strike before China becomes a major nuclear power. A nuclear war between major powers, like the Soviet Union and China, could escalate into a world war. That is why it is in the interests of the United States and the West to welcome, not oppose, efforts on the part of the Soviet Union and the People's Republic of China to reduce tensions.

The least likely danger of nuclear war is a Soviet nuclear attack on Western Europe or the United States. The Soviet leaders are and will continue to be dedicated to extending communist domination over non-communist nations. But they are not madmen, and they are not fools. No matter how confident they are that they can win a nuclear war, it would be at the risk of great destruction to the Soviet homeland. Having Europe and the United States reduced to nuclear wastelands would be the bitter fruit of such a "victory." World war has become obsolete as an instrument of policy between the two superpowers. That is why the primary danger, as far as the United States and Western Europe are concerned, is not destruction in war but surrender to nuclear coercion.

Reducing the danger of nuclear war involves arms control, but it is a mistake to support arms control as desirable in itself and to believe that any agreement is better than none. The primary purpose of arms control is to reduce the danger of war. It is not the existence of arms, but political differences that lead to their use, which leads to war. A bad agreement that opens the way to Soviet superiority increases the danger of war. Even a good agreement will not prevent war if political differences lead to armed conflict. Thus, an agreement reducing arms but not linked to restraints on political conduct would not contribute to peace. If political differences escalate into war, it is no comfort to know that each side has the capacity to destroy the other only two times rather than twenty times.

President Reagan has been unfairly criticized for adhering to the SALT II (Strategic Arms Limitation Talks) treaty negotiated by President Jimmy Carter but not approved by the Senate. The critics contend that the reason the Soviet Union is ahead and that we are behind in land-based strategic missiles is because the Soviets are cheating on the arms control agreements and because those agreements restricted our strategic programs. There is no question that the Soviets will do all that is allowed under an arms control agreement and will stretch it to the outer limits and indeed will cheat if they can get away with it. But they gained their superiority in strategic land-based missiles not because of what *they* did in violation of arms control agreements but because of what *we* did *not* do within the limits allowed by the agreements. We must also face up to the hard reality that without a credible arms control initiative, it would be impossible to get congressional approval for adequate defense budgets to match the Soviet effort or to retain the support of our allies.

It is contended that because of the flaws in the agreements and the Soviet practice of violating them, the United States would be better off without any agreement. Yet, while there is strong evidence that the Soviet Union is probably violating provisions of SALT I and SALT II, it is complying with the limits on the fractionation of warheads agreed to in SALT II. If President Reagan had decided not to continue complying with SALT II, the Soviet Union would not consider itself to be bound by these provisions and limitations either; it could attach 30 warheads to each of its 300 giant SS-18 intercontinental ballistic missiles rather than the 10 allowed under the treaty. This would mean an increase of 6,000 warheads in the Soviet arsenal. The United States has no missiles of this size which would allow us to match such an action by the Soviets.

Looking to the future, without a new arms control agreement, even if the United States were to continue its own arms program at the levels requested by President Reagan rather than the far lower levels approved by Congress, and if the Soviets were to continue their programs at current levels, the Soviet Union will be further ahead in nuclear missiles in 1990 than it is today.

If we are to prevent otherwise inevitable Soviet superiority, our only option is to negotiate a new, verifiable arms control agreement based on strict parity that denies a first-strike capability to the Soviet Union as well as to ourselves. What is most urgent is to remove the threat of the SS-18s and the new ICBMs, the SS-24 and SS-25, which are designed not to attack our cities in retaliation for an attack on the Soviet Union but for a decisive first strike against our missile sites. Many senators and congressmen have voted for the 40 MX missiles in the hope that they would be an effective bargaining chip in the Geneva negotiations. But the Soviets are not philanthropists. They will not cut back their 300 SS-18s to only 40 without getting something in return.

That is why, contrary to the critics' contention, the President's Strategic Defense Initiative (SDI) is indispensable to arms control. Without it, the Soviet Union would have no incentive to limit its offensive weapons. It is important, however, to distinguish among three different defensive systems.

A defensive system to protect our entire population would make nuclear weapons obsolete and thus replace deterrence as our defense against nuclear weapons. But for such a system to be effective against an all-out Soviet attack, it would have to be virtually leakproof. In view of the dramatic scientific breakthroughs made in my lifetime, I do not contend, as some do, that this is impossible. But we cannot base our *current* strategic planning on a system which, at best, will not be ready for full deployment until the next century.

A system that defends our missile sites, however, is possible in ten years or less. Even if it is only 30-percent effective, it would effectively deny the Soviet Union a first-strike capability against our missile sites. The purpose of such a defensive system would be not to replace deterrence but to strengthen it.

The third kind of system, a thin population defense, which would not be adequate against an all-out Soviet attack but *would* be effective against an accidental launch or an attack by a minor nuclear power, is also feasible within the next ten years. This is an area where the Soviet Union could agree with us that developing and deploying such a limited system is in their interest as well as ours.

President Reagan is correct in insisting that research on all aspects of the SDI is not negotiable, both because a ban on research is not verifiable and because if there is even a remote chance to develop a total population defense it should be a priority goal of our defense establishment. We also must have in mind that the Soviet Union is spending twice as much as we are on defense against nuclear weapons.

But deployment, as distinguished from research, for defense of our missile fields is the ultimate bargaining chip, just as was the case with SALT I. We should agree to limit our deployment of defensive weapons *only* if the Soviets significantly reduce and limit their offensive weapons. The choice is Gorbachev's. Either the Soviets cut back on their offensive forces or we will deploy defensive forces to match their buildup.

III

Arms control and political issues must go forward together. Progress on arms control can lead to stability and the reduction of political tensions. Reduction of political tensions can lead to a better climate for reaching an arms control agreement that is fair to both sides. Those who contend that we should seek arms control regardless of what happens on political issues should bear in mind that what destroyed any chance for Senate approval of the SALT II treaty was the Soviet invasion of Afghanistan. Today, there is no chance that the Senate would approve an arms control treaty at a time when the Soviet Union is supporting anti-U.S. forces in El Salvador and Nicaragua.

A summit agenda, therefore, should have as its first priority not arms control but the potential flash points for U.S.-Soviet conflicts. It is highly doubtful that we would have agreed to SALT I in 1972 had we not settled in the Berlin Agreement of 1971 those issues which had led to so many crises since the end of World War II. A similar opportunity is presented in the Middle East and Central America today.

The most difficult and potentially dangerous issue which brings the two nations into confrontation is the Soviet policy of supporting revolutionary movements against non-communist governments in the Third World. The Brezhnev Doctrine of 1968, announced after Soviet troops crushed a rebellion against the communist government of Czechoslovakia, proclaimed that Soviet conquests in Eastern Europe were irreversible. Putting it simply, Brezhnev said, "what's mine is mine." By Soviet probes in Latin America, Africa, the Persian Gulf and the Mideast against allies and friends of the United States, that doctrine has been extended to mean "what's yours is mine." The Soviet leaders must be made to understand that it would be both irrational and immoral for the United States and the West to accept the doctrine that the Soviet Union has a right to support wars of liberation in the non-communist world without insisting on our right to defend our allies and friends under assault and to support true liberation movements against pro-Soviet regimes in the Third World.

We cannot expect the Soviets to cease being communists, dedicated to expanding communist influence and domination in the world. But we must make it clear to the Soviets that military adventurism will destroy the chances for better relations between the United States and the Soviet Union. We must also make it clear that the revised Brezhnev Doctrine of not only defending but extending communism will be answered by a Reagan Doctrine of defending and extending freedom. Our only common interest is to conduct ourselves in such a way that such conflicts do not escalate into nuclear confrontation.

In view of the danger of proliferation of nuclear weapons, both nations have a mutual interest in working together to combat international terrorism, whether promoted by states or individuals. With the progress that is being made in the technology of miniaturization, the time is not far off when the danger of breaking the nuclear threshold will come from individuals and not only nations. If the nuclear genie gets out of the bottle, the fallout could affect all nations and particularly those which have nuclear weapons. The Soviets should be asked to join us in a declaration that terrorists and those who give aid and comfort to terrorists are guilty of an international crime and should be dealt with accordingly.

While we should hold the Soviets accountable for the actions they take that are opposed to our interests, we should recognize that they are not responsible for all of the troubles in the world. The income gap beween nations that produce raw materials and those that consume them, famine due to climatic causes, radical Muslim fundamentalist and terrorist movements emanating from Libya and Iran—all of these problems would exist even if the Soviet Union did not exist. But rather than exploiting such problems, the Soviet Union should join the United States and other Western nations in combating them. The Soviets should be especially concerned about the rise of Muslim fundamentalism not only because one-third of the population of the Soviet Union is Muslim, but also because the Muslim revolution competes with the Soviet revolution for the support of people in Third World nations.

There is one phase of our competition which should be brought under control—competing with each other in fueling the arms race in the Third World. U.S. and Soviet arms sales to Third World countries run to billions of dollars. Most of these countries are desperately poor, and they need economic assistance far more than they need additional arms. For the Soviet Union to arm India, while the United States arms Pakistan, can only end in tragedy for the people of both countries. Even though these are only non-nuclear arms, they are instruments of war, and small wars always have the potential of escalating into nuclear wars. There is no prospect for reducing arms sales soon, if at all, but both the United States and the U.S.S.R. have an interest in controlling them and not letting them drag us into conflict.

IV

Turning to collateral issues, while it is an illusion that trade by itself will lead to peace, an increase in unsubsidized trade in nonmilitary items can provide a strong incentive for the Soviet Union to avoid conduct that increases political tensions between our two countries. Trade and political issues are inexorably linked. For the United States to increase trade, which the Soviets need and want, at a time when they are engaging in political activities that are opposed to our interests, would be stupid and dangerous. No nation should subsidize its own destruction.

One of the most widely held misconceptions is that person-to-person programs and cultural exchange will significantly reduce tensions. As a longtime supporter of such programs, I must reluctantly point out that this is not the case. "Getting to know you" is not the issue between the Soviet Union and the United States. What are called the three Cs—consular, cultural and commercial issues—will and should receive appropriate attention at summit meetings. But since Soviet authorities

decide who is to go to the United States and what and whom
foreigners can see in the Soviet Union, no one should be under
any illusion that agreements in such peripheral areas by themselves have any significant effect on the nature of the conflict
between the two superpowers.

The most highly charged emotional issue is that of human
rights abuses in the Soviet Union. The Soviets insist that under
no circumstances will they allow their internal policies to be a
subject for negotiation with another government. We should
make human rights a top-priority *private* issue but not a *public*
issue. We saw this principle in practice in 1972. In my summit
conversations with Brezhnev, I privately urged that he lift
limitations on Jewish emigration in order to gain support for
détente in the United States. A record 37,000 exit visas were
granted in that year. The following year, the Jackson-Vanik
Amendment to the trade bill put public pressure on the Soviets
to increase Jewish emigration. The Soviets reacted by sharply
reducing the number of visas rather than *increasing* them.

V

For the past five years I have strongly urged holding annual
summit meetings. Such meetings can serve useful purposes
apart from reaching any major substantive agreements. Most
important, they can substantially reduce the risk of war from
miscalculation. This will be the case not because the two leaders
will charm each other or find that they like each other but
because they will understand each other's interests, respect
each other's strength, and know the limits beyond which they
cannot go without running the risk of armed conflict. This was
a factor after the 1973 summit which probably helped to
convince Brezhnev that I was not bluffing later in the year
(October 1973) when I ordered an alert of our forces to back
up our demand that he not intervene unilaterally in the Middle
East war.

Moreover, when a summit meeting is scheduled, it inhibits
one side from engaging in actions that would be clearly against
the interests of the other during the period before the meeting;
thus each party will have an incentive to avoid conduct which
might poison the atmosphere. This factor probably also played
a role in cooling the 1973 crisis.

A summit meeting is also a very useful tool to get a bureaucracy moving. The Soviet bureaucracy is notoriously and mad-
deningly slow, rigid and inflexible. The U.S. bureaucracy is

not free of such faults. There is nothing like the deadline of a summit to knock heads together and to shape up a bureaucracy. The danger which must be avoided is pressure, especially from the bureaucracy, for agreements for agreements' sake to ensure the success of the summit. It is far better to have no agreement at all than to negotiate a bad one.

VI

One hundred and fifty years ago, Alexis de Tocqueville observed with incredible foresight:

> There are at the present time two great nations in the world which seem to bend toward the same end although they start from different points: I allude to the Russians and the Americans—the Anglo-American relies upon personal interest to accomplish his ends and gives free scope to the unguided exertions and common sense of the citizens; the Russian centers all the authority of society in a single arm: the principal instrument of the former is freedom, of the latter servitude. Their starting point is different and their courses are not the same; yet each of them seems to be marked out by the will of heaven to sway the destinies of half the globe.

This was written long before the communists came to power in Russia. We must recognize that while Russians and Americans can be friends, our governments are destined by history to be adversaries. Yet while we are destined to be adversaries, we have a mutual interest in avoiding becoming enemies in a suicidal war. This requires a candid and honest recognition of our irreconcilable and permanent differences, not a superficial glossing-over of them. A difference not recognized can be dangerous. A difference recognized can be controlled.

The one absolute certainty about the Soviet-American relationship is that the struggle in which we are engaged will last not just for years but for decades. In such a struggle, one advantage the Soviet Union has over the United States is that its foreign policy has consistency and continuity. The leaders change but the policies remain the same. Khrushchev wore short-sleeved shirts and Brezhnev wore French cuffs, but both set the same foreign policy goals: the extension of Soviet domination and influence in the world.

Every eight years and sometimes every four years, American policy, with bipartisanship virtually ended by the Vietnam War, oscillates between extremes of underestimating and overestimating the Soviet threat. What is needed is a steady, consistent policy with bipartisan support that does not change from one administration to another. This is a long struggle with no end in sight. Whatever their faults, the Soviets will be firm, patient and consistent in pursuing their foreign policy goals. We must match them in this respect. Gorbachev, at 54, is a man who does not need to be in a hurry. He may live long enough to deal with as many as five American presidents. We must not give him the opportunity to delay making a deal with one president in the hope that he might get a better one from the president who is to succeed him.

Michael Mandelbaum

THE LUCK OF THE PRESIDENT

Asked what kind of generals he preferred to have leading his armies, Napoleon is said to have replied "lucky ones." Ronald Reagan has been a lucky president, especially in relations with the rest of the world.

During the five years of his stewardship American foreign policy has been largely successful. One test of success for any sovereign state is the level of its power and prestige, its general standing in the international community. America's standing has improved since 1981. Another important measure of success is the avoidance of war; this, too, Mr. Reagan has managed. The interest of a great power committed to the international status quo, like the United States, is served by averting geopolitical setbacks. On this score as well, Mr. Reagan's record is a good one. There has been no Vietnam or Iran during the past five years. By these standards, the President has conducted what is perhaps the most successful American foreign policy of the last 25 years.

The success that the United States has enjoyed since 1981 has been due in large part to circumstances having little direct connection with the efforts of the Reagan Administration. It has been the result of forces and trends outside the control of the United States and of measures undertaken by others and occasionally even opposed by Mr. Reagan. He owes his success abroad at least as much to good fortune as to good policies.

II

America's chief adversary has been disadvantaged in its leadership for most of Mr. Reagan's term of office. Until Mikhail Gorbachev's assumption of power in March 1985, the leaders of the Soviet Union were in poor health and unable to exercise decisive leadership for all but a few months of Mr. Reagan's presidency. At the same time, the Soviet Union has been in the grip of a severe economic downturn, limiting to

Michael Mandelbaum is a Senior Fellow and Director of the Project on East-West Relations at the Council on Foreign Relations.

some degree its taste for contesting American interests abroad. The first half of the 1980s also turned out to be a time of significant resistance at the extremities of the Soviet empire. Soviet imperial reach extended to places where the tanks of the Soviet army were of little use in imposing order. In Afghanistan, Southeast Asia and southern Africa, Soviet clients and even Soviet troops came under fire. These outbreaks of resistance handicapped the Soviet Union in its rivalry with the United States—and they arose independently of American policies.

In the ongoing nuclear competition with the Soviets, the Reagan Administration benefited from the work of others. The previous administration had negotiated a series of limits on offensive weapons that were encoded in the second Strategic Arms Limitations Talks (SALT II) treaty. As presidential candidate and as President, Mr. Reagan opposed the treaty. The Senate has not ratified it. But early in 1981, the Reagan Administration declared that it would abide by the relevant limitations of the SALT II treaty as long as the Soviet Union did so.[1] Without these restrictions the Soviet Union might have fielded many more weapons than it has since 1981. If it had done so the United States would have had to decide how to respond. The decision would not have been an easy one: matching the Soviets would have been difficult and expensive; doing nothing would have been controversial. SALT II has spared the President having to make such a decision.

SALT II has conditioned the Reagan Administration's conduct of arms control negotiations as well. The two sides have not come close to reaching agreement on a new treaty, but there has been little urgency to do so because the SALT II restraints have remained safely in place. The United States and the Soviet Union could each afford to make proposals unlikely to meet with the other's approval, secure in the knowledge that neither party's position would deteriorate in the absence of a new accord. Mr. Reagan has enjoyed both the benefits of limits negotiated by others and the luxury of criticizing these limits for not being sweeping enough.

The foreign policies of recent administrations have encountered greatest difficulty in the Middle East. It is the most

---

[1] On June 10, 1985, the White House announced that the President had decided to dismantle a Poseidon submarine in order to remain in compliance with the provisions of the treaty.

treacherous part of the world, one that is politically unstable and where, unlike other equally volatile regions, the two great powers both have important interests. The 1973 Middle East war began the undoing of the relationship that President Nixon was trying to forge with the Soviet Union. The Iranian revolution left a blight on Mr. Carter's presidency. Here, too, Mr. Reagan has enjoyed great good fortune.

The war between Iraq and Iran continued throughout the first five years of Mr. Reagan's term in office. If either country had overcome the other it would have dominated the region and threatened the neighboring oil states that are important to the West. Indeed, if there had been no war at all, both would have been free to seek influence at the expense of the United States. But the bloody stalemate along the Iran-Iraq border continued through 1985. This state of affairs nicely, if perversely, served American interests.[2]

The Iran-Iraq war reduced the oil available from both countries. In the 1970s this would have harmed the Western economies. The oil shocks of 1973–74 and 1979 had their origins in a drop in production in the Middle East; in each case this led to a sharp rise in price that caused enormous economic damage in the rest of the world and gave the oil-producing countries potential influence over Western policies. At the end of the 1970s it seemed that the price of oil was destined to rise steadily and that the members of OPEC would acquire an ever-tighter grip on the foreign policy of the United States.[3]

Neither development occurred. Mr. Reagan had the good luck to enter office at a moment when the world oil market was undergoing a historic shift: for the first time in the postwar period, overall oil consumption decreased. Production outside the OPEC countries increased. OPEC's share of oil consumption in the West dropped sharply and the worldwide price of oil fell. These trends shielded the United States and its allies from economic damage and political blackmail.

[2] The opposite outcome worked to American advantage in the Falklands conflict of 1982. Then it was two countries allied with, rather than hostile to, the United States that went to war. For the Administration to side with either would alienate the other; to stand aloof would antagonize both. The American interest, therefore, lay in the shortest possible war and, indeed, the British did win quickly. America's good fortune continued when the Argentine regime, which would undoubtedly have remained bitter against the United States for supporting Britain, fell from power and was replaced by a democratic government with no responsibility for the war.

[3] "There is no doubt that the Saudis have the capacity to wield the oil weapon with cruel effect—and selectively." George W. Ball, "Reflections on a Heavy Year," *Foreign Affairs*, America and the World 1980, p. 492.

This happy outcome was the result not so much of national policies as of the impersonal operation of market forces. When the price of something rises consumers use less and producers provide more: the combination of reduced demand and increased supply lowers the price. So it was with oil during the first half of the 1980s, to the great benefit of the United States.

The chronic problem for American policy in the Middle East has been the Arab-Israeli conflict. It was the 1973 war that led to the first oil shock and briefly threatened to draw the United States and the Soviet Union into a military confrontation with each other as well. The Reagan Administration did not have to contend with the prospect of another major round of that conflict, again thanks to the work of others. The efforts of the three previous administrations helped to produce the Camp David peace accords between Israel and Egypt, the largest and most important Arab country. As long as that treaty holds, Egypt will not take part in a war against Israel. Without Egypt, other Arab states are not likely to go to war. Without the threat of war, American policy in the Middle East since 1979 has enjoyed an unfamiliar and welcome margin of safety.

During its first term, the Reagan Administration conducted an active Middle East policy, sponsoring two major initiatives. In September 1982, the President proposed the "Reagan Plan," calling for Palestinian self-rule on the West Bank of the Jordan River in association with the kingdom of Jordan. It also committed troops and diplomatic capital to an effort to reconstruct a peaceful, united Lebanon favorably disposed to the West. Both initiatives failed decisively. Jordan and Israel rejected the Reagan Plan. American forces were withdrawn from Lebanon, the country remained in a state of ongoing civil war, and it is Syria, not the United States, that has emerged as the most influential foreign presence there. Neither failure had a drastic effect on American interests in the region, however, which were protected by the changes in the oil market and by the Camp David accords.

In historical perspective, the most momentous international event of the Reagan years may turn out to be the dramatic passage of the People's Republic of China from a planned, centralized economic system toward an economy operated according to market principles. The sweeping changes that China inaugurated at the end of the 1970s constitute a cultural and political, as well as an economic, revolution. They were endorsed in an official economic blueprint unveiled in Beijing in September of 1985. They had nothing to do with American foreign policies; they were undertaken by the Chinese for their own reasons. Their ultimate consequences cannot be known and may not even be favorable for the United States. Nonetheless, in the short term they have an unmistakable symbolic significance that favors the West. They show that the world's oldest and most populous nation has decided that its interests are served by becoming more like the United States and less like the Soviet Union.

The essence of luck is good timing. Mr. Reagan has been in the right place at the right time. He has profited from political capital accumulated by others. He has drawn particular benefit from the labors of his immediate predecessor. It was Mr. Carter, after all, whose administration negotiated the SALT II treaty and the Camp David accords.[4] It was he who took the politically difficult decision to begin the decontrol of U.S. energy prices, which reinforced the trends in international markets that have proved so favorable to the United States. It was he who started what became a substantial increase in defense spending and who began to send assistance to the Afghan resistance in 1980. History will be grateful to Mr. Carter, although his contemporaries were not.

Luck, both good and bad, is an underappreciated element in public affairs. Those who enjoy good fortune naturally impute their success to their own talents. Those who are unlucky risk sounding churlish and sour if they invoke fate to account for their failures. Modern historians and commentators without partisan interests usually resist using luck as an analytical category for fear of seeming frivolous. It was not always so. Machiavelli, as clear-eyed an analyst of politics as ever addressed the subject, placed great emphasis on the role of fortune in shaping human affairs. But even he did not consider it all important.[5] "Luck is the residue of design," said an authority in a very different field, Branch Rickey, the baseball executive who was assembling winning teams in St. Louis at about the time that young "Dutch" Reagan was broadcasting the games of his archrivals, the Chicago Cubs.

[4] To these might be added the Panama Canal Treaties, but for which, it could be argued, the canal might have become the focal point of Central American hostility to the United States, the inspiration for large demonstrations, and even the object of sabotage or direct military assault.
[5] "I think it may be true that fortune is the rule of half our actions. . . ." *The Prince*, Chapter XXV.

Napoleon, although impressed with the role of forces beyond human control in warfare, also observed that God is almost invariably on the side with the bigger battalions. The Reagan foreign policy owes its success to good luck, but not to good luck alone.

III

At the very least, the favorable trends in international politics vindicate the President's view of the world. If the Soviet Union's economy has faltered, if its efforts to spread its influence have provoked resistance, this bears out Mr. Reagan's understanding of the direction in which history is moving.[6] If energy supplies are safer and cheaper, thanks to the magic of the market, and if China has discovered the value of free enterprise, few figures in American public life in the last half century have been as devoted to the virtues of the laws of supply and demand as the President. This has been one of the principal themes of his public career. Whatever his responsibility for them, the favorable developments of the last five years can have come as no surprise to Mr. Reagan. But even this gives him too little credit for the success of American foreign policy since he took office.

It was once put to the great physicist Ernest Rutherford that he had been fortunate to "ride the wave" of discoveries in his field in the early part of the century. "But I made the wave, didn't I?" he replied. Mr. Reagan did not make the wave himself; the tides of history, like those in the natural world, cannot be summoned by politicians. But he has helped the wave along. His Administration has provided assistance to rebels against Soviet clients in the Third World. It has presided over most of the increase in defense spending of the last six years. It has carried through the process of decontrolling energy prices that the Carter Administration began.

Not least important for the promotion of the nation's purposes abroad, the Reagan Administration has demonstrated, in limited but significant ways, that it is willing to send American armed forces into action as part of its foreign policy. The shooting down of two Libyan jets in 1981, the eviction of a government friendly to Cuba from the tiny Caribbean island

---

[6] "I firmly believe (that) the tide of history is moving away from Communism and into the warm sunlight of human freedom." Quoted in Madeleine G. Kalb, "Where Consensus Ends," *The New York Times Magazine*, Oct. 27, 1985, p. 104.

of Grenada in 1983, the launching of an air attack on Syrian positions in Lebanon in the same year, and the capture of the hijackers of the Italian liner *Achille Lauro* in 1985 were all minor military operations.[7] Collectively, however, they helped to create the impression of a President prepared to use force in support of American interests. Although it cannot be proven, it is not unreasonable to suppose that this impression has entered the calculations of others from time to time over the last five years, to the advantage of the United States.

Each of Mr. Reagan's contributions to the favorable tides in international affairs has been a measured one; this is another way in which he himself has had some responsibility for America's success abroad since 1981. His policies have been informed by a sense of proportion, of limits, of how far they could be pressed without taxing the prudence of other countries and exhausting the goodwill of the American public. This sense of limits was on vivid display on those occasions when Mr. Reagan changed course or retreated from positions previously staked out, in order to adjust to international realities or to the shape of public opinion at home, or both.

For all his hostility to the Soviet Union (and his Administration's reservations about summit conferences), he arranged the Geneva meeting with Mr. Gorbachev in November 1985. In 1982 Mr. Reagan imposed sanctions on European companies participating in the Siberian gas pipeline under American license. The European governments protested and he removed the sanctions. In the first year of the Administration, Secretary of State Alexander Haig suggested that the way to set things right in Central America was to "go to the source" of the trouble, that is, to Cuba. The Administration has, of course, done no such thing.

Mr. Reagan entered office with a long-held affection for Taiwan. This did not sit well with Beijing, which made restrictions on arms sales to the island a test of the Sino-American relationship that three administrations had worked to create. Mr. Reagan chose a policy that the People's Republic could tolerate. Despite principled opposition to government interference in economic affairs, the Administration has acted to help prevent Third World countries from defaulting on their loans

---

[7] Mr. Reagan also sent a contingent of American marines to Lebanon in 1982. Their mission, however, was to help keep the peace, and so was not, strictly speaking, a military operation.

and to bring down the international value of the dollar. Most
recently, after declaring his opposition to the idea several times,
Mr. Reagan reversed himself in September 1985, under pressure from the Congress, and imposed limited economic sanctions on South Africa as a mark of American disapproval of
the continuing system of apartheid.

The President has demonstrated an unerring sense of just
how far to go. This is an invaluable, indeed an essential, political
skill. A leader in a democracy must present himself as a person
of firm principles. He or she must, however, compromise those
principles in order to govern. A leader without any guiding
precepts is spineless and aimless; one who will never bend them
is a fanatic. The successful statesman is the one who can
navigate between the two extremes, earning a reputation for
being principled but not bullheaded. Mr. Reagan has that
reputation.[8] His predecessor did not. That difference is not
just a matter of luck.

IV

The mixture of good luck and adept statecraft that has
characterized the Reagan foreign policy was in evidence in one
of the most dramatic episodes of 1985, the hijacking of an
American commercial airliner to Beirut and the holding hostage of a number of its passengers for 17 days in the second
half of June. After leaving Athens the plane was seized by two
members of a shadowy group of Lebanese Shia Muslims. They
ordered it flown to Beirut, then to Algiers, then back to Beirut.
Early on they murdered an American navy diver who was
traveling on the flight. The majority of the passengers and
crew were released, but 40 were held captive. Most of them
were taken off the aircraft and moved to hiding places around
Beirut. The largest Lebanese Shia organization, Amal, took
control of the plane and of most of the American prisoners. Its
leader, Nabih Berri, became the focal point of efforts to release
the hostages. He gave a number of interviews on American
television. The hostages also made several appearances. Finally,
they were taken across the Syrian border to Damascus and
flown home.

The outcome of the hijacking was an undoubted success for

<hr>
[8] "For all his compromises, he still manages to look like a man of unbending principle."
Leslie H. Gelb, "The Mind of the President," *The New York Times Magazine*, Oct. 6, 1985, p.
21.

the Reagan Administration. The Americans were released in a reasonable period of time without any obvious concessions being made to their captors by the United States or indeed by Israel, which was the object of their original demands.[9]

The Beirut hijacking was an instance of the President's luck. While it has some claim to being the worst crisis of the first five years of his Administration, by the standards of the past 25 years it was scarcely a crisis at all. The stakes were not remotely as high as they had been in Berlin in 1961, or in the Caribbean during the Cuban missile crisis of 1962, or in the Middle East in 1973. Nor were they as high as they had been when American personnel were held hostage in Teheran. As in Lebanon, the American captives in Iran from 1979 to 1981 became caught up in an internal struggle for power. But the Iranian struggle was consequential for American interests. Iran has both oil and a strategic location, bordering on the Persian Gulf and the Soviet Union; it is important for the United States. Lebanon is not.

Even so, the hijacking could have damaged the Administration had it dragged on as the Iranian affair did, paralyzing the highest levels of the American government. Mr. Reagan tried to keep his distance from the events as they unfolded. He could not have stood apart indefinitely, but he did not have to. In contrast with the episode in Teheran, the parties in control of events in Beirut—the leadership of Amal, the government of Syria, and perhaps also Syria's patron, the Soviet Union—found it in their respective interests to end the affair promptly rather than to prolong it. The factions in control of the American hostages in Teheran apparently came to the opposite conclusion.

The release of the Americans in Beirut was probably not, however, merely a matter of luck. Amal, Syria and perhaps the Soviets may well have reckoned that the Administration's patience might at some point wear thin, that it would be moved to take military action, and that this would make life more difficult for all of them. Mr. Reagan had, after all, sent marines once to Lebanon. Those in control of the hostages certainly did not want American troops to return. They obviously de-

---

[9] They demanded that 766 men taken prisoner in southern Lebanon and held in Israel be released. The Israeli government had previously announced that it would release them gradually. Some were let go while the Americans were being held. The rest were sent home afterward.

cided that whatever benefit they drew from holding the hostages would be outweighed by the costs of confronting an angry American President. It is possible that their deliberations were shadowed by the fear that the United States would not be restrained indefinitely. If such a concern did hover at the back of their minds, it was Ronald Reagan who, by his deeds, helped to put it there.

Another of Mr. Reagan's skills was in evidence in the hijacking episode: his sense of just how far to go in doing what he has said he is willing to do. Before June 1985 he had said, more than once, that he would act forcefully against terrorists. He entered office promising "swift and effective retribution." He and his secretary of state repeated the pledge on several occasions afterward. In response to the Beirut hijacking, as to the bombing of the American embassy and the destruction of the marine barracks in Lebanon in 1982, the American government did nothing.

The Administration might have done what Israel has long made it national policy to do in response to terrorism: it could have punished, if not the terrorists themselves, then those in a position to control them. It could have attacked selected targets in Lebanon or Syria or even Iran. It could thereby have put pressure on the governments involved or, in the case of Lebanon, the military and political organizations, to police their own territory. Swift and effective retribution is a way of holding people in authority responsible for activities that originate where their writ runs.

Such a response would have been costly. If it had been undertaken while the hostages were still being held, it would no doubt have forfeited their lives. If reprisal raids had been conducted after their release, people having no connection with terrorism probably would have been killed. American reprisals would likely have set off a renewed cycle of violence as those injured sought to retaliate against the United States. The American government would then have had to be ready to respond once more. To carry out a strategy of swift and effective retribution requires following the cycle to its end, no matter how much blood is shed along the way. The capture of the four hijackers of the *Achille Lauro* was the exception that proved the rule. The perpetrators themselves were caught. No harm came to anybody else. The hijackers will be brought to trial in a Western judicial system. These circumstances had not been present in previous episodes of terror and are not likely to recur often.

The attacks in the Rome and Vienna airports over the Christmas season that killed several Americans raised anew the question of how to respond to terrorism. The Administration publicly charged Libya with assisting those responsible, and once again hinted at some kind of retaliation. In response to the Beirut hijacking, however, the Reagan Administration chose not to retaliate. Despite the outcry in the United States, this decision was in keeping with the basic sentiments of the American public. This is not because Americans' moral scruples are more refined than those of Israelis. The American people were willing to have their armed forces kill thousands of civilians in military operations undertaken in Germany and Japan in 1944 and 1945. For the United States then and for Israel now, however, the stakes were supremely high. The operations in each case were undertaken in response to what were seen as mortal threats.

Americans do not see terrorism that way. In the public mind it has something like the same status as crime in the United States. It provokes outrage. It is reprehensible. It is taken as a sign of the decline in civic standards, and precautions to prevent it are regarded as necessary. More serious measures, however, are not considered to be in order. Three centuries ago thieves were hanged in Europe. No one suggests that this practice be resumed or that civil liberties be suspended and the nation turned into a police state to stop crime. Similarly, there is no real consensus in favor of serious military reprisals against the agents and sponsors of terrorism that will kill others as well. No doubt this makes the United States a more attractive target than countries that are less reticent about shedding blood. It is perhaps the price to be paid for living in a nation whose citizens do not like to kill innocent people.

In 1985 enduring terrorism abroad was, for the United States, like suffering crime at home. It was the cost of being a liberal great power, just as putting up with a certain crime rate is the by-product of maintaining an open society.

The President might not put it in quite that way, but he plainly understood the country's feelings on the matter and acted in deference to them. His well-developed sense of the public's wishes has also contributed to his success. No one can have a successful foreign policy without the opportunity to

conduct it, which in the United States requires the authorization of the electorate. Mr. Reagan has received it twice.

V

President Reagan has not been as popular in the rest of the
world as at home. He has been particularly unpopular in the
Soviet Union. A campaign of personal vilification of Mr.
Reagan in the Soviet press reached a crescendo with a series of
pointed comparisons to Hitler. Still, the Soviet leaders' disenchantment with him did not keep them away from the November summit meeting, which was held despite the lack of any
serious business to transact or ratify.

There is a point beyond which United States relations with
the Soviet Union cannot be allowed to deteriorate. The first
duty of any American President is to keep the ongoing rivalry
between the two great powers from sliding into nuclear disaster. But the success of a leader's foreign policy cannot fairly be
judged by the extent to which he is warmly regarded by those
whose designs it is a central object of that policy to resist. If
the low esteem in which Mr. Reagan was held in Moscow for
most of his term was not necessarily a badge of honor, it was
not exactly a mark of disgrace either.

The President has also been unpopular in friendlier capitals.
The West Europeans, while not of one mind in this as in other
matters, did not, on the whole, think well of him during his
first five years in office. The American President, after all, has
the ultimate say over Europe's destiny, but Europeans have no
constitutional voice in his policies. Their nervousness deriving
from this fact takes two particular forms, which are inherent
in all alliances but are especially pronounced in NATO. They
fear that the alliance will not work and that they will be
abandoned by the United States in their hour of need, and
they fear that it will work too well and they will be entrapped
in a conflict they wish to avoid.[10]

The issue that preoccupied the Atlantic alliance for much of
Mr. Reagan's first term, the stationing of American-controlled
intermediate-range nuclear missiles in Europe, illustrates both
concerns. The plan for deploying them had its origins in the
European fear during the 1970s that the growing Soviet ad-

---

[10] The concepts of abandonment and entrapment, as used here, are considered at length
in Michael Mandelbaum, *The Nuclear Revolution: International Politics before and after Hiroshima.*
New York: Cambridge University Press, 1981, pp. 147–75.

vantage in this category of weaponry would "decouple" the United States from the continent, weaken the deterrent power of American forces, and raise the chances that the United States would abandon its allies in a crisis. The sharp Soviet denunciation of the plan aroused the Europeans' other fear: a superpower confrontation involving them. The Europeans were unhappy at risking the improved relations with the Eastern bloc that they had nurtured. First they wanted the missiles to avoid being abandoned; then they did not want them for fear of being entrapped in a new cold war.[11] These fears did not begin with the Reagan presidency. They are perennial, arising from the basic structure of the alliance.

Not all the President's difficulties with the allies, however, are reruns of NATO's chronic internal disputes. He has had to contend with a widening divergence of views on the most important issue of all, the question of the proper policies toward the Soviet Union. For West Europeans, especially the Germans, the détente of the 1970s is the ideal. Trade between East and West expanded then; human contacts across the political and military divisions of the continent multiplied. Relations with the Soviets were cordial, in comparison with the first quarter century after 1945. The United States' European allies would like to keep them cordial.

For the United States the period of détente was also the time when the Soviet Union steadily expanded its military forces, repressed efforts at liberalization within its domain and energetically extended its influence in places such as Southeast Asia and Afghanistan. A firmer policy toward the Soviets than the Europeans wanted has therefore seemed necessary to Americans.

The difference in outlook between the two wings of the Atlantic alliance goes deeper than the personalities of the national leaders at any particular moment. It stems from different interests that are based on differing national roles and, ultimately, on the critical difference in geography. The Euro-

[11] A telling example of the complementary fears of abandonment and entrapment can be seen in the American government's deliberations during the Cuban missile crisis of 1962, as reported by Theodore Sorensen. Asked what the European reaction would be to alternative responses to the emplacement of the missiles, Secretary of State Dean Rusk replied that if the United States did nothing the allies would be unhappy on the grounds that, if the senior partner in the alliance would not act firmly so close to home, it could not be depended on to defend people thousands of miles away; and that, if the American response was a firm one, the Europeans would be unhappy at the prospect of being dragged into war over an issue that had nothing to do with them. *Kennedy*, New York: Harper & Row, 1965, pp. 681–82.

peans are unavoidably concerned, above all, with what happens in Europe. The last decade and a half has been a peaceful period there. They want it to continue. The United States concerns itself not only with Europe but also the rest of the world, which has been less peaceful. The Soviets have been pushing outward. Americans have been disposed to resist them.

These differences are likely to be a continuing source of friction within NATO. The task of the American President is not to avoid contention—that is not possible—but to manage it so as to limit the damage to the alliance. From this perspective the Reagan record is not at all bad.

European discomfort with the President, however, goes beyond the political differences that preceded and will outlast his presidency. It has, as well, a personal basis. He appears to Europeans to be ill equipped for the responsibility that he bears, a kind of cowboy figure, bellicose, ignorant, with a simplistic view of the world pieced together from journals of right-wing opinion and old Hollywood movies.[12]

By the standards of the postwar presidencies, Mr. Reagan's has not been bellicose. He has, however, regularly appeared to be ill informed about things he ought to know. In 1985 he defended his decision to visit a German military cemetery at Bitburg, where members of the notorious ss were buried, with the explanation that these men were as much victims of the war as those who had perished in the death camps. He also expressed the view that segregation in South Africa had been eliminated. These misstatements were at best dismaying. Perhaps more alarming was the evidence that, at least during his first term, the President's grasp of the main principles of nuclear strategy and arms control was shaky.[13]

As for his picture of the world, it is evidently simple, but it is not patently wrong. The President attracted unfavorable comment in both Europe and the United States for calling the Soviet Union an "evil empire." This phrase may have been

[12] The European unhappiness was forcefully described in these pages two years ago by David Watt, "As A European Saw It," *Foreign Affairs*, America and the World 1983, pp. 521–32.
[13] The evidence is in Strobe Talbott, *Deadly Gambits: The Reagan Administration and the Stalemate in Arms Control*. New York: Alfred A. Knopf, 1984, pp. 132, 237, 250, 263, 273 and 274. During the first term, the Administration was deeply divided on the positions to adopt in the negotiations with the Soviet Union. To get an agreement, Mr. Reagan would have to choose among the competing preferences of the relevant agencies of government—the State and Defense Departments, the Joint Chiefs of Staff and the Arms Control and Disarmament Agency. To do that, he would have had to know the issues in some detail.

impolitic; it was surely not inaccurate. The Bolshevik holdings in Europe and central Asia are as much an empire as were those of the Romanovs, the Hapsburgs and the Ottoman Turks before them. If the Soviet Union and its satellites do not constitute an empire, the term has no meaning. And while the use of the word "evil" to describe it is perhaps debatable, were the Poles, Czechs, Lithuanians, Armenians and others who live involuntarily within its boundaries asked to select a more appropriate term it is unlikely that they would choose to call it "benign." Mr. Reagan's view of the world is like a caricature. It is a picture that is neither rich nor detailed, that emphasizes a few salient features, but that is nonetheless a universally recognizable version of the original.

His elementary sense of the rest of the world and ignorance in important areas are not the fatal handicaps for the President that they would be for European leaders. His job is different from theirs. It is not to defend a detailed program of legislation in give-and-take with the political opposition from the commanding heights of a clear parliamentary majority. It is rather to muster ad hoc coalitions on behalf of a few major issues in a political system where power is constitutionally divided and has been further fragmented by the decline in importance of the two major political parties. The American President must arouse popular enthusiasm for his program in order to get his way. This requires not mastery of legislative detail but the capacity to make broad themes compelling to a mass audience. Presidential power, in Richard Neustadt's famous phrase, is the power to persuade.[14] It has become the power to command several hours of prime-time television each year to try to persuade the American public of the wisdom of a few selected initiatives. At this Mr. Reagan is adept. His simple, clear approach to complex matters is essential to his success.

VI

The success of the Reagan foreign policy is provisional, as success in public affairs always is. Policies have consequences—often unforeseen and unwanted—long after their creators have departed. Even when the consequences are fully apparent they are not easy to judge. Then it is the judgment of history that matters, and those who write it are seldom of one mind. Was

[14] *Presidential Power.* New York: John Wiley & Sons, 1960, chapter three.

Woodrow Wilson a thwarted, unappreciated visionary or a naïve bumbler? Even now there is no consensus. Still, the success of the Reagan foreign policy is unusually provisional; it rests less on the President's having mastered great challenges to American interests than on his having been spared any such tests.

Challenges can appear suddenly, however, sometimes in the form of an unwelcome change of government somewhere in the world. Discontent and unrest gather force over many years, revolution erupts, people hostile to the United States take power. Whoever is President at the time must cope with them. Mr. Kennedy was not responsible for Fidel Castro's victory in Cuba but he became preoccupied with its consequences. Mr. Carter did not create the conditions in which the Ayatollah Khomeini came to power in Iran but found himself entangled in a painful and protracted conflict with the new Iranian regime. Other countries might follow the same course during the balance of Mr. Reagan's term. The Philippines and South Africa are, perhaps, the leading candidates.

Mr. Reagan and his associates, moreover, have not been content simply to serve as passive caretakers of the nation's relations with other countries. They have launched several major foreign policy initiatives. It is on the fate of these undertakings that the success of the Reagan foreign policy will ultimately depend. The outcome of the three most important of them—the Reagan Doctrine, the Strategic Defense Initiative, and the arms buildup—remain quite uncertain.

The Reagan Doctrine goes beyond the long-standing American policy of resisting the spread of Soviet influence; it advocates providing assistance to groups fighting governments that have aligned themselves with the Soviet Union. The Administration has continued the assistance to the Afghan resistance begun by President Carter. It has broached the idea of sending aid to non-communist groups fighting the Vietnamese occupiers of Kampuchea. In 1985 Congress repealed the Clark Amendment prohibiting military involvement of any kind in Angola, thus clearing the way for assistance to forces opposing the Luanda government and its contingent of Cuban troops.

The most significant instance of the Reagan Doctrine has been in Nicaragua, where the United States has supported a sizable insurgency against the Sandinista regime. The Nicaraguan "contras" have mounted a visible challenge to the government without bringing it close to collapse—but without appreciable cost to the United States either. The future of the insurgency, and of the American role in it, are not at all clear. What the President and his officials have said does not add up to an unambiguous statement of their goals. Is the Reagan Administration seeking to overthrow the regime, or simply to force it to permit greater political freedom? Is its aim to affect Nicaraguan foreign policy—to compel the Sandinistas to leave neighboring countries alone, or to cut their ties with Cuba, or with the Soviet Union, or some combination of these? How far is the Administration prepared to go in pursuit of whatever goals it sets? At some point these questions will have to be addressed.

When they are, the Reagan Administration, or its successor, will confront the risk of the two principal American failures in Vietnam: making a commitment that is more costly than the public will sustain, and permitting the defeat of forces with which the United States is closely identified.

Similar uncertainty surrounds the effort to make nuclear weapons "impotent and obsolete" through the development of defenses against ballistic missile attack. The best imaginable result of the Strategic Defense Initiative would, of course, be the creation of a perfect system of defense, a kind of leakproof dome that would cover the United States and friendly countries as well. This would be a strategic revolution as profound as the one that the creation of the atomic bomb itself represented. It would give the United States military superiority over the Soviet Union, which is the reason the Soviets have not been shy about letting it be known that they do not like the scheme.

While a perfect defense would be a great thing for the United States and the West, almost nobody believes that it can be achieved in the foreseeable future. Less-than-perfect defensive systems might still be worth having. They could protect not cities and people but rather American missile silos against a preemptive attack. This, however, would not put an end to the mutual hostage relationship between the two great nuclear powers, as the President wishes. It would in fact reinforce that relationship.

It is conceivable that the Soviet Union will ultimately wish to expand the very modest system of defense against missiles that it now has and that the Anti-Ballistic Missile Treaty of 1972 permits. If, for example, the spread of nuclear weapons proceeds more swiftly over the next two decades than it has in the past two, if the new nuclear nations make Soviet territory their target, and if the Soviets fear that their existing systems of defense against missiles and manned aircraft provide inadequate protection, it is possible that they will agree to allow American defensive systems in return for American acceptance of larger defenses of their own. That is not, however, their present attitude. Adamant opposition to the American strategic defense program was apparently the burden of Mr. Gorbachev's presentations at Geneva.

If the Soviets hold to this view, the Strategic Defense Initiative could in the end make Americans less rather than more secure. It might cause the Soviets to field many more nuclear weapons than they now have. Since defensive systems would be partly based in space, the immunity from attack that reconnaissance satellites have thus far enjoyed might end, to the great disadvantage of the West. The United States might be worse off having embarked on an effort to defend itself against missile attack than it would have been had it never tried to do so.

The most expensive foreign policy undertaking of the Reagan years has been the defense buildup. The defense budget has increased more since 1981 than in any comparable period in peacetime. The Reagan defense program has added to American strength in virtually every military category. But the completion of the program requires continuing high levels of appropriations. The passage of the Gramm-Rudman Bill to balance the federal budget by 1991 makes it highly unlikely that such sums will be available. Cuts in the program, perhaps drastic cuts, will then be necessary. There is no sign that the Administration has decided how to minimize damage to the nation's military standing.

It is distinctly possible that the character of the program, especially the distribution of funds already allocated, will produce a defense posture skewed in ways inadvisable on purely strategic grounds. The direction of American defense spending into the 1990s may well emphasize naval and air forces rather than the army; but it is the army, after all, that will have to meet the brunt of a Soviet attack in the center of Europe, where for a generation it has been considered most likely. Over the next decade, limits on available resources may yield a military establishment rich in powerful, complicated, expensive weapons but poor in spare parts for them, short of the funds to exercise and maintain these armaments, and, because of insufficient pay scales, without skilled personnel to operate them.[15] What Robert E. Osgood wrote in these pages four years ago about the sharp increase in defense spending remains true: "This tangible expression of national will might be the most important achievement of Reagan's defense policy, but in the long run it would be an empty achievement if increased expenditures were not translated into increased capabilities related to a coherent strategy."[16]

The amount of money the Congress will make available for defense in the years ahead will depend on the health of the American economy. That will turn on the fate of the President's macroeconomic policies and their consequences, especially the large deficit in the federal budget. There are two schools of thought on this subject. One holds that, as the requirements rise for public borrowing and for paying back with interest what has already been borrowed, the country will have to accept large tax increases and severe reductions in spending of the sort that the Reagan Administration has so far conspicuously avoided. The Gramm-Rudman Bill suggests that this point of view has carried the day in Congress.

The other school considers drastic measures unnecessary and counts on continued economic growth, coupled with appropriate monetary policies, to keep the gap between income and expenditures at a manageable size. This is not the place to rehearse the arguments on both sides, but it is worth noting a parallel between the President's economic and foreign policies. Each has brought appreciable benefits at little cost. The economist's axiom states that there is no such thing as a free lunch. Both at home and abroad this Administration thus far has come close to providing just that.[17]

The price of harassing the Soviet empire on its flanks, of aspiring to a revolutionary transformation of the strategic nuclear balance, and of building up American armed forces has been remarkably low by historical standards. What will happen if that price goes up? The question really has two parts. Will the cost of Reagan's major initatives rise appreciably during the next three years, forcing choices that the President

[15] On this subject the interested reader is referred to two valuable pamphlets by William W. Kaufmann, *The Defense Budget 1985* and *The Defense Budget 1986*, Washington: The Brookings Institution, 1984 and 1985 respectively; and to an article by Richard Stubbing, "The Defense Program: Buildup or Binge," *Foreign Affairs*, Spring 1985, pp. 848–72.

[16] Robert E. Osgood, "The Revitalization of Containment," *Foreign Affairs*, America and the World 1981, p. 478.

[17] A good discussion of this point is in Robert W. Tucker, "Toward a New Détente," *The New York Times Magazine*, Dec. 9, 1984, p. 90.

has not yet had to make? If so, what will Mr. Reagan do? Will he press ahead to the point of either complete success or disaster? Or will he be disposed to compromise, cut his losses and accept less than what he has sought?

Will he be ready to strike a bargain with the Sandinistas, easing the pressure on them in exchange for concessions in their domestic and foreign policies that the United States desires? Will he agree to place limits on American programs of strategic defense in return for reduction in offensive weaponry on both sides, or, what is not necessarily the same thing, for a more stable balance of nuclear forces? Will he join with the Congress in adjusting the pace of the defense buildup in a way acceptable to both branches of government?

Mr. Reagan has compromised and retreated in the past. But his commitments to assuring American interests in Central America, to strategic defense and to large military investment are apparently powerful. Moreover, to change course too soon can be as costly as holding to it too long. If the Administration were to make concessions on Nicaragua, the Strategic Defense Initiative or the defense budget prematurely, it would forfeit leverage that persisting in the original policies could have brought. If political fortune, like the prices of stocks, bonds and commodities, is cyclical, the essence of statecraft is to sense when the market has reached a peak and act accordingly.

This requires both luck and political skill. Mr. Reagan has had a generous share of both for five years. The trend lines have gone up. Like most people, he has done well in a bull market. He has ridden the crest of the wave without slipping. That is the Reagan record of the last five years. What the record does not tell us is how he will fare if the tide goes out.

John G. Tower

CONGRESS VERSUS THE PRESIDENT: THE FORMULATION AND IMPLEMENTATION OF AMERICAN FOREIGN POLICY

> The President is the sole organ of the nation in its external relations, and its sole representative with foreign nations.
>
> —John Marshall
> March 7, 1800
> 6th Congress

One of the oldest conflicts in the American system of government is that between Congress and the President over the right to formulate and implement foreign policy. Is the President solely responsible for the conduct of external relations? Is the Congress an equal partner? Or does Congress have the right to shape U.S. policy by enacting legislation which proscribes a President's flexibility? These are not just debating points for historians and constitutional lawyers, but critical issues which need to be addressed if we are to see the successful exercise of American diplomacy in the 1980s. Our effectiveness in dealing with the problems ahead, especially U.S.-Soviet competition in the Third World, will depend to a significant degree on our ability to resolve the adversary relationship between the President and Congress.

The struggle for control of foreign policy came to the fore in the twentieth century, with America's reluctant entry into world affairs, two World Wars, and a smaller, but more complex, postwar bipolar world characterized by the increasing interdependence of nations. The first significant Congressional challenge to the Executive's foreign policy prerogative occurred during the interwar years. After the Senate rejected President Wilson's Versailles Treaty in 1920, Congress continued to assert itself in the formulation of foreign policy. By the 1930s, a strong Congress was able to prevent presidential initiative in the critical prewar years. The almost universal consensus today is that this Congressional intrusion had been a disaster and had inhibited the United States from playing a useful role in Europe that might have prevented World War II.

John G. Tower was U.S. Senator from Texas from 1961 until 1985. He served as U.S. Negotiator on Strategic Nuclear Arms in 1985–86, and in 1986–87 chaired the President's Special Review Board, which studied the role and functions of the National Security Adviser and the NSC.

Following the Japanese attack on Pearl Harbor and our entry into the Second World War, Congress and the President stood in agreement over the direction of American foreign and military policy. Congressional intervention all but ceased.

The post-World War II period was marked by a reasonable balance between Congress and the President in the foreign policy decision-making process. In fact, Presidential foreign policy initiatives were generally accepted and reinforced by bipartisan support on Capitol Hill. American foreign policy was fairly coherent and consistent through changing complexions of the body politic. The United States was perceived as a reliable ally and its leadership generally accepted with a high degree of confidence by the non-communist world. But the relative stability between Congress and the President began to erode in the early 1970s with Congressional disenchantment over the Vietnam War. By mid-decade the two branches were locked in a struggle for control of American foreign policy. To a certain extent Congress won, and the balance between Congress and the President has swung dangerously to the legislative side with unfavorable consequences for American foreign policy.

If the balance is not soon restored, American foreign policy will be unable to meet the critical challenges of the 1980s. We are entering an era of fast change and increasing volatility in world affairs. Political instability and regional conflict are on the rise, especially in the Third World. Developing nations in many parts of the world are being torn apart by civil wars between pro-West and Soviet-supported factions, subverted by externally supported insurrection, or subjected to radical or reactionary anti-Western pressures. The industrialized economies of the West are ever more dependent on a lifeline of resources from an increasingly vulnerable part of the world. The Soviet Union has pursued an aggressive interventionist policy on its periphery and abroad, supported by its emerging global force projection capability and its successful use of less direct means of projecting power.

We may well be in a situation today which is analogous to that of the late 1930s, when America's inability to play a more active role in world affairs helped permit the Axis to realize its objectives without serious challenge. During this period Congress tied the President's hands, with disastrous consequences. Now we are back in the same situation, and risk making the same mistakes. If the United States is prevented from playing an active role in countering Soviet and Soviet proxy involvement in the Third World, the 1990s could well find a world in which the resource-rich and strategically important developing nations are aligned with the Soviet Union.

II

What is the proper balance between Congress and the President in the formulation and implementation of foreign policy? Although the bulk of opinion argues for strong Executive authority in the conduct of external relations, the Constitution itself offers no clear definition as to where legislative authority ends and Presidential prerogative begins. The Constitution would appear to have vested war powers in both the Executive and Legislative branches. Although it conferred the power to declare war and raise and support the armed forces on Congress (Article I, Section 8), the Constitution also made the President Commander-in-Chief of the armed forces (Article II, Section 2). Nowhere in the Constitution is there unambiguous guidance as to which branch of government has the final authority to conduct external relations. Nonetheless, there is the strong implication that the formulation and implementation of foreign policy is a function of the Executive Branch, both as a practical necessity and as an essential concomitant of nationality.

John Jay argues this point in the *Federalist Papers* (Number 64, March 5, 1788):

The loss of a battle, the death of a Prince, the removal of a minister, or other circumstances intervening to change the present posture and aspect of affairs, may turn the most favorable tide into a course opposite to our wishes. As in the field, so in the cabinet, there are moments to be seized as they pass, and they who preside in either, should be left in capacity to improve them. So often and so essentially have we heretofore suffered from the want of secrecy and dispatch, that the Constitution would have been inexcusably defective if no attention had been paid to those objects. Those matters which in negociations usually require the most secrecy and the most dispatch, are those preparatory and auxiliary measures which are not otherwise important in a national view, than as they tend to facilitate the attainment of the objects of the negociation. For these the president will find no difficulty to provide, and should any circumstance occur which requires the advice and consent of the senate, he may at any time convene them.

The Supreme Court has forcefully upheld Executive authority in foreign relations. In 1935 Justice Sutherland, in the case of *U.S. v. Curtiss-Wright Export Corporation et al.* (299 U.S. 304), cited a series of previous Court decisions in arguing that the powers of "internal sovereignty" lay with the individual states, but those of "external sovereignty" were with the national government.

[There are fundamental differences] between the powers of the federal government in respect to foreign or external affairs and those in respect to domestic or internal affairs. . . . Not only . . . is the federal power over external affairs in origin and essential character different from that over internal affairs, but participation in the exercise of the power is significantly limited. In this vast external realm, with its important, complicated, delicate and manifold problems, the President alone has the power to speak or listen as a representative of the nation. He *makes* treaties with the advice and consent of the Senate; but he alone negotiates. Into the field of negotiation the Senate cannot intrude; and Congress itself is powerless to invade it.

It is quite apparent that if, in the maintenance of our international relations, embarrassment—perhaps serious embarrassment—is to be avoided and success for our aims achieved, congressional legislation which is to be made effective through negotiation and inquiry within the international field must often accord to the President a degree of discretion and freedom from statutory restriction which would not be admissible were domestic affairs alone involved.

In addition to the constitutional, judicial and historical arguments against Congressional intervention in foreign policy, there is an even more clear-cut issue of the efficacy of Congressional involvement in foreign policy. To the extent that Congress often represents competing regional and parochial interests, it is almost impossible for it to forge a unified national foreign policy strategy and to speak with one voice in negotiating with foreign powers. Because of the nature of the legislative process a law may be passed in response to a certain set of events, yet remain in effect long after the circumstances have changed. The great danger of Congressional intervention in foreign affairs is that enacted legislation becomes an institutional rigid "solution" to a temporary problem.

The President, along with the Vice President, is the only officer of government who is elected by and responsible to the nation as a whole. As such, only he possesses a national mandate. As head of the Executive Branch, the President can formulate a unified foreign policy, taking into consideration how each aspect of it will fit into an overall strategy. He and his advisers can formulate their strategy with the necessary confidentiality not only among themselves, but between the United States and foreign powers. The President has the information, professional personnel, operational experience, and national mandate to conduct a consistent long-range policy.

The legislative body, on the other hand, is elected to represent separate constituencies. Congress must of necessity take a tactical approach when enacting legislation, since the passage of laws is achieved by constantly shifting coalitions. This serves us well in the formulation of domestic policy, where we proceed by voting on one discrete piece of legislation at a time. Although many of us may have our own long-term strategies in mind as we vote on specific legislative matters, the overall effect is a body of legislation passed piece by piece by a changing majority of legislators. We build domestic policy one step at a time to the end that the final product of domestic legislation is reflected in a consensus of various coalitions. If we later find out we have made an error in a specific piece of domestic legislation, we can change it. For example, if we determine that we have underfunded housing subsidies we can increase them the next year. But the process by which generally accepted domestic policy is arrived at does not lend itself to the formulation of a long-term, coherent, foreign policy. Once we alienate a friendly government, perhaps through shortsighted legislation, it may take years for us to rebuild that relationship and recoup the loss.

A foreign policy should be an aggregate strategy, made up of separate bilateral and multilateral relationships that fit into a grander scheme designed to promote the long-term national interests. With a comprehensive design in mind, those who execute foreign policy can respond to changes in the international environment, substituting one tactic for another as it becomes necessary, but retaining the overall strategy.

In 1816, the Senate Foreign Relations Committee put the argument this way:

The President is the constitutional representative of the United States with regard to foreign nations. He manages our concerns with foreign nations and must necessarily be most competent to determine when, how, and upon what subjects negotiation may be urged with the greatest prospect of success. ... The Committee ... think the interference of the Senate in the direction of foreign negotiations are calculated to diminish that responsibility and thereby to impair the best security for the national safety. The nature of transactions with foreign nations, moreover, requires caution and unity of design, and their success frequently depends on secrecy and dispatch.

Five hundred and thirty-five Congressmen with different philosophies, regional interests and objectives in mind cannot forge a unified foreign policy that reflects the interests of the United States as a whole. Nor can they negotiate with foreign powers, or meet the requirement for diplomatic confidentiality. They are also ill equipped to respond quickly and decisively to changes in the international scene. The shifting coalitions of Congress, which serve us so well in the formulation and implementation of domestic policy, are not well suited to the day-to-day conduct of external relations. An observer has compared the conduct of foreign relations to a geopolitical chess game. Chess is not a team sport.

III

The 1970s were marked by a rash of Congressionally initiated foreign policy legislation that limited the President's range of options on a number of foreign policy issues. The thrust of the legislation was to restrict the President's ability to dispatch troops abroad in a crisis, and to proscribe his authority in arms sales, trade, human rights, foreign assistance and intelligence operations. During this period, over 150 separate prohibitions and restrictions were enacted on Executive Branch authority to formulate and implement foreign policy. Not only was much of this legislation ill conceived, if not actually unconstitutional, it has served in a number of instances to be detrimental to the national security and foreign policy interests of the United States.

The President's freedom of action in building bilateral relationships was severely proscribed by the series of *Nelson-Bingham Amendments*, beginning with the 1974 Foreign Assistance Act (P.L. 93-559). This legislation required the President to give advance notice to Congress of any offer to sell to foreign countries defense articles and services valued at $25 million or more and empowered the Congress to disapprove such sales within 20 calendar days by concurrent resolution. In 1976, the Nelson-Bingham Amendment to the Arms Export Control Act (P. L. 94-329) tightened these restrictions to include advance notification of any sale of "major" defense equipment totaling over $7 million. Congress is now given 30 days in which to exercise its legislative veto.

The consequence of these laws is that for the past seven years every major arms sale agreement has been played out amidst an acrimonious national debate, blown out of all proportion to the intrinsic importance of the transaction in question. Often the merits of the sale and its long-term foreign policy consequences are ignored, since legislators are put into the position of posturing for domestic political considerations. The debate diverts the President, the Congress and the nation from focusing on vital internal matters. Finally, because arms sales debates command so much media attention, legislators are inclined to give impulsive reaction statements before they have an opportunity for informed deliberation. They thereby often commit themselves to positions that, on cool reflection, they find untenable but difficult to recant.

The recent debate over the sale of AWACS (Airborne Warning and Control System) surveillance aircraft to Saudi Arabia is a classic case in point. Under such circumstances, it becomes extremely difficult for elected legislators to ignore constitutent pressures and decide an issue on its merits. For example, Congressman Dan Rostenkowski (D-Ill.) said following the House vote to reject the AWACS sale that he voted against selling AWACS to Saudi Arabia for political reasons, despite his view that the sale should go through on its merits.

Such a situation raises the possibility that should the Congressional decision do ultimate violence to our national interest, the nation whose perceived interests have been sustained by successful lobbying will pay a price later. My colleague, Senator William Cohen (R-Maine), who opposed the sale on its merits, felt compelled to vote for it because he feared its defeat would precipitate an American backlash against Israel:

If the sale is rejected, [Israel] ... will be blamed for the dissolution of the peace process ... when the crisis comes, ... when everyone is pointing an accusatory finger looking for a scapegoat, I do not want to hear any voices in the United States say—if only they had not been so intransigent, if only they had agreed not to interfere, if only they had not brought this mess—this death—upon themselves.

In some cases Congress allows a sale to go through, but only after a series of trivial and humiliating restrictions are placed on the purchasing nation. This tends to negate whatever goodwill the sale was designed to achieve. For example, in 1975 the President agreed to sell HAWK surface-to-air mobile missiles to Jordan. After a national brouhaha filled with many insults to King Hussein and questions about the stability of his regime, the sale finally went through, but only in "compromise" form—we took the wheels off. Presumably, HAWK missiles without wheels would allow the Jordanians to use them in fixed positions to protect the capital and key military locations, but prevent them from moving the missiles to the front line to be used against Israel. King Hussein later asked then Secretary of State Henry Kissinger why Congress had insisted on such a trivial point. It was never a question of whether the HAWKs would be mobile or not—we knew the Jordanians would be able to buy the wheels on the international market if they decided to violate the terms of the sale. The end result was that rather than cement our friendly relations with Jordan, we succeeded in humiliating a longtime friend.

Such actions are not soon forgotten. In his recent visit to Washington, King Hussein indicated that Jordan is considering turning to the Soviet Union for its new air defense missiles. This attitude clearly stems in part from his unhappiness over Congressional restrictions on U.S. arms sales to Jordan. According to a State Department spokesman, the 1975 HAWK missile sale "still rankles" in Jordan.

The *Turkish Arms Embargo* was a case where Congress tied the President's hands in negotiations. After the Turkish invasion of Cyprus on July 19–20, 1974, the Administration became involved in negotiations aimed at reconciling our two NATO allies, Greece and Turkey. After two days, a cease-fire was achieved, with Turkey controlling 25 percent of Cyprus.

Yet Congress was moving on a path of its own. On August 2, the House introduced two measures demanding the immediate and total removal of Turkish troops from Cyprus. After the second Turkish assault on August 14, the Senate Foreign Relations Committee prompted a State Department inquiry into possible Turkish violations of U.S. arms restrictions.

At one point, Prime Minister Ecevit of Turkey privately communicated his willingness to settle on terms representing a significant improvement over the status quo. The Administration was concerned that Congressional action would make it harder for Turkey to follow a conciliatory policy and thus destroy any hopes of a negotiated settlement. In an attempt to discourage a Turkish embargo, the White House invited several of my colleagues to attend briefings on the possibility of negotiations. Even after being shown evidence that a negotiation likely to improve Greece's position was in the making, these Congressmen continued to call for an arms embargo; soon, all hopes for a negotiated settlement vanished. On September 16, Ecevit's moderate government collapsed, and on October 17, the Congress imposed a Turkish arms embargo on a "very, very reluctant" President Ford. The embargo began on February 5, 1975; by that time, Turkey controlled 40 percent of the island. On June 17, 1975, Turkey responded to the embargo by placing all U.S. bases and listening posts on provisional status. On July 24, 1975, the House rejected a motion to partially lift the embargo; two days later, Turkey announced it was shutting down all U.S. bases and posts on its territory.

Thus, instead of reaching an agreement with a moderate Turkish government that controlled one-quarter of Cyprus, the United States had severely strained relations with an angry Turkish government that controlled two-fifths of the island. Furthermore, the aid cutoff weakened Turkey militarily, jeopardizing the southern flank of NATO and putting at risk our strategic listening posts in that country.

In a society such as ours, with its heterogeneous mix of various national and ethnic groups, strong lobbies are inevitable. But to submit American foreign policy to inordinate influence by these groups—often emotionally charged—is to impair a President's ability to carry out a strategy which reflects the interests of our nation as a whole. The Nelson-Bingham Amendments and the Turkish Arms Embargo were two pieces of legislation conducive to such a situation.

A second major area where Congressional intervention contributed to foreign policy disasters was the series of anti-war amendments. Throughout the early 1970s Congress proposed a series of acts aimed at forcing the United States into early withdrawal from Southeast Asia and cutting off American aid to Vietnam, Laos and Cambodia. The *Cooper-Church Amendment*, which became law in early 1971, cut off funds for U.S. troops, advisers and air support in and over Cambodia. The *Eagleton Amendment* (1973) called for American withdrawal from Laos and Cambodia. The *McGovern-Hatfield Amendment* (1970–71) set deadlines for American withdrawal from Indochina. Even though these two latter anti-Vietnam amendments did not become law, the pattern was clear by the early 1970s. My Senate colleagues would introduce one amendment after another, making it clear to the North Vietnamese that we would eventually legislate ourselves out of Vietnam. The Administration lost both credibility and flexibility in the peace negotiations. By making it clear to the North Vietnamese that Congress would prevent the President from further pursuing the war, or from enforcing the eventual peace, Congress sent a clear signal to our enemies that they could win in the end. The North Vietnamese were encouraged to stall in the Paris Peace Talks, waiting for American domestic dissent to provide them with the victory their military forces had been unable to achieve. After the Paris Agreements, aid to South Vietnam was throttled.

Finally, on July 1, 1973, we destroyed any hope of enforcing the Paris Peace Accords. The *Fulbright Amendment* to the Second Supplemental Appropriations Act for FY 1973 prohibited the use of funds "to support directly or indirectly combat activities in . . . or over Cambodia, Laos, North Vietnam and South Vietnam." As I said in Congressional debate over the Eagleton Amendment, the forerunner to the Fulbright Amendment:

It has tremendous significance because it marks the placing on the President of an . . . inhibition in the conduct of foreign relations, in the negotiating of agreement and treaties, and in the implementation and enforcement of those agreements once arrived at. . . . What we have in effect done in the Eagleton Amendment is said to [the North Vietnamese]: 'You may do whatever you please. Having concluded this agreement, we intend to walk away from it, and we don't care whether you violate those provisions or not.'

I believed then and still believe that our failure to enforce the Paris Accords was a principal contributor to Communist victory in Indochina and the resulting horrors we have seen since in Laos, Cambodia and Vietnam. Reasonable men may argue whether or not we were right in being in Vietnam in the first place. I remain convinced that we made many mistakes that led us there, and that our direct involvement was ill conceived. But to deny a President the military means to enforce a negotiated agreement guaranteed that all the sacrifices that came before it would be in vain. Just because a peace agreement is signed or a cease-fire agreed to is no guarantee that both sides will live up to it. After World War II we enforced the peace with Germany and Japan by occupation forces. We guaranteed the Korean cease-fire by the continued presence of U.N. troops at the Demilitarized Zone. The Fulbright Amendment prohibited our enforcing the Paris Accords. We bought a settlement in Vietnam with 50,000 American lives that gave South Vietnam, Cambodia and Laos a chance to survive—a chance that was thrown away when we refused to be guarantors to that settlement.

The *War Powers Act* (P.L. 93–148) is probably the most potentially damaging of the 1970s legislation, although we have yet to experience a crisis where its effects are felt. The War Powers Act (1973) grew out of Congress' frustration with the war in Vietnam and its desire to prevent such a situation from ever happening again. Although President Nixon vetoed the Act on October 24, 1973, terming it "unconstitutional," his veto was overridden two weeks later by the House and Senate.

The act provides that before American troops are introduced "into hostilities or into situations where imminent involvement in hostilities is clearly indicated by the circumstances" the President is to consult with Congress "in every possible instance." The President must notify Congress and submit a report within 48 hours after armed forces are sent abroad, "setting forth the circumstances necessitating the introduction of U.S. forces" and the "estimated scope and duration of the hostilities or involvement." After this initial two-day period, the President has 60 days to withdraw those forces or receive Congressional authorization for an extension, or a declaration of war.

This act jeopardizes the President's ability to respond quickly, forcefully and if necessary in secret, to protect American interests abroad. This may even invite crises. Although the act does not specify whether the report to Congress must be unclassified, there remains the possibility that a confidential report would become public knowledge. In many cases the more urgent the requirement that a decision remain confidential, the greater the pressures for disclosure. Thus, by notifying Congress of the size, disposition and objectives of U.S. forces dispatched in a crisis, we run the risk that the report may get into the public domain. If this information becomes available to the enemy, he then knows exactly what he can expect from American forces and thus what risks he runs in countering American actions. This removes any element of surprise the U.S. forces might have enjoyed and eliminates any uncertainties the adversary might have as to American plans.

It is interesting to speculate on just how damaging the legislation could prove to be at some future point. For that matter, what if the Iranian rescue attempt had gone somewhat differently? On April 26, 1980, President Carter reported to Congress the use of armed forces in the unsuccessful attempt to rescue American hostages in Iran on April 24, in full compliance with the 48-hour notification requirement of the War Powers Act. In this case, the rescue operation was over by the time the report was submitted, so there was no longer a need for secrecy nor a need for Congress to consider whether forces should be authorized or withdrawn. But what if the rescue attempt had bogged down or been planned as a longer effort? No doubt the details would have gotten out almost immediately, leaving little doubt in the minds of the Iranians just what the Americans were up to. While the framers of the War Powers Act intended it to prevent another Vietnam, their legislation has the effect of severely limiting the President's ability to respond quickly, forcefully and in secret to a foreign crisis.

In addition to the questionable wisdom of the reporting and consulting requirements of the War Powers Act, there are also doubts as to whether the legislative veto contained in the act is constitutional. Section 5 of the Act allows Congress the right to terminate any use of force, at any time, that has not been specifically authorized by either a declaration of war or similar legislation, by a concurrent resolution passed by a simple majority of both Houses. The legislative veto contained in the War Powers Act would appear to be in violation of Article 1, Section 7 of the Constitution. This so-called presentation clause clearly stipulates that an act can become law only if it is passed by a majority of both Houses of Congress followed by the President's assent, or by a two-thirds vote in each Chamber to override the President's veto.

After the Indochina debacle, there was a raft of Vietnam-syndrome legislation that sought to prevent the President from getting us involved in "future Vietnams." The *Tunney Amendment* to the Defense Appropriations Act of 1976 (P.L. 94-212), which passed the Senate on December 19, 1975, prohibited the use of "funds appropriated in this Act for any activities involving Angola other than intelligence gathering."[1] My colleagues feared that President Ford's attempts to offer minimal assistance to the pro-West UNITA (National Union for the Total Independence of Angola) and FNLA (National Front for the Liberation of Angola) factions would somehow embroil us in "another Vietnam." The domestic debate over whether we should become involved in Angola sent a clear signal to the Soviets and their Cuban proxies. They knew that the risk of U.S. intervention was low, and the possibility of continued U.S. assistance to the pro-Western factions slim.

Although the Soviet-Cuban airlift halted temporarily in December with President Ford's stern warning to the Soviet Ambassador, the airlift resumed with a vengeance following passage of the Tunney Amendment on December 19, 1975. The number of Cubans in Angola doubled as they began flying in fresher troops for what was to become an all-out offensive against pro-Western forces. By January the Soviet Union had increased its military assistance to the MPLA (Popular Movement for the Liberation of Angola) and stationed Soviet warships in the vicinity of Angola. They began extensive ferrying operations for Cuban troops. It was clear that the United States had lost whatever leverage it might have had to persuade Soviet leaders to reduce Soviet and Cuban involvement in Angola.

With Angola the Soviet Union entered a new phase; never before had it or its surrogate Cuban army attempted such large-scale operations in Africa or anywhere else in the Third World. Their successful intervention in Angola bestowed on the Soviet Union and Cuba the image of dependable allies and supporters of radical movements in southern Africa. The United States by

---

[1] The Clark Amendment to the Arms Export Control Act of 1976 (Sec. 404, P.L. 94-329), which became law on June 30, 1976, further tightened the restriction by prohibiting "assistance of any kind . . . for the purpose, or which would have the effect, of promoting or augmenting, directly or indirectly, the capacity of any nation, group, organization, movement, or individual to conduct military or paramilitary operations in Angola."

contrast was portrayed as having lost its taste for foreign involvement after Vietnam, and as being domestically divided over a foreign policy strategy. The moderate black African states lost confidence in America's willingness to stem the tide of Soviet involvement in the region.

After being reduced to sporadic guerrilla engagements for over a year, in July 1977 the pro-West UNITA faction declared its intention to renew the fight. Following this announcement, the Soviets and Cubans increased their efforts. As of late 1979, there were some 19,000 Cuban troops, 6,000 Cuban civilian technicians and 400 to 500 Soviet advisors in Angola. Although the guerrilla war continues, the Clark Amendment prohibits the United States from offering any aid to the pro-Western faction. The Clark Amendment prevents us from responding to Soviet and Cuban involvement in Angola, and leaves open to them the mineral-rich, strategically important region of southern Africa.

Finally, two of the most damaging Congressional intrusions into national security policy were the Senate Select Committee to Study Governmental Operations with Respect to Intelligence Activities (the so-called *Church Committee*) and the *Hughes-Ryan Amendment* to the Foreign Assistance Act (P.L. 93–189). As vice-chairman of the Church Committee (1975–76) I sought to limit the damage to our intelligence community, although to little avail. By conducting a public inquiry into the CIA we exposed not only its supposed blunders and malfeasance but also important information as to how the CIA is organized, how it gathers intelligence and what kinds of sources and methods it uses.

The Hughes-Ryan Amendment, which became law on December 30, 1974, prohibited any CIA activities abroad that are not directly related to intelligence gathering, "unless and until the President finds that each such operation is important to the national security of the United States and reports, in a timely fashion, a description and scope of such operations to the appropriate committees of Congress." By 1977 information about covert intelligence activities was available to eight Congressional committees, for a total of 200 members or roughly 40 percent of Congress.[2]

This, plus the Church Committee hearings, confirmed to our adversaries that clandestine operations would be severely curtailed in the future. It sent a signal to our adversaries that they could

[2] In one of the few reversals of the 1970s legislation, in October 1980 the President signed into law an amendment to the National Security Act (P.L. 96–450), which stipulates that he must report covert operations to only two Congressional Committees, the House and Senate Select Committees on Intelligence.

proceed with impunity in the "back alleys of the world." These actions also shook the confidence of those friendly states which had cooperated with us in intelligence gathering, and caused many of them to reassess their relationship with the U.S. intelligence community. They feared Congressional investigations of the CIA would expose their own intelligence sources and methods. In private conversations with officials of friendly intelligence agencies, I have been told that the Church Committee raised doubts about the wisdom of their cooperating with the United States in the future. This has also adversely affected our cooperation with countries that for political reasons take a publicly hostile attitude toward the United States, but who privately cooperate with us on some matters of mutual interest. They fear the publicity generated by a Congressional investigation would expose what is essentially a private relationship, and lead to unfavorable domestic political consequences for them. Finally, either through leaks or publicly released data, the Church Committee titillated the press with daily helpings of some of our nation's most treasured secrets.

IV

If we are to meet the foreign policy challenges facing us in the 1980s, we must restore the traditional balance between Congress and the President in the formulation and implementation of foreign policy. To do so, much of the legislation of the past decade should be repealed or amended.

Many in Congress are coming to this conclusion and are working toward a reversal of the imbalance. The 1980 modification of the Hughes-Ryan Amendment to require notification of covert actions to only the two Intelligence Committees is one such step, as is the Senate's October 22, 1981, vote to repeal the Clark Amendment. Further efforts in this direction are essential if we are to have the maximum flexibility required to respond to a fast-changing world.

In addition to reversing much of this legislation, we should also look at new legislation which may be appropriate. There are strong arguments in favor of creating an unspecified contingency fund for economic and military assistance. One of the consequences of the 1970s legislation was that such funds which had previously existed were either abolished or severely curtailed. Reestablishment of such funds would grant the President the flexibility he needs to be able to respond quickly to help new friends that emerge unexpectedly, or old friends who are suddenly endangered. While disbursement of these funds should be made with appropriate notification to Congress, the inevitable delays involved in waiting for new Congressional authorization should be avoided.

For example, when Zimbabwe became independent on April 18, 1980, the new government was strongly anti-Soviet, pro-West and in need of economic assistance. On the day he took office, President Mugabe invited the United States to be the first nation to establish diplomatic relations with and open an embassy in Zimbabwe. We responded with a pledge of economic assistance, but due to the lack of funds for such contingencies, were able to grant only $2 million. We had to wait almost ten months, until the next appropriations cycle could be completed, to grant Zimbabwe the amount of economic assistance it needed.

We face a similar situation in northern Africa today. In the confusion cast over the area in the wake of the Sadat assassination, Libyan President Qaddafi has heightened threats against the anti-Soviet government of Sudan. The Libyan army appears to be on an alerted posture. Were Libya to attack Sudan tomorrow, there is very little the United States could do right away to assist President Nimeiry.

As legislation now stands the President has certain limited flexibility to grant military assistance to respond quickly to unplanned situations. The Foreign Assistance Act of 1961, as amended, permits the President, in the interests of national security, to draw on U.S. military stocks, defense services, or military education and training, up to $50 million in any fiscal year for foreign use. In 1981 the Reagan Administration requested that new contingency funds totalling $350 million be established for emergency economic and military assistance. As of mid-November 1981 Congressional action on this request is still pending, although it appears that both Houses are moving to reduce significantly the size of these contingency funds.

In supporting such discretionary authority and appropriations, and urging the repeal of the excessively restrictive legislation of the 1970s, I am in effect proposing a return to the situation that prevailed in the 1950s and 1960s.

At that time the Congress did provide discretionary authority and substantial contingency funds for the use of Presidents Truman, Eisenhower, Kennedy and Johnson. Each of these Presidents employed his authority to act quickly and decisively in ways which, on balance, served the national interest—especially in new and unforeseen situations emerging in what we now call the Third World. The basic authority of the Congress to appropriate funds for the armed forces and foreign activities remained constant.

Indeed, the Congress from time to time expressed its views forcefully as to the desirability of support for nations that acted in ways prejudicial to American interests. (An early example of such legislation was the Hickenlooper Amendment, which for many years expressed Congress' general opposition to continue aid to countries that nationalized private American companies without adequate compensation.) The crucial difference is that such expressions of Congressional sentiment almost invariably contained a saving clause that permitted the President to go ahead if he certified to the Congress that the action was necessary for overriding national security reasons. This is a perfectly sound and reasonable practice, and one that avoids the immense complications and possible unconstitutionality of the legislative vetoes introduced by the various amendments of the 1970s.

In short, what I propose above is vastly more effective than the present situation, sounder from every constitutional standpoint, and fully in keeping with past precedents.

v

Finally, in reconsidering the legislation of the 1970s, it is useful to reexamine it and its causes in a more dispassionate light than that of the period. At the time, much of this legislation was considered a necessary response to counter the excesses of the presidency. Since the Vietnam War had never been formally declared by Congress, it was seen as the President's war. Watergate, along with the war, was considered to be the result of a Presidency grown too authoritarian. If the war were ever to end, and if future Vietnams were to be prevented, the President's foreign policy authority would have to be proscribed. As Arthur Schlesinger put it, the theory "that a foreign policy must be trusted to the executive went down in flames in Vietnam. . . . Vietnam discredited executive control of foreign relations as profoundly as Versailles and mandatory neutrality had discredited congressional control."[3]

If this legislation was motivated by an "Imperial Presidency," whose ultimate manifestation was an undeclared war, then the motivation is flawed. Blame for Vietnam can be laid at many doors: a series of American Presidents, and those in the civilian leadership who advocated gradual escalation and limited rules of

---

[3] Arthur M. Schlesinger, Jr., *The Imperial Presidency*, Boston: Houghton Mifflin, 1973, pp. 282–83.

engagement. But Congress was not blameless. The war in Vietnam, while undeclared by Congress in a formal sense, had de facto Congressional support. Beginning in the mid-1960s the Administration sent defense authorization and appropriations bills to Congress—legislation which clearly designated certain men and monies for the war effort. Year after year Congress acquiesced in the Vietnam War, by authorizing and appropriating resources for it. As former Senator J. William Fulbright remarked, "It was not a lack of power which prevented the Congress from ending the war in Indochina but a lack of will." With waning public support for a war which seemed to drag on forever, many in Congress and the media looked to a single explanation—for a scapegoat who could be held accountable for an unpopular war. Blame for the war in Vietnam was attributed to the usurpation of power by the President.

In the early 1970s Congress reversed itself and belatedly attempted to use its appropriation authority to end the war. While this was certainly within its prerogative, the timing was of questionable wisdom. Our efforts to disengage from Vietnam and to negotiate with the North Vietnamese were made more difficult by Congressional intervention. Congressional action made a settlement all the more difficult to achieve and, ultimately, impossible to enforce. The view that the Vietnam War discredited forever Executive control of foreign policy was an emotional reaction, driven by the passion of the moment. Because of it, Congress embarked on a course to limit not only President Nixon's flexibility, but also that of future Presidents. Congress prescribed a cure for a nonexistent disease. The lasting effect was that Congress institutionalized its foreign policy differences with the President by legislating permanent solutions for a temporary situation.

As Cyrus Vance said at the 1980 Harvard commencement, "Neither we nor the world can afford an American foreign policy which is hostage to the emotions of the moment." The authority to conduct external relations should not vacillate between Congress and the President as a result of failed or unpopular initiatives. The whole point of a written constitution and body of judicial opinion is to establish a consistent mechanism for apportioning authority. Whereas the Constitution confers on the Senate the duty of advice and consent in the making of treaties, on the Congress the power to appropriate monies for armed forces and to declare war, and special authority in the field of trade, it confers on Congress no other special rights in the field of external affairs.

The cumulative effect of this legislation is that, as the United States enters a period when the greatest flexibility is required of an American President to deal with fast-changing situations in the world, Congress has inhibited the President's freedom of action and denied him the tools necessary for the formulation and implementation of American foreign policy. We know that the Soviet Union maintains clandestine operations which are well organized, well disciplined, well financed, well trained and often well armed, in virtually every Third World country. They are in a position to exploit many restive political situations which they may or may not originate. To inhibit the United States in its ability to conduct covert operations, to provide military assistance to pro-West governments or groups, and to respond quickly to military crises is to concede an enormous advantage to the Soviet Union and its proxies.

It is my sincere hope that Congress will reexamine its role in the conduct of foreign policy and repeal or amend, as necessary, the legislation of the 1970s. The end towards which we should work is to do whatever is necessary to strengthen America's ability to formulate and implement a unified, coherent and cohesive foreign policy to face the challenges of the 1980s.

McGeorge Bundy
George F. Kennan
Robert S. McNamara
Gerard Smith

THE PRESIDENT'S CHOICE: STAR WARS OR ARMS CONTROL

T he reelection of Ronald Reagan makes the future of his Strategic Defense Initiative the most important question of nuclear arms competition and arms control on the national agenda since 1972. The President is strongly committed to this program, and senior officials, including Secretary of Defense Caspar W. Weinberger, have made it clear that he plans to intensify this effort in his second term. Sharing the gravest reservations about this undertaking, and believing that unless it is radically constrained during the next four years it will bring vast new costs and dangers to our country and to mankind, we think it urgent to offer an assessment of the nature and hazards of this initiative, to call for the closest vigilance by Congress and the public, and even to invite the victorious President to reconsider. While we write only after obtaining the best technical advice we could find, our central concerns are political. We believe the President's initiative to be a classic case of good intentions that will have bad results because they do not respect reality.

This new initiative was launched by the President on March 23, 1983, in a surprising and quite personal passage at the end

---

McGeorge Bundy was Special Assistant to the President for National Security Affairs from 1961 to 1966 and President of the Ford Foundation from 1966 to mid-1979. He is currently Professor of History at New York University.

George F. Kennan is Professor Emeritus at the Institute for Advanced Study, Princeton. He was U.S. Ambassador to the Soviet Union, 1952, and to Yugoslavia, 1961–63. He is the author of *Soviet-American Relations, 1917–20* (2 Vols.) and *Memoirs* (2 Vols.), and has contributed over a dozen articles to *Foreign Affairs*.

Robert S. McNamara was Secretary of Defense from 1961 to 1968 and President of the World Bank from 1968 to mid-1981.

Gerard Smith was Chief of the U.S. Delegation to the Strategic Arms Limitation Talks from 1969 to 1972, and is the author of *Doubletalk: The Story of SALT I*.

of a speech in praise of his other military programs. In that passage he called on our scientists to find means of rendering nuclear weapons "impotent and obsolete." In the briefings that surrounded the speech, Administration spokesmen made it clear that the primary objective was the development of ways and means of destroying hostile missiles—meaning in the main Soviet missiles—by a series of attacks all along their flight path, from their boost phase after launch to their entry into the atmosphere above the United States. Because of the central position the Administration itself gave to this objective, the program promptly acquired the name Star Wars, and the President's Science Advisor, George Keyworth, has admitted that this name is now indelible. We find it more accurately descriptive than the official "Strategic Defense Initiative."[1]

II

What is centrally and fundamentally wrong with the President's objective is that it cannot be achieved. The overwhelming consensus of the nation's technical community is that in fact there is no prospect whatever that science and technology can, at any time in the next several decades, make nuclear weapons "impotent and obsolete." The program developed over the last 18 months, ambitious as it is, offers no prospect for a leak-proof defense against strategic ballistic missiles alone, and it entirely excludes from its range any effort to limit the effectiveness of other systems—bomber aircraft, cruise missiles, and smuggled warheads.

The President's hopes are entirely understandable. There must be very few Americans who have never shared them. All four of us, like Mr. Reagan, grew up in a world without nuclear weapons, and we believe with passion that the world would be a much safer place without them. Americans should be constantly on the alert for any possibilities that can help to reduce

[1] There has been an outpouring of technical comment on this subject, and even in a year and a half the arguments have evolved considerably. Two recent independent analyses on which we have drawn with confidence are *The Reagan Strategic Defense Initiative: A Technical, Political, and Arms Control Assessment*, by Sidney D. Drell, Philip J. Farley and David Holloway, A Special Report of the Center for International Security and Arms Control, July 1984, Stanford: Stanford University, 1984; and *The Fallacy of Star Wars* (based on studies conducted by the Union of Concerned Scientists and co-chaired by Richard L. Garwin, Kurt Gottfried, and Henry W. Kendall), John Tirman, ed., New York: Vintage, 1984.

the nuclear peril in which we all live, and it is entirely natural that a hope of safety like the one the President held out should stir a warmly affirmative first response. But false hope, however strong and understandable, is a bad guide to action.

The notion that nuclear weapons, or even ballistic missiles alone, can be rendered impotent by science and technology is an illusion. It reflects not only technological hubris in the face of the very nature of nuclear weapons, but also a complete misreading of the relation between threat and response in the nuclear decisions of the superpowers.

The first and greatest obstacle is quite simply that these weapons are destructive to a degree that makes them entirely different from any other weapon in history. The President frequently observes that over the centuries every new weapon has produced some countervailing weapon, and up to Hiroshima he is right. But conventional weapons can be neutralized by a relatively low rate of kill, provided that the rate is sustained over time. The classic modern example is defense against nonnuclear bombing. If you lose one bomber in every ten sorties, your force will soon be destroyed. A pilot assigned to fly 30 missions will face a 95-percent prospect of being shot down. A ten-percent rate of kill is highly effective.

With nuclear weapons the calculation is totally different. Both Mr. Reagan's dream and his historical argument completely neglect the decisive fact that a very few nuclear weapons, exploding on or near population centers, would be hideously too many. At today's levels of superpower deployment—about 10,000 strategic warheads on each side—even a 95-percent kill rate would be insufficient to save either society from disintegration in the event of general nuclear war. Not one of Mr. Reagan's technical advisers claims that any such level of protection is attainable. They know better. In the words of the officer in charge of the program, Lieutenant General James Abrahamson, "a perfect defense is not a realistic thing." In response to searching questions from Senator Sam Nunn of Georgia, the senior technical official of the Defense Department, Under Secretary Richard DeLauer, made it plain that he could not foresee any level of defense that would make our own offensive systems unnecessary.

Among all the dozens of spokesmen for the Administration, there is not one with any significant technical qualifications who has been willing to question Dr. DeLauer's explicit statement that "There's no way an enemy can't overwhelm your defenses if he wants to badly enough." The only senior official who continues to share the President's dream and assert his belief that it can come true is Caspar Weinberger, whose zealous professions of confidence are not accompanied by technical support.

The terrible power of nuclear weapons has a second meaning that decisively undermines the possibility of an effective Star Wars defense of populations. Not only is their destructive power so great that only a kill rate closely approaching 100 percent can give protection, but precisely because the weapons are so terrible neither of the two superpowers can tolerate the notion of "impotence" in the face of the arsenal of the opponent. Thus any prospect of a significantly improved American defense is absolutely certain to stimulate the most energetic Soviet efforts to ensure the continued ability of Soviet warheads to get through. Ever since Hiroshima it has been a cardinal principle of Soviet policy that the Soviet Union must have a match for any American nuclear capability. It is fanciful in the extreme to suppose that the prospect of any new American deployment which could undermine the effectiveness of Soviet missile forces will not be met by a most determined and sustained response.

This inevitable Soviet reaction is studiously neglected by Secretary Weinberger when he argues in defense of Star Wars that today's skeptics are as wrong as those who said we could never get to the moon. The effort to get to the moon was not complicated by the presence of an adversary. A platoon of hostile moon-men with axes could have made it a disaster. No one should understand the irrelevance of his analogy better than Mr. Weinberger himself. As secretary of defense he is bound to be familiar with the intensity of our own American efforts to ensure that our own nuclear weapons, whether on missiles or aircraft, will always be able to get through to Soviet targets in adequate numbers.

The technical analyses so far available are necessarily incomplete, primarily because of the very large distance between the President's proposal and any clearly defined system of defense. There is some truth in Mr. Weinberger's repeated assertion that one cannot fully refute a proposal that as yet has no real content. But already important and enduring obstacles have been identified. Two are systemic and ineradicable. First, a Star Wars defense must work perfectly the very first time, since it can never be tested in advance as a full system. Second, it must be triggered almost instantly, because the crucial boost phase of Soviet missiles lasts less than five minutes from the moment of launch. In that five minutes (which new launch technology can probably reduce to about 60 seconds), there must be detection, decision, aim, attack and kill. It is hard to imagine a scheme further removed from the kind of tested reliability and clear presidential control that we have hitherto required of systems involving nuclear danger.

There are other more general difficulties with the President's dream. Any remotely leak-proof defense against strategic missiles will require extensive deployments of many parts of the system in space, both for detection of any Soviet launch and, in most schemes, for transmission of the attack on the missile in its boost phase. Yet no one has been able to offer any hope that it will ever be easier and cheaper to deploy and defend large systems in space than for someone else to destroy them. The balance of technical judgment is that the advantage in any unconstrained contest in space will be with the side that aims to attack the other side's satellites. In and of itself this advantage constitutes a compelling argument against space-based defense.

Finally, as we have already noted, the President's program offers no promise of effective defense against anything but ballistic missiles. Even if we assume, against all the evidence, that a leak-proof defense could be achieved against these particular weapons, there would remain the difficulty of defense against cruise missiles, against bomber aircraft, and against the clandestine introduction of warheads. It is important to remember here that very small risks of these catastrophic events will be enough to force upon us the continuing need for our own deterrent weapons. We think it is interesting that among the strong supporters of the Star Wars scheme are some of the same people who were concerned about the danger of the strategic threat of the Soviet Backfire bomber only a few years ago. Is it likely that in the light of these other threats they will find even the best possible defense against missiles a reason for declaring our own nuclear weapons obsolete?

Inadvertent but persuasive proof of this failing has been given by the President's science adviser. Last February, in a speech in Washington, Mr. Keyworth recognized that the Soviet response to a truly successful Star Wars program would be to "shift their strategic resources to other weapons systems," and he made no effort to suggest that such a shift could be prevented or countered, saying: "*Let* the Soviets move to alternate weapons systems, to submarines, cruise missiles, advanced technology aircraft. Even the critics of the President's defense initiative agree that *those* weapons systems are far more stable deterrents than are ICBMs [land-based missiles]." Mr. Keyworth, in short, is willing to accept all these other means of warhead delivery, and he appears to be entirely unaware that by this acceptance he is conceding that even if Star Wars should succeed far beyond what any present technical consensus can allow us to believe, it would fail by the President's own standard.

The inescapable reality is that there is literally no hope that Star Wars can make nuclear weapons obsolete. Perhaps the first and most important political task for those who wish to save the country from the expensive and dangerous pursuit of a mirage is to make this basic proposition clear. As long as the American people believe that Star Wars offers real hope of reaching the President's asserted goal, it will have a level of political support unrelated to reality. The American people, properly and sensibly, would like nothing better than to make nuclear weapons "impotent and obsolete," but the last thing they want or need is to pay an astronomic bill for a vastly intensified nuclear competition sold to them under a false label. Yet that is what Star Wars will bring us, as a closer look will show.

III

The second line of defense for the Star Wars program, and the one which represents the real hopes and convictions of both military men and civilians at the levels below the optimistic President and his enthusiastic secretary of defense, is not that it will ever be able to defend *all our people*, but rather that it will allow us to defend *some of our weapons and other military assets*, and so, somehow, restrain the arms race.

This objective is very different from the one the President has held out to the country, but it is equally unattainable. The Star Wars program is bound to exacerbate the competition between the superpowers in three major ways. It will destroy the Anti-Ballistic Missile (ABM) Treaty, our most important arms control agreement; it will directly stimulate both offensive and defensive systems on the Soviet side; and as long as it continues it will darken the prospect for significant improvement in the currently frigid relations between Moscow and

Washington. It will thus sharpen the very anxieties the President wants to reduce.

As presented to Congress last March, the Star Wars program calls for a five-year effort of research and development at a total cost of $26 billion. The Administration insists that no decision has been made to develop or deploy any component of the potential system, but a number of hardware demonstrations are planned, and it is hoped that there can be an affirmative decision on full-scale system development in the early 1990s. By its very nature, then, the program is both enormous and very slow. This first $26 billion, only for research and development, is not much less than the full procurement cost of the new B-1 bomber force, and the timetable is such that Mr. Reagan's second term will end long before any deployment decision is made. Both the size and the slowness of the undertaking reinforce the certainty that it will stimulate the strongest possible Soviet response. Its size makes it look highly threatening, while its slowness gives plenty of time for countermeasures.

Meanwhile, extensive American production of offensive nuclear weapons will continue. The Administration has been at pains to insist that the Star Wars program in no way reduces the need for six new offensive systems. There are now two new land-based missiles, two new strategic bombers, and two different submarine systems under various stages of development. The Soviets regularly list several other planned American deployments as strategic because the weapons can reach the Soviet homeland. Mr. Reagan recognized at the very outset that "if paired with offensive systems," any defensive systems "can be viewed as fostering an aggressive policy, and no one wants that." But that is exactly how his new program, with its proclaimed emphasis on both offense and defense, is understood in Moscow.

We have been left in no doubt as to the Soviet opinion of Star Wars. Only four days after the President's speech, Yuri Andropov gave the Soviet reply:

On the face of it, laymen may find it even attractive as the President speaks about what seem to be defensive measures. But this may seem to be so only on the face of it and only to those who are not conversant with these matters. In fact the strategic offensive forces of the United States will continue to be developed and upgraded at full tilt and along quite a definite line at that, namely that of acquiring a first nuclear strike capability. Under these conditions the intention to secure itself the possibility of destroying with the help of the ABM defenses the corresponding strategic systems of the other side, that is of rendering it unable of dealing a retaliatory strike, is a bid to disarm the Soviet Union in the face of the U.S. nuclear threat.[2]

The only remarkable elements in this response are its clarity and rapidity. Andropov's assessment is precisely what we should expect. Our government, of course, does not intend a first strike, but we are building systems which do have what is called in our own jargon a prompt hard-target kill capability, and the primary purpose of these systems is to put Soviet missiles at risk of quick destruction. Soviet leaders are bound to see such weapons as a first-strike threat. This is precisely the view that our own planners take of Soviet missiles with a similar capability. When the President launches a defensive program openly aimed at making Soviet missiles "impotent," while at the same time our own hard-target killers multiply, we cannot be surprised that a man like Andropov saw a threat "to disarm the Soviet Union."[3] Given Andropov's assessment, the Soviet response to Star Wars is certain to be an intensification of both its offensive and defensive strategic efforts.

Perhaps the easiest way to understand this political reality is to consider our own reaction to any similar Soviet announcement of intent. The very thought that the Soviet Union might plan to deploy effective strategic defenses would certainly produce a most energetic American response, and the first and most important element of that response would be a determination to ensure that a sufficient number of our own missiles would always get through.

Administration spokesmen continue to talk as if somehow the prospect of American defensive systems will in and of itself lead the Soviet government to move away from strategic missiles. This is a vain hope. Such a result might indeed be conceivable if Mr. Reagan's original dream were real—if we could somehow ever deploy a *perfect* defense. But in the real world no system will ever be leak-proof; no new system of any sort is in prospect for a decade and only a fragmentary capability for years thereafter; numerous powerful countermeasures are readily available in the meantime, and what is at stake

[2] Cited in Sidney Drell *et al.*, *op. cit.*, p.105.
[3] Richard Nixon has analyzed the possible impact of new defensive systems in even more striking terms: "Such systems would be destabilizing if they provided a shield so that you could use the sword." *Los Angeles Times*, July 1, 1984.

from the Russian standpoint is the deterrent value of their largest and strongest offensive forces.

In this real world it is preposterous to suppose that Star Wars can produce anything but the most determined Soviet effort to make it fruitless. Dr. James Fletcher, chairman of an Administration panel that reviewed the technical prospects after the President's speech, has testified that "the ultimate utility . . . of this system will depend not only on the technology itself, but on the extent to which the Soviet Union agrees to mutual defense arrangements and offense limitations." The plain implication is that the Soviet Union can reduce the "utility" of Star Wars by refusing just such concessions. That is what we would do, and that is what they will do.

Some apologists for Star Wars, although not the President, now defend it on the still more limited ground that it can deny the Soviets a first-strike capability. That is conceivable, in that the indefinite proliferation of systems and countersystems would certainly create fearful uncertainties of all sorts on both sides. But as the Scowcroft Commission correctly concluded, the Soviets have no first-strike capability today, given our survivable forces and the ample existing uncertainties in any surprise attack. We believe there are much better ways than strategic defense to ensure that this situation is maintained. Even a tightly limited and partially effective local defense of missile fields—itself something vastly different from Star Wars—would require radical amendment or repudiation of the ABM Treaty and would create such interacting fears of expanding defenses that we strongly believe it should be avoided.

The President seems aware of the difficulty of making the Soviet Union accept his vision, and he has repeatedly proposed a solution that combines surface plausibility and intrinsic absurdity in a way that tells a lot about what is wrong with Star Wars itself. Mr. Reagan says we should give the Russians the secret of defense, once we find it, in return for their agreement to get rid of nuclear weapons. But the only kind of secret that could be used this way is one that exists only in Mr. Reagan's mind: a single magic formula that would make each side durably invulnerable. In the real world any defensive system will be an imperfect complex of technological and operational capabilities, full understanding of which would at once enable any adversary to improve his own methods of penetration. To share this kind of secret is to destroy its own effectiveness. Mr.

Reagan's solution is as unreal as his original dream, and it rests on the same failure of understanding.

There is simply no escape from the reality that Star Wars offers not the promise of greater safety, but the certainty of a large-scale expansion of both offensive and defensive systems on both sides. We are not here examining the dismayed reaction of our allies in Europe, but it is precisely this prospect that they foresee, in addition to the special worries created by their recognition that the Star Wars program as it stands has nothing in it for them. Star Wars, in sum, is a prescription not for ending or limiting the threat of nuclear weapons, but for a competition unlimited in expense, duration and danger.

We have come this way before, following false hopes and finding our danger greater in the upshot. We did it when our government responded to the first Soviet atomic test by a decision to get hydrogen bombs if we could, never stopping to consider in any serious way whether both sides would be better off not to test such a weapon. We did it again, this time in the face of strong and sustained warning, when we were the first to deploy the multiple warheads (MIRVs) that now face us in such excessive numbers on Soviet missiles. Today, 15 years too late, we have a consensus that MIRVs are bad for us, but we are still deploying them, and so are the Russians.

IV

So far we have been addressing the question of new efforts for strategic defense with only marginal attention to their intimate connection with the future of the most important single arms control agreement that we and the Soviet Union share, the Anti-Ballistic Missile Treaty of 1972. The President's program, because of the inevitable Soviet reaction to it, has already had a heavily damaging impact on prospects for any early progress in strategic arms control. It has thrown a wild card into a game already impacted by mutual suspicion and by a search on both sides for unattainable unilateral advantage. It will soon threaten the very existence of the ABM Treaty.

That treaty outlaws any Star Wars defense. Research is permitted, but the development of space-based systems cannot go beyond the laboratory stage without breaking the Treaty. That would be a most fateful step. We strongly agree with the finding of the Scowcroft Commission, in its final report of March 1984, that "the strategic implications of ballistic missile defense and the criticality of the ABM Treaty to further arms control agreements dictate extreme caution in proceeding to engineering development in this sensitive area."

The ABM Treaty stands at the very center of the effort to limit the strategic arms race by international agreements. It became possible when the two sides recognized that the pursuit of defensive systems would inevitably lead to an expanded competition and to greater insecurity for both. In its underlying meaning, the Treaty is a safeguard less against defense as such than against unbridled competition. The continuing and excessive competition that still exists in offensive weapons would have been even worse without the ABM Treaty, which removed from the calculations of both sides any fear of an early and destabilizing defensive deployment. The consequence over the following decade was profoundly constructive. Neither side attempted a defensive deployment that predictably would have given much more fear to the adversary than comfort to the possessor. The ABM Treaty, in short, reflected a common understanding of exactly the kinds of danger with which Star Wars now confronts the world. To lose the Treaty in pursuit of the Star Wars mirage would be an act of folly.

The defense of the ABM Treaty is thus a first requirement for all who wish to limit the damage done by the Star Wars program. Fortunately the Treaty has wide public support, and the Administration has stated that it plans to do nothing in its five-year program that violates any Treaty clause. Yet by its very existence the Star Wars effort is a threat to the future of the ABM Treaty, and some parts of the announced five-year program raise questions of Treaty compliance. The current program envisions a series of hardware demonstrations, and one of them is described as "an advanced boost-phase detection and tracking system." But the ABM Treaty specifically forbids both the development and the testing of any "spaced-based" components of an anti-ballistic missile system. We find it hard to see how a boost-phase detection system could be anything but space-based, and we are not impressed by the Administration's claim that such a system is not sufficiently significant to be called "a component."

We make this point not so much to dispute the detailed shape of the current program as to emphasize the strong need for close attention in Congress to the protection of the ABM Treaty. The Treaty has few defenders in the Administration—the President thought it wrong in 1972, and Mr. Weinberger thinks so still. The managers of the program are under more pressure for quick results than for proposals respectful of the Treaty. In this situation a heavy responsibility falls on Congress, which has already shown this year that it has serious reservations about the President's dream. Interested members of Congress are well placed to ensure that funds are not provided for activities that would violate the Treaty. In meeting this responsibility, and indeed in monitoring the Star Wars program as a whole, Congress can readily get the help of advisers drawn from among the many outstanding experts whose judgment has not been silenced or muted by co-option. Such use of independent counselors is one means of repairing the damage done by the President's unfortunate decision to launch his initiative without the benefit of any serious and unprejudiced scientific assessment.

The Congress should also encourage the Administration toward a new and more vigorous effort to insist on respect for the ABM Treaty by the Soviet government as well. Sweeping charges of Soviet cheating on arms control agreements are clearly overdone. It is deeply unimpressive, for example, to catalogue asserted violations of agreements which we ourselves have refused to ratify. But there is one quite clear instance of large-scale construction that does not appear to be consistent with the ABM Treaty—a large radar in central Siberia near the city of Krasnoyarsk. This radar is not yet in operation, but the weight of technical judgment is that it is designed for the detection of incoming missiles, and the ABM Treaty, in order to forestall effective missile defense systems, forbade the erection of such early warning radars except along the borders of each nation. A single highly vulnerable radar installation is of only marginal importance in relation to any large-scale breakout from the ABM Treaty, but it does raise exactly the kinds of questions of intentional violation which are highly destructive in this country to public confidence in arms control.

On the basis of informed technical advice, we think the most likely purpose of the Krasnoyarsk radar is to give early warning of any attack by submarine-based U.S. missiles on Soviet missile fields. Soviet military men, like some of their counterparts in our own country, appear to believe that the right answer to the threat of surprise attack on missiles is a policy of launch-under-attack, and in that context the Krasnoyarsk radar, which fills an important gap in Soviet warning systems, becomes understandable. Such understanding does not make the radar anything else but a violation of the express language of the

Treaty, but it does make it a matter which can be discussed and resolved without any paralyzing fear that it is a clear first signal of massive violations yet to come. Such direct and serious discussion with the Soviets might even allow the two sides to consider together the intrinsic perils in a common policy of launch-under-attack. But no such sensitive discussions will be possible while Star Wars remains a non-negotiable centerpiece of American strategic policy.

Equal in importance to defending the ABM Treaty is preventing hasty overcommitment of financial and scientific resources to totally unproven schemes overflowing with unknowns. The President's men seem determined to encourage an atmosphere of crisis commitment to just such a manner of work, and repeated comparisons to the Manhattan Project of 1942–45, small in size and crystal-clear in purpose by comparison, are not comforting. On the shared basis of conviction that the President's dream is unreal, members of Congress can and should devote themselves with energy to the prevention of the kind of vested interest in very large-scale ongoing expenditures which has so often kept alive other programs that were truly impotent, in terms of their own announced objectives. We believe that there is not much chance that deployments remotely like those currently sketched in the Star Wars program will ever in fact occur. The mere prospect of them will surely provoke the Russians to action, but it is much less likely that paying for them will in the end make sense to the American people. The larger likelihood is that on their way to oblivion these schemes will simply cost us tens and even hundreds of billions of wasted dollars.[4]

In watching over the Star Wars budget the Congress may find it helpful to remember the summary judgment that Senator Arthur Vandenberg used to offer on programs he found wanting: "The end is unattainable, the means hare-brained, and the cost staggering." But at the same time we believe strongly in the continuation of the long-standing policy of maintaining a prudent level of research on the scientific possibilities for defense. Research at a level ample for insurance

---

[4] The Russians have their own program, of course. But they are not about to turn our technological flank in the technologies crucial for ABM systems. "According to the U.S. Department of Defense, the United States has a lead in computers, optics, automated control, electro-optical sensors, propulsion, radar, software, telecommunications, and guidance systems." Drell *et al.*, *op. cit.*, p. 21.

against some Soviet surprise can be continued at a fraction of the cost of the present Star Wars program. Such a change of course would have the great advantage of preventing what would otherwise be a grave distortion of priorities not only in defense research but in the whole national scientific effort.

V

This has not been a cheerful analysis, or one that we find pleasant to present. If the President makes no major change of course in his second term, we see no alternative to a long, hard, damage-limiting effort by Congress. But we choose to end on a quite different note. We believe that any American president who has won reelection in this nuclear age is bound to ask himself with the greatest seriousness just what he wants to accomplish in his second term. We have no doubt of the deep sincerity of President Reagan's desire for good arms control agreements with the Soviet Union, and we believe his election night assertion that what he wants most in foreign affairs is to reach just such agreements. We are also convinced that if he asks serious and independent advisers what changes in current American policy will help most to make such agreements possible in the next four years, he will learn that it is possible to reach good agreements, or possible to insist on the Star Wars program as it stands, but wholly impossible to do both. At exactly that point, we believe, Mr. Reagan could, should, and possibly would encourage the serious analysis of his negotiating options that did not occur in his first term.

We do not here explore these possibilities in detail. They would certainly include a reaffirmation of the ABM Treaty, and an effort to improve it by broadening its coverage and tightening some of its language. There should also be a further exploration of the possibility of an agreement that would safeguard the peaceful uses of space, uses that have much greater value to us than to the Soviets. We still need and lack a reliable cap on strategic warheads, and while Mr. Reagan has asked too much for too little in the past, he is right to want reductions. He currently has some advisers who fear all forms of arms control, but advisers can be changed. We are not suggesting that the President will change his course lightly. We simply believe that he does truly want real progress on arms control in his second term, and that if he ever comes to understand that he must choose between the two, he will choose the pursuit of agreement over the demands of Star Wars.

We have one final deep and strong belief. We think that if there is to be a real step away from nuclear danger in the next four years, it will have to begin at the level of high politics, with a kind of communication between Moscow and Washington that we have not seen for more than a decade. One of the most unfortunate aspects of the Star Wars initiative is that it was launched without any attempt to discuss it seriously, in advance, with the Soviet government. It represented an explicit expression of the President's belief that we should abandon the shared view of nuclear defense that underlies not only the ABM Treaty but all our later negotiations on strategic weapons. To make a public announcement of a change of this magnitude without any effort to discuss it with the Soviets was to ensure increased Soviet suspicion. This error, too, we have made in earlier decades. If we are now to have renewed hope of arms control, we must sharply elevate our attention to the whole process of communication with Moscow.

Such newly serious communication should begin with frank and explicit recognition by both sides that the problem of nuclear danger is in its basic reality a *common* problem, not just for the two of us, but for all the world—and one that we shall never resolve if we cannot transcend negotiating procedures that give a veto to those in each country who insist on the relentlessly competitive maintenance and enlargement of what are already, on both sides, exorbitantly excessive forces.

If it can ever be understood and accepted, as a starting point for negotiation, that our community of interest in the problem of nuclear danger is greater than all our various competitive concerns put together, there can truly be a renewal of hope, and a new prospect of a shared decision to change course together. Alone among the presidents of the last 12 years, Ronald Reagan has the political strength to lead our country in this new direction if he so decides. The renewal of hope cannot be left to await another president without an appeal to the President and his more sober advisers to take a fresh hard look at Star Wars, and then to seek arms control instead.

Caspar W. Weinberger

U.S. DEFENSE STRATEGY

The Reagan Administration took office in 1981 committed to rebuilding American military power. We are encouraged by the results of the past four years. The Reagan defense program is having its intended effect on the Soviet Union.

The sequence of annual Soviet aggression against new targets that began in the mid-1970s in Angola, and culminated in the invasion of Afghanistan in late 1979, has ceased. After walking out of the Geneva negotiations in protest over NATO's deployment of theater nuclear weapons in November 1983, the Soviet delegation is back at the bargaining table. Just prior to the recent meeting between President Reagan and General Secretary Mikhail Gorbachev, the Soviets began for the first time to talk seriously about deep cuts in strategic offensive forces. Indeed, the Soviet Union now appears to be moving toward President Reagan's "zero option" proposal for eliminating land-based intermediate range nuclear forces—a proposal that was dismissed in 1981 by most American arms control advocates as a propaganda ploy.

In 1980 the crucial issue was whether the United States could afford to acquiesce in the Soviet Union's attempt to achieve a position of global military superiority. The answer from the American electorate was clear. We agreed to pay the price for military strength to deter war.

My purpose in this article is not to review all of the programs and policies of this Administration. Rather, I want to describe U.S. defense strategies and to summarize the major changes we have made in our thinking at the Department of Defense over the past five years.

II

When the Reagan Administration entered office in 1981 it inherited strategic concepts formulated more than a quarter-century ago. Consider the list: nuclear deterrence, extended deterrence, escalation control, strategic stability, offensive dominance, counterinsurgency, limited war, and escalation lad-

---

Caspar W. Weinberger is Secretary of Defense.

ders. The dominant features of the 1950s, when most of these ideas were first formulated and applied, can be summarized in two phrases: American nuclear preeminence and American military superiority. In the nuclear arena we had a decisive advantage. Across the board in military forces we invested more than the Soviets and had a margin of superiority in most military dimensions.

That era has vanished. The Soviet Union has become a military superpower through an effort that has consumed more than twice as large a percentage of its gross national product as U.S. defense spending does. Whether the United States should be willing to accept a position of parity in military power with the Soviet Union over the longer run can (and should) be debated. But about our current defense programs there should be no illusions. We are not trying to regain the earlier margin of advantage. Rather, we are struggling to win the resources necessary to enable us to maintain sufficient military strength to ensure deterrence.

What does this transformation of the military balance between the United States and the Soviet Union imply for the relevance of our basic strategic concepts? Should ideas formulated in an era of American military predominance apply with equal validity in an era of parity?

The world has changed profoundly since the 1950s and early 1960s, when most of our conceptual arsenal was formulated— so profoundly that some of these concepts are now obsolete. Thus, as we reaffirm the central concepts of postwar American policy, we are reformulating others and reaching out for new ideas in a search for ways to make our deterrent more effective. In 1981 we could not delay rebuilding American military strength while we conducted a lengthy conceptual debate. There could be but one overriding priority: to reestablish the balance of military power necessary for stable deterrence. But even as we moved decisively to restore military parity with the Soviet Union, we also began to reassess those strategic concepts inherited from past policymakers.

Now, five years later, I believe we have made significant progress both in strengthening our military forces and in modernizing our defense strategy and policy. Neither task is complete. But as we address the agenda for the remaining years of the Reagan Administration, it should be useful to state succinctly the core of our defense strategy.

Our strategy is simple. We seek to prevent war by maintaining forces and demonstrating the determination to use them, if necessary, in ways that will persuade our adversaries that the cost of any attack on our vital interests will exceed the benefits they could hope to gain. The label for this strategy is deterrence. It is the core of our defense strategy today, as it has been for most of the postwar period. Moreover, this strategy is working. It has succeeded in winning for the United States and our allies four decades of peace with our primary adversary—a period nearly twice as long as the time-span between World War I and World War II.

To be effective, deterrence must continue to meet four tests: *Survivability*: our forces must be able to survive a preemptive attack with sufficient retaliatory strength to threaten losses that outweigh gains. *Credibility*: our threatened response to an attack must be of a form that the potential aggressor believes we could and would carry out. *Clarity*: the action to be deterred must be sufficiently clear to our adversaries so that the potential aggressor knows what is prohibited. *Safety*: the risk of failure through accident, unauthorized use, or miscalculation must be minimized.

Beyond these aims, a more complex concept of deterrence places a greater emphasis on three interrelated ideas. First, effective deterrence must address not just the objective facts of the military balance sheet, but also Soviet leaders' *perceptions* of those facts. It is not sufficient for us to believe that the costs we will impose in response to an attack will exceed the benefits the Soviet leadership hopes to achieve. Interpreting the facts within their own framework, the Soviet leaders must conclude *they* cannot advance *their* objectives by attacking us.

Recognition that an adversary's perceptions are an essential dimension of deterrence is not a new idea. As the Scowcroft Commission's report stated: "Deterrence is the set of beliefs in the minds of the Soviet leaders, given their own values and attitudes, about our capabilities and our will. It requires us to determine, as best we can, what would deter them from considering aggression, even in a crisis—not to determine what would deter us."[1]

Because of our relative ignorance of Soviet perceptions, U.S. planners tend to rely on their own calculations. But all the evidence we have suggests that preparing to deter an attack only by assembling forces adequate to deter us under similar

---

[1] *Report of the President's Commission on Strategic Forces*, April 1983, p. 3.

conditions could provide too little to deter the Soviets. For example, many strategic analysts have opposed this Administration's modernizaton of strategic nuclear forces with the argument that such investments are "sterile," since the marginal gain in attack and retaliation calculations is relatively small for the level of investment. The issue for a strategy of deterrence that takes perceptions seriously, however, is whether the Soviet leadership shares the judgment that additional expenditures are pointless. The fact that for the past decade Soviet investment in strategic forces (as measured in dollars) has been two to three times the size of our own investment would suggest that they do not share this judgment. Moreover, our forces must be adequate not only to deter Soviet aggression, but also to be seen by our allies as sufficient.

The *second* element is risk, the key issue in defense planning. Unfortunately, many discussions of deterrence are led astray by a misunderstanding of this concept. For example, consider the argument that because our current capabilities are insufficient to meet all our commitments, we must cut back our commitments. Our commitments are based on our interests. We can never afford to buy the capabilities sufficient to meet all of our commitments with one hundred percent confidence. The critical questions are: What risk of failure are we prepared to accept in our plans for meeting particular contingencies? How much are we prepared to pay to reduce this risk?

The *third* point is that deterrence is a multilayered concept. The way in which we persuade the Soviet leaders that the costs of an attack would exceed any benefits they might hope to achieve includes three layered components: defense, escalation and retaliation.

If the adversary calculates that his aggression is likely to fail in its own terms, he will not attack. Further, he must know that even if his aggression should succeed in achieving its immediate objectives, he faces the threat of escalation to hostilities that would exact a higher cost than he is willing to pay. In addition to defense and escalation, the third layer is retaliation: if the adversary confronts a credible threat that aggression will trigger attacks by a surviving U.S. retaliatory capability against the attacker's vital interests that result in losses exceeding any possible gains, he will not attack.

Of these three layers of deterrence, the safest and most reassuring is defense. Our "warfighting" capability to defeat an attack and restore the peace is therefore not something separate from our strategy of deterrence. In fact, it forms the foundation of effective deterrence. If an adversary believes that his attack could be defeated at a low level of violence, and at low risk, why would he attack? We understand that the costs of maintaining the capability to meet every contingency effectively on its own terms can be prohibitive. Thus the United States must maintain a credible threat both of escalation and of retaliation to secure deterrence across the spectrum of potential conflict.

The Reagan Administration has reaffirmed the basic U.S. defense strategy of deterrence. In challenging ourselves, our colleagues in the Administration, and the broader strategic community to reassess the conceptual arsenal of the 1960s and reach out for new ideas, our aim is to find ways to make this strategy of deterrence more effective. Our principal difference with our immediate predecessor arose from our judgment that it was urgent to fund defense at levels adequate to restore our neglected military so that we could maintain deterrence and to do so as quickly as possible. We have accomplished a great deal, but we still confront major Soviet advantages in capital assets purchased since the 1970s and a continuing Soviet military buildup. In light of U.S. congressional demands that deficit reduction be given highest priority, maintaining forces adequate for the missions essential to our vital interests remains our largest challenge.

To the basic defense policies that have guided defense planning since the 1950s, the Reagan Administration has made a number of revisions and additions. We have added four pillars of defense policy for the 1990s that attempt to address the most important changes in the strategic environment that have occurred since the 1960s. These four pillars are: the Strategic Defense Initiative and secure nuclear deterrence; uses of military force and secure conventional deterrence; a strategy for reducing and controlling arms; and competitive strategies.

In the sections that follow I will discuss each policy.

III

The President's Strategic Defense Initiative (SDI) stunned many traditional thinkers because, as so often is the case with the President's proposals, it flew in the face of conventional wisdom. In fact, strategic defense represents a change of strategy, but it is motivated by the search for a more secure deterrent. It offers a far safer way to keep the peace.

Critics of strategic defense are, in most cases, proponents of the concept of mutual assured destruction (MAD). This concept describes a condition in which, after suffering an all-out nuclear first strike, either superpower would retain the nuclear capability to retaliate and destroy its opponent as a modern society. It is a mutual suicide pact. Currently, both the United States and the Soviet Union have the capacity to destroy each other. And according to advocates of MAD, this mutual suicide pact is the bedrock of strategic stability. Because each has the capability to destroy the other's society, it is argued, neither can contemplate war, and war is therefore deterred. Indeed, some proponents of MAD advocate actions to make nuclear war as horrible as possible, since that makes it as unthinkable as possible. Many oppose any defense, from civil defense to strategic defense. Some even attempt to rewrite the history of U.S. policy to claim that the United States embraced MAD and based its deterrent in the 1960s and early 1970s on retaliating against Soviet cities. This, of course, was never the case, and for good reason.

This MAD logic ignores three fundamental questions. First, is a strategy that amounts to a suicidal response sufficiently credible to deter *all* Soviet attacks? Second, what form of retaliatory threat would be the most moral and effective deterrent? And third, while secure retaliatory deterrence is necessary today, can we not move to a safer world in the future?

Is a nuclear deterrent that simply threatens the end of modern society credible? If the Soviet leadership believed that in response to a nuclear attack by them, we would be forced to choose between suicide and surrender, might they not conclude that we would decide not respond to an attack at all? Would deterrence not be gravely weakened? To avoid that dilemma, every president and every secretary of defense since the early 1960s has said we should maintain the capability to respond to a range of possible Soviet attacks with a range of appropriate options. Our Administration has accelerated the development of more selective, discriminate and controlled responses, and, most important, has sought and been voted much of the resources to accomplish this. Such limited options both pose a more credible threat to meet any level of Soviet attack, and increase the likelihood that escalation could be controlled and collateral damage minimized.

Misguided critics have sometimes confused our efforts to create credible response options for the purpose of deterring

Soviet aggression with a malign intention to fight limited nuclear wars. Some have even gone so far as to confuse prudent planning for deterrence with insensitivity to the horrors of nuclear war. This is nonsense—springing from either ignorance of our policies, or a desire to search for any means to attack our policies. No one who has received as many briefings on nuclear weapons or participated in crisis exercises as I have could hold any doubts about the absolute necessity of avoiding nuclear war. It is precisely because of this necessity that the United States must have a secure deterrent. Moreover, developing selective, discriminate responses is manifestly moral.

It is not in our interest to inform the Soviets precisely how we would respond to every possible contingency. Nor is it possible to be certain that our efforts to limit escalation and terminate a conflict once begun would succeed. But it is imperative that we take every step possible both to deter war and to limit the destruction of any conflict. Without these credible limited options, our critics' view that any response to a Soviet attack would automatically lead to mutual suicide could become a tragic self-fulfilling prophecy. In short, while our policy cannot guarantee success, our critics' policy can only guarantee failure.

The knowledge that any conflict between the United States and the Soviet Union might escalate to nuclear catastrophe is certainly part of deterrence today. But that knowledge also impels us to ask whether there is not a better way to provide for the defense of the West. Because nuclear deterrence is necessary today, we must seek to make it secure; yet because it poses dangers, we must seek better alternatives for the future. The President and I believe that the answer lies in the Strategic Defense Initiative.

We hope that strategic defense will eventually render nuclear missiles obsolete. That is our long-range vision. But we have already rendered obsolete one of the concepts of the MAD logic: the belief that deterrence must rest on the threat to destroy a certain high percentage of the Soviet population. We do not, in fact, plan our retaliatory options to maximize Soviet casualties or to attack deliberately the Soviet population. Indeed, we believe such a doctrine would be neither moral nor prudent.

It is not moral because the Soviet people should not deliberately be made the victims of any U.S. retaliation to an attack launched by the Soviet leadership—a leadership for which the Soviet people are not responsible and cannot control. It is not prudent because secure deterrence should be based on the threat to destroy what the Soviet leadership values most highly: namely, itself, its military power and political control capabilities, and its industrial ability to wage war.

The U.S. government knows that a nuclear war cannot be won. Our nuclear doctrine is designed to ensure that the Soviet Union's leadership cannot escape this same conclusion: that a nuclear war can never be won—however they choose to define victory—and therefore must never be fought.

IV

It seems to me there are three irrefutable arguments for President Reagan's SDI—any one of which would be sufficient for the research program we have undertaken, and all three of which are, in fact, valid. They can be summarized as: Soviet breakthrough, Soviet breakout and the very real possibility that American science and technology will achieve what appears to some to be an impossible dream. Let me say more about each.

Since the Anti-Ballistic Missile Treaty of 1972, the Soviet Union has spent as much on strategic defense as on its extraordinary strategic nuclear offensive buildup. Soviet air defenses now include nearly 12,000 launchers for surface-to-air missiles, and a formidable array of radars and interceptors. The Soviet Union has exploited the one ABM system permitted by the ABM treaty—the system around Moscow—to upgrade, test and gain experience in the operation of an effective full-scale defense against ballistic missiles. Moreover, for more than two decades, the Soviets have been investing heavily in precisely those technologies encompassed by our own SDI program. While the Congress funded only 74 percent of our FY 1986 budget request for SDI research, the Soviet Union continued to spend ten times our level of effort on strategic defense.

Evidence of the Soviet program leads us to conclude that the Soviet leaders have never accepted the theory of mutual assured vulnerability so favored by many American strategists, a theory that served as the foundation of the ABM treaty. Indeed, the Soviet leaders have made a vigorous, sustained effort to reduce the vulnerability of their country, and especially of themselves. Not only are the Soviets ahead of us today in the development and deployment of strategic defenses, but they have invested so much more on these technologies, and in so many different areas, that our SDI research program would be justified as a prudent hedge against a Soviet breakthrough—even if that were the only consideration.

Concern about a Soviet breakout follows directly from this. The Soviet commitment to strategic defense is so unswerving that we must consider the possibility of a real Soviet breakout from the ABM treaty. If they could deploy today a strategic defense that significantly advanced their interests, who doubts that they would do so, despite the treaty and their criticism of our program? What prevents the Soviets from abrogating the ABM treaty is their calculation of what each of us would do in its absence. A vigorous American strategic defense research program is thus essential to ensure that we do not awake some day to find the Soviets rushing to full-scale ABM deployment.

The third and, in my view, most conclusive argument for our strategic defense research program is the very real possibility that science and technology can in fact create a future in which nuclear missiles become less and less capable of their awful mission.

This journey to a safer world will not be easy, or short. Our research program is the necessary *first* step. But given the past record of experts' declarations about what could not be done in the future, I am dismayed by the absolute assurance with which some distinguished American scientists and others declare the President's dream to be impossible. Recall that Albert Einstein predicted in 1932: "There is not the slightest indication that [nuclear] energy will ever be obtainable. It would mean that the atom would have to be shattered at will." Such distinguished errors only strengthen my belief that we should not be dissuaded from a vigorous research program. The President's purpose and resolve are, quite simply, to do all we can to help create a much safer world for generations to come.

If we could defend our people, who would prefer to avenge them? If we could live secure in the knowledge that our survival did not rest upon the threat of retaliation to deter a Soviet attack, would this not be a preferable moral position? The search for something beyond reliance on retaliation is neither cynical nor naïve. From the outset, we have insisted that progress toward an effective SDI will have to proceed hand in hand with regaining an effective offensive deterrent and, paradoxically enough, with arms reduction as well. A persistent and patient dialogue with the Soviet Union is a necessary condition for life in today's world.

Indeed, in pursuing SDI, we are aware of alternative modes

of delivering nuclear weapons. Even a thoroughly reliable shield against ballistic missiles would still leave us vulnerable to other modes of delivery, or perhaps even to other devices of mass destruction. Despite an essentially leakproof missile defense, we might still be vulnerable to terrorist attacks against our cities. Our vision of SDI therefore calls for a gradual transition to effective defenses, including deep reductions in offensive nuclear weapons. Thus, SDI is part of the President's larger goal to reduce reliance on nuclear weapons and the role of nuclear weapons in international politics.

For the foreseeable future, however, nuclear weapons will be part of the inescapable backdrop of U.S.-Soviet relations. Even if at some future point the United States and the Soviet Union were to abolish their nuclear weapons, we cannot eradicate the knowledge of how to make them, nor the fact that other nations and terrorist organizations have that capability. These facts make it absolutely essential that we should undertake every feasible effort to reduce to the lowest possible level the risk of nuclear war.

V

I have elsewhere outlined six major tests that should be applied by the United States in deciding to commit U.S. conventional military forces to combat.[2] I argued that U.S. military forces have an essential, but circumscribed and necessarily limited, role in the larger framework of national power. That speech spawned a continuing debate inside and outside the government. In light of that continuing commentary, let me now reiterate the key points I made.

According to theories developed in the 1950s and early 1960s, limited war was essentially a diplomatic instrument—a tool for bargaining with the enemy. As such, it had to be centrally directed by the political leadership and applied with precise control. The gradual application of American conventional power, combined with the threat of incremental increases in the application of that power, would, according to the theorists, persuade America's opponents to accept a settlement while they avoided strategic defeat.

The fatal flaw of these theories of the 1950s was their neglect

[2]"The Uses of Military Power," address to the National Press Club, Washington, D.C., Nov. 28, 1984. Reprinted in the January 1985 issue of *Defense*, a Department of Defense publication.

of the domestic political realities of American democracy. Both these theories and the actual experience of Lyndon Johnson in Vietnam in the 1960s applied an eighteenth-century approach to war. In that period, as Clausewitz noted: "War was still an affair for governments alone, and the people's role was simply that of an instrument."

The framers of the American Constitution rejected this concept of war. Our Constitution reserves for the Congress alone, as representative of the people, the right to declare war. In fact, prior to Korea and Vietnam, except for occasional short excursions, presidents worked hard to build public support before taking America to war. From 1939 to 1941, Franklin Roosevelt worked and waited to build a consensus, even though Europe was under siege. He had no other feasible option. Though he would have preferred to do so, President Roosevelt never considered sending American forces into combat without the approval of the Congress and the assurance of support of the American people. In Korea, and then Vietnam, America went to war without a strong consensus or support for our basic purposes and, as it turned out, without the firm commitment to win. Indeed, as one of my predecessors, Secretary Robert McNamara, once observed: "The greatest contribution Vietnam is making—right or wrong is beside the point—is that it is developing an ability in the United States to fight a limited war, to go to war without the necessity of arousing the public ire."[3] As successive administrations discovered, the American people had the final word. The "public ire" was aroused as perhaps never before—and never again should the imperative of public support be ignored.

Despite our best efforts to deter or prevent such developments, situations will arise in which it may be appropriate to commit U.S. military forces to combat. From our reading of the postwar period, this Administration derives several lessons that can be stated as tests to be applied in facing such choices. These tests cannot be applied mechanically or deductively. Weighing the evidence in specific cases will always require judgment. But applying these tests to the evidence will make it clear that while there are situations in which U.S. troops are

[3] Quoted in Douglas H. Rosenberg, "Arms and the American Way: The Ideological Dimension of Military Growth," in Bruce M. Russett and Alfred Stepan, eds., *Military Force and American Society*, New York: Harper & Row, 1973, p. 170.

required, there are even more situations in which U.S. combat forces should *not* be used. These tests are:

—The United States should not commit forces to combat unless our vital interests are at stake. Our interests, of course, include vital interests of our allies.

—Should the United States decide that it is necessary to commit its forces to combat, we must commit them in sufficient numbers and with sufficient support to win. If we are unwilling to commit the forces or resources necessary to achieve our objectives, or if the objective is not important enough so that we must achieve it, we should not commit our forces.

—If we decide to commit forces to combat, we must have clearly defined political and military objectives. Unless we know precisely what we intend to achieve by fighting, and how our forces can accomplish those clearly defined objectives, we cannot formulate or determine the size of forces properly, and therefore we should not commit our forces at all.

—The relationship between our objectives and the size, composition and disposition of our forces must be continually reassessed and adjusted as necessary. In the course of a conflict, conditions and objectives inevitably change. When they do, so must our combat requirements.

—Before the United States commits combat forces abroad, the U.S. government should have some reasonable assurance of the support of the American people and their elected representatives in the Congress. Of course, this does not mean we should wait upon a public opinion poll. The public elects a president as a leader, not a follower. He takes an oath to protect and defend the Constitution. The people also expect a Congress sworn to the same principles and duties. To that end, the president and the leadership of the Congress must build the public consensus necessary to protect our vital interests. Sustainability of public support cannot be achieved unless the government is candid in making clear why our vital interests are threatened, and how, by the use, and only by the use of American military forces, we can achieve a clear, worthy goal. U.S. troops cannot be asked to fight a battle with the Congress at home, while attempting to win a war overseas. Nor will the American people sit by and watch

U.S. troops committed as expendable pawns on some grand diplomatic chessboard.

—Finally, the commitment of U.S. forces to combat should be a last resort—only after diplomatic, political, economic and other efforts have been made to protect our vital interests.

Each of these tests deserves lengthy discussion. For present purposes, several limited comments must suffice.

American interests are nowhere etched in stone. We should never succumb to the temptation to define a perimeter of vital interests, as Dean Acheson did in early 1950, in effect announcing that certain areas are "beyond our strategic perimeter." This virtually, albeit unintentionally, invited North Korea, with Stalin's approval, to invade South Korea. Judgments about our vital interests will sometimes depend on the circumstances of the specific case and trends, as well as on intrinsic values. Our vital interests can only be determined by ourselves and our definition of the threat. In his discussion of "the common defense" in *The Federalist Papers*, Alexander Hamilton argued that "it is impossible to foresee or define the extent and variety of national exigencies, or the correspondent extent and variety of the means which may be necessary to satisfy them. The circumstances that endanger the safety of nations are infinite." For this reason, we not only can never say never; we can never *think* never.

When using force, the necessity to win requires a clearly defined, achievable objective on which there is clear agreement. In Korea, we paid the full cost of this lesson—though this lesson still eludes many. There, our original purpose had been to defeat North Korean aggression and restore South Korea's territorial integrity. But we had divided counsels: many thought this could only be done if we eliminated the unnatural division between North and South Korea. We crossed the 38th Parallel and pushed forward to the Chinese border. But we were not united or determined to achieve the objective of uniting Korea. Again in Vietnam, failure to define a clear, achievable goal, and a belief that we could achieve what some wanted without a military victory, led to confusion, public frustration and eventual withdrawal.

When we define a clear objective, we must commit the forces necessary to achieve it. Gradualism is inherently attractive to some, but almost always a mistaken way to achieve military success. It exaggerates the illusion of control, violates the strategic principle of concentration of force, and encourages underestimation of the domestic political costs entailed by any use of American military forces abroad. If combat forces are required, they should be introduced rapidly and in the strength necessary to achieve our objective at the least possible cost. Where force has been committed to a peacekeeping buffer role, as in Lebanon, and circumstances change so that the original objective cannot be achieved, there will always be those who discover some further objective that might be served by a continued American presence. But a peacekeeping buffer force cannot always achieve a wholly different objective quickly, if at all. If, for example, a peacekeeping force, sized accordingly, cannot fulfill its mission because there is no peace to keep, then it should be withdrawn. And this was our decision in Lebanon.

No aspect of the doctrine I have enunciated for determining the use of force has received more comment and criticism than the requirement that we have reasonable assurance of the support of the American people. There can be no such assurance, the critics say. A government forced to wait for its people will be paralyzed in international politics. Recognizing this handicap, our adversary will be emboldened. One critic put it this way: even if Secretary Weinberger had a favorable public opinion poll for using force, who could guarantee that the public would not change its mind?

My purpose is not to wish away the frustrations of leadership in a democracy. Perhaps if President Roosevelt had been willing to defy the opinion polls and act on his own authority in 1939, 1940 or 1941, the enormous losses of World War II could have been reduced. But perhaps only by waiting until the full force of American public opinion was clearly mobilized behind the necessity of winning an all-out war was President Roosevelt able, with our allies, to secure the unconditional surrender of both the Nazis and the Japanese.

It is not necessary for me to argue that the considered judgment of the American people is always correct. My thesis is more modest, but more important. It is that American democracy is constructed on the principle, not that the American people will always be right, but that there exists no better guide to a wise policy. Our government, therefore, constructs a process that forces the president and the Congress to lead and argue, to seek and win the support of the American people in order to sustain a course of action. The inherent assumption here is that this process will, in the long run, produce wiser choices than any other mechanism yet discovered. Our Constitution does not say that this will be easy. But as Churchill once remarked: "Democracy is the worst form of government known to man—except for all the others." Our government is founded on the proposition that the informed judgment of the people will be a wiser guide than the view of the president alone, or of the president and his advisers, or of any self-appointed elite.

Taken together, these tests remind us of our most important and precious political feature: we are a democracy. Nothing distinguishes us more sharply from our Soviet adversary than the fact that whether at home or abroad, our government policy can be challenged and vindicated or reversed by a majority of our citizens. Any U.S. government that attempts to fight where our vital interests are not at stake, when we have no good reason to suppose there will be continuing public support, committing military forces merely as a regular and customary adjunct to our diplomatic efforts, invites the sort of domestic turmoil we experienced during the Vietnam War. Such a government has no grounds for expecting any less disastrous result.

The caution sounded by these six tests for the use of military force is intentional. The world consists of an endless succession of hot spots in which some U.S. forces could play, or could at least be imagined to play, a useful role. The belief that the mere presence of U.S. troops in Lebanon, or Central America or Africa or elsewhere could be useful in some way is not sufficient for our government to ask our troops to risk their lives. We remain ready to commit our lives, fortunes and sacred honor when the cause warrants it. But the hope that a limited U.S. presence might provide diplomatic leverage is not sufficient.

It has been said that I am relentless in building up our military strength on the one hand, but reluctant to use our military forces on the other. I have noticed that our commanders who would lead our men into battle and who sometimes have to order them to their deaths are equally determined that the need for such ultimate sacrifices must be fully warranted. Some critics will charge that commitments both to strength and caution are inconsistent. I believe that together they express a vital truth and a profound paradox. Recognition of our democracy's inherent reluctance about asking our troops to die for their country places an even larger premium on the need to have the military power required to deter opponents. The central thread in the Reagan Administration's policy is to combine sufficient military strength with such a clear determination to resist aggression that we discourage challenges. By preventing the attack that would make necessary an American commitment of forces in response, we achieve our objectives without war. Thus, peace through strength is more than a motto—it is a fact.

What fires this Administration's determination to build up our conventional military capabilities, emphasize readiness and sustainability, and reduce reliance upon nuclear weapons is our commitment to make conventional deterrence work. The stronger our conventional deterrent, the less likely an attack, and the lower the risk of war. The more vigorous our conventional deterrent, the less we must rely on the threat of nuclear retaliation.

VI

Reviewing the results of the first SALT interim agreement and the ABM and SALT II treaties, we can see why President Reagan has labeled this "pseudo arms control." The two premises behind the ABM treaty were that both sides would keep only limited defenses, and that both would sharply reduce offensive forces. Neither of these premises proved true. The United States chose not to deploy the full ABM system permitted by the 1972 ABM treaty and the 1974 Protocol—and in fact dismantled its one ABM site in 1975. But the Soviets not only have improved and upgraded significantly their Moscow ABM system over the past several years, they also have invested as heavily in their strategic defense programs since 1972 as they have in their offensive buildup.

In the mid-1960s, the United States ceased building silos for its land-based ICBMs. In contrast, the Soviets leaped ahead in numbers and far ahead in missile throw-weight. In submarine-launched ballistic missiles, we stopped building; again they raced ahead. Only in the area of total strategic nuclear warheads, a basically irrelevant category since it does not consider modernization of launchers, accuracy or any other factors, did the United States maintain a lead. Soviet programs may finally overtake that. Harold Brown once summarized the phenomenon of constant Soviet additions: "When we build, they build. When we stop, they build."

Misinformed arms control advocates continue to talk about

a "spiraling" arms race. Yet the facts are significantly different. Today, the U.S. stockpile of strategic offensive and theater nuclear forces has some 25 percent *fewer* weapons than it did in 1967. The megatonnage of this diminished stockpile is approximately 70 percent lower than it was in 1967. Moreover, in October 1983, the NATO alliance agreed to reduce by 1,400 the number of nuclear warheads deployed in Europe. These reductions are under way and, together with the 1,000 warheads previously withdrawn, will reduce the number of nuclear weapons in the alliance stockpile to the lowest level in 20 years.

While we cannot give similar precise estimates for the Soviet nuclear stockpile, we do know that the Soviets have *added* more than 7,000 *new* warheads to their strategic offensive systems since 1967—6,500 of them since 1972, when the SALT I agreements were signed. Even with the SALT II restraints, the Soviet Union has built more warheads capable of destroying our missile silos than we had initially predicted they would build *without* any SALT agreement.

Treaty compliance—or noncompliance—is another verse in the same song. It was assumed that while the Soviets might exploit ambiguities in an agreement, they would avoid blatant cheating. But even in the case of the ABM treaty, the Soviets have engaged in gross violations.

Ignoring Soviet violations of arms control agreements will not make them go away. Indeed, reluctance on our part to respond can only encourage further Soviet noncompliance. The United States will continue to inform the Soviet Union of discoveries of its violations and give it the opportunity to discuss ambiguous situations. But when we have determined that the Soviet actions are deliberate and dangerous, we must respond. Arms control treaties are not like domestic laws, which can be enforced by civil authorities. Instead, arms control violations must be met by firm American reactions. But U.S. responses should be proportionate (though not necessarily identical in nature), and clearly in the United States' interests. The Soviet leadership must understand that the United States has no intention of accepting one-sided compliance with arms control agreements. Progress on this issue is essential if arms control is to remain a useful component of our national security policy. Without exaggerating past mistakes, we must nevertheless learn from this experience of Soviet violations of past treaties.

The Reagan Administration's approach to arms control is

quite different from that of its predecessors. Let me underscore four key differences.

First, President Reagan has insisted that we focus steadily on the goal of how to prevent nuclear war and build a more secure world so that this generation, and future generations, will live in peace with freedom.

The President's proposition—"A nuclear war cannot be won and must never be fought"—not only bears repetition but deserves contemplation. The President's determination to ensure that a nuclear war will never be fought is the mandate for our defense program and arms reduction initiatives. Our goal can be stated simply: to ensure that the defense of America's vital interests never *requires* the United States to fight a nuclear war. In our approach to arms reduction, as in our overall defense programs, we seek to protect and defend vital U.S. interests by reducing the risk of nuclear war to the lowest possible level.

Second, arms reduction is a component of our larger national security policy—not an isolated objective or independent instrument.

Arms reduction is one of the ways in which we pursue our national security objectives. Recognition that arms control negotiations and agreements are but a strand in the overall relationship between the United States and the Soviet Union brings into sharp focus a major dimension of any effective strategy for achieving arms reductions. This dimension—Soviet incentives—was entirely neglected in the previous approach. What are the Soviets' incentives to agree to useful, effective agreements for real reductions? Even more vital, what are the Soviets' incentives to *comply* with what they have agreed to?

In strengthening U.S. forces and acquiring arms while simultaneously negotiating with the Soviet Union, we are creating the necessary incentives for them to reach agreements that meet our interests. Why should the Soviets agree to reductions, if we reduce voluntarily without any corresponding Soviet reduction? Why should they comply, if we accept their violations? Ask yourself: Why is General Secretary Gorbachev now beginning to consider real reductions in strategic nuclear forces? Why are the Soviets beginning to move on INF negotiations? Quite simply, it is the new strength and resolve we have demonstrated. Not only should we negotiate from strength— this is in fact the only way we can negotiate effectively. It is not

Soviet goodwill, but our strength, that is bringing about their changes.

Third, negotiated, structural arms agreements must reduce arms, not legitimize increases.

President Reagan has identified the primary criteria for acceptable, negotiated arms reduction agreements. They must significantly reduce the number of offensive systems, bring us to parity (measured not just by numbers of warheads but by effectiveness) at much lower levels than each side has now, be effectively verifiable, and contribute to a broad policy of strengthening peace and stability. In view of past and current Soviet violations of arms control agreements, it is essential that future agreements establish comprehensive verification regimes that reverse the current Soviet pattern of denial of information essential to verification, facilitate U.S. monitoring and deter Soviet cheating. Without such an effective verification regime, an arms control agreement will serve only to limit U.S. options and programs without providing assurance that the other party has been similarly constrained.

Fourth, beyond negotiated agreements on forces lies an array of initiatives to control nuclear arms and reduce the risks that they might ever be used.

These initiatives focus on factors that could prevent accidents or unauthorized escalation; improve communication capabilities; and remove ambiguities, misperceptions and misunderstandings. This part of our arms negotiation agenda includes a large number of actions that the United States can take independently—without Soviet concurrence or agreement—but in ways that will actually reduce the risk of accidents, unauthorized use or inadvertent escalation. Continuing improvements in our command, control and communication (C^3) and in our warning systems will reduce even further the already low risk that the Soviets might somehow come to believe that a surprise attack might succeed and the equally low risk that weapons could be used accidentally or in an unauthorized fashion. As we modernize our arsenal, we seek to improve weapons' safety and command and control procedures.

Operational arms control also includes a number of bilateral and multilateral actions—sometimes referred to as confidence-building measures—that seek to reduce the possibility of conflict through accident, miscalculation or failure of communications. During our first term, we proposed several new initiatives to the Soviet Union. Some of them have met with success.

In June 1985, both countries agreed to clarify their obligations under the 1971 "Accidents Measures" agreement to consult in the event of a nuclear incident involving terrorists. In October 1985, technical testing of the upgraded Moscow-Washington hotline was successfully conducted, and operational testing of the new capability to send facsimiles began in January 1986. In November in Geneva, President Reagan and Secretary Gorbachev agreed that both governments will examine the possibility of creating risk-reduction centers to lessen the chances of miscalculation or accidental conflicts. We also have conducted a series of policy-level discussions on regional issues.

VII

Implementation of our overarching strategy of secure deterrence requires an array of strategies that capitalize on our advantages and exploit our adversaries' weaknesses. Even when U.S. military investment was substantially larger than that of the Soviets, it would have been advantageous to have more explicit strategies for competing. After a decade in which the cumulative Soviet military investment has been 50 percent greater than our own, it is essential that we rebuild our forces in ways that emphasize our specific comparative advantages.

Exploiting our comparative advantages requires a purposeful direction of research, development and procurement programs, as well as adaptations of doctrine, operational concepts and changing organizations. This effort also means we will have to pay greater attention to the timing and phasing of U.S. initiatives, for example, the introduction of new weapons or major modifications of weapons or tactics.

The potential impact of competitive strategies is illustrated by the decisive advantage achieved by the combination of American technology and Israeli tactics in the 1983 air war between Israel and Syria. The "score" in that air war was 86 to 1 against Soviet MiGs. Another example is our new technology popularly referred to as "stealth." If American technology were able to create airplanes, ballistic missiles and cruise missiles essentially invisible to current Soviet radar technology, massive Soviet investments in defense against aircraft over the battlefield in Europe would become obsolete. Or, if the United States had a capability to reach into the Soviet Union and destroy selective, highly valued targets, Soviet confidence in its nuclear warfighting plan would perforce be greatly reduced.

While specific details of this technology are appropriately classified, publicly available evidence should suggest that these possibilities are by no means fanciful.

We are not likely to regain the position we had in the 1950s. Even now, we are just matching the Soviet levels of weapons procurement (measured in dollars), and it will be the mid-1990s before the "dollar cost" of our weapons stock roughly matches that of the Soviets. Soviet research, development, testing, evaluation and military construction programs remain substantially larger than ours, as do a wide variety of nominally "civilian" programs designed to create a stock of militarily useful assets. In these circumstances, well thought out strategies for competing effectively with the Soviets are no longer something that it would be "nice" to have. They have become a clear necessity.

An intelligent and sensible use of competitive strategies will allow us to maintain an effective force even if our overall budget is constrained. It should enable us to retain a secure deterrent without having to match the Soviets plane for plane, ship for ship, and tank for tank. Even without much systematic effort in the past, we were able to benefit from such an approach. For example, our shift to a strategy of low-level penetration by our bombers forced a large diversion of Soviet resources into air defense. This was certainly preferable to allowing Soviet investment of those resources in offensive forces.

Another area where competitive strategy has produced beneficial results is in antisubmarine warfare. Our ASW capability has reinforced the Soviet navy's defensive orientation, keeping it close to the Soviet homeland in order to protect its ballistic-missile submarine fleet. This limits the Soviet navy's threat to our sea lines of communication with our European and Asian allies in the early period of a war.

In the future, we must vigorously expand the number of areas in which we compete. We must develop thoughtful strategies based on areas of natural, sustainable U.S. advantage. Where possible, we should adopt strategies that make obsolete past Soviet defense investments. We should devise programs for which an effective Soviet response would be far more costly than the programs we undertake. If possible, we should try to move the competition into areas in which we have natural advantages and to channel Soviet defense efforts into areas that are less threatening to us and less destabilizing to the overall military balance.

In order to capitalize on these opportunities and implement competitive strategies more effectively, we must also gain a better understanding of Soviet programs and policies. This Administration has already committed significant funds to, and is making progress in, rebuilding our intelligence capabilities. We must make a concerted effort to improve our understanding of Soviet perceptions, to identify Soviet weaknesses and to assess trends in the military balances. We will not only know our enemy better, we will be able to attend to his weaknesses more effectively.

In sum, I have decided to make competitive strategies a major theme of the Department of Defense during the remainder of this Administration. There are a number of reasons for believing we can successfully develop strategies for competing more effectively in selected areas. We are entering into a period of rapid technological change that can work to our advantage. We have superior skills in the development of military systems embodying some of the leading technologies and superior manufacturing techniques and skills. And having at last realized the danger of giving critical technologies to the Soviets, or allowing them to steal them, we are now more effectively slowing that flow.

VIII

The central lesson of World War II and the past four decades is this: American military power is the prerequisite of peace. Strength is the price for peace. If peace seems expensive, consider the alternatives. By scrimping on strength we will reduce our security and increase the risks of war. But if we fail to keep the peace, the costs will be incalculable.

In 1981, with broad bipartisan support, this Administration began rebuilding American military strength. As I said in my first appearance before the Congress, the road to recovery of a secure deterrent would be neither short nor easy. To reverse the results of a decade in which U.S. defense efforts declined by 20 percent in the face of a 50-percent increase in Soviet military strength required a long-term program. Our urgent need was to regain sufficient military strength to persuade the Soviets that we would allow them no significant exploitable military advantage against our vital interests.

Looking back on the first five years of our rebuilding program, the prime result is that, unquestionably, U.S. military forces are stronger, readier, better trained, better equipped and therefore more capable than at any previous time in our peacetime history. The consequences of this are profound. Our rebuilding of American military strength is redefining the terms of the U.S.-Soviet relationship. Rather than dealing from weakness (and the prospect of greater relative disadvantage), the United States is now beginning to deal from strength and the promise of greater relative strength. Now we must persuade the Soviets that this is not a short-term commitment. Nothing could so enhance the prospects for peace as Soviet acceptance of the proposition that they can achieve no significant, exploitable military advantage over us. Denying the Soviet Union exploitable military advantage cannot by itself guarantee peace. But if we allow the Soviet Union such advantages as they had in 1980, we can be assured that we will then be tested in ways that risk war.

Seventy-five years ago, Theodore Roosevelt enjoined Americans to "speak softly and carry a big stick." His counsel of caution is as relevant today as then. But we must also carry a stick as powerful as our adversary's, for our strength is the foundation of our strategy for peace.

Stephen S. Rosenfeld

THE GUNS OF JULY

On a long hot day last June and then three straight days in early July, American foreign policy clicked into a new phase whose implications the nation is only beginning to explore. In rapid succession, the House of Representatives, dominated by the Democrats and until then an off-and-on check on the bent of a Republican President and Senate, took four signal votes.

The House dramatically reversed itself and voted "humanitarian" aid to the contras in Nicaragua. It initiated the first open American assistance to the non-communist resistance in Cambodia. It repealed a ten-year-old legislative ban on military aid to antigovernment guerrillas in Angola. And for the first time it publicly voted funds to sustain the resistance in Afghanistan.

The notion that the United States should sponsor putatively democratic forces striving to unseat Soviet-supported regimes had been gaining momentum for several years. These votes to aid the world's four leading anti-communist insurgencies, however, gave the so-called Reagan Doctrine a sharp new profile and a powerful new thrust. I propose to examine how the Reagan Doctrine came to be, what it might become, and what its progress tells us about the kind of nation we are. This is an inquiry into what might be called the guns of July.

II

At first glance the Reagan Doctrine has a familiar look; it appears to fit easily into the United States' 40-year quest for containment of the Soviet Union.[1] Actually it is different. As

---

[1]For friendly analyses of the Reagan Doctrine, see Jeane J. Kirkpatrick, "The Reagan Doctrine and U.S. Foreign Policy," Washington: The Heritage Foundation, 1985; "Implementing the Reagan Doctrine," National Security Record No. 82, Washington: The Heritage Foundation, August 1985; Michael Ledeen, "Fighting Back," *Commentary*, August 1985; Charles Krauthammer, "The Poverty of Realism," *The New Republic*, Feb. 17, 1986. For skeptical analyses, see Robert W. Tucker, "Intervention and the Reagan Doctrine," New York: The Council on Religion and International Affairs, 1985, and Robert H. Johnson, "'Rollback' Revisited: A Reagan Doctrine for Insurgent Wars?" Washington: Overseas Development Council, January 1986.

Stephen S. Rosenfeld is deputy editorial page editor of *The Washington Post*.

practiced by Presidents Truman, Eisenhower, Nixon and Carter, whose names have embellished previous "doctrines," containment is a defensive theory referring to efforts to limit the further spread of Soviet power.

The Reagan Doctrine goes over to the offensive. It upholds liberation, the goal of trying to recover communist-controlled turf for freedom. In theory, its reach is universal. In practice, the places to which the Reagan Doctrine has been applied are a particular set of Third World countries where the Marxist grip is relatively recent and therefore presumably light. This puts Ronald Reagan firmly in the older American anti-communist tradition of Woodrow Wilson, who, preaching nonintervention, put American troops ashore at Archangel and Vladivostok. That effort to strangle the Russian Revolution conferred a Wilsonian pedigree on subsequent attempts to undo Marxist regimes.

These attempts include the operations associated with the Inchon landing in Korea; the CIA's part, during the Truman Administration, in putting emigrés ashore in Albania; John Foster Dulles' public toying with the idea of liberation in Eastern Europe; and John Kennedy's landing of Cuban emigrés at the Bay of Pigs. All of these operations were disasters. Their implicit residual significance, to conservatives, is less as a model for emulation than as a caution against the halfhearted pursuit of such undertakings.

It was not, however, a sense of history that produced the Reagan Doctrine. It was an event in history, the appearance during the 1970s of a third wave of newly declared or alleged Marxist states, following the earlier waves launched by the two world wars. South Vietnam, Cambodia and Laos fell to communism and traditionally Western positions were lost in Angola, Mozambique, Ethiopia, South Yemen, Nicaragua, Grenada, Suriname and Afghanistan. On the American left, these developments tended at first to be viewed as coincidental and discrete and as not especially damaging to American interests, Afghanistan excepted. On the right, however, they were immediately received as the integrated and consequential reflection of a new global imbalance brought on by a default of American will—the "Vietnam syndrome"—and by the Kremlin's sure-handed orchestration of Soviet troops, arms and surrogates.

After the Soviet invasion of Afghanistan in 1979, these currents tended to merge. A Soviet juggernaut, it seemed even to people of different persuasions, was truly on the move. Moscow appeared to be in a stage of territorial and political expansion the likes of which had not been seen since the end of World War II, and then only on a much more geographically restricted and strategically modest basis. The danger ever more widely perceived was that even if Moscow had not inspired and directed these convulsions, the affected countries would tend to gravitate toward Moscow and to create major new difficulties for the United States and its friends.

It was precisely here that the Brezhnev Doctrine of 1968 assumed a new life in the American mind. Strictly speaking, the original Soviet doctrine of national liberation—any state is fair game for the revolution—was and is the more fundamental and the more menacing to the West. Nonetheless, the Brezhnev version of this doctrine—once in the Soviet bloc, always in— came to be seen as particularly insidious and objectionable for its felt implication that the West had to sit by with arms folded as the Soviet Union gobbled up one new place after another in its own good time. No longer was the Brezhnev Doctrine taken just as an outrageous alibi framed to justify an imperial act, the subordination of Czechoslovakia. If, as it seemed, it was being invoked by the Kremlin to put its new acquisitions of the 1970s beyond Western challenge, then it somehow had to be confronted head on. Otherwise the West would have ratified by its inaction a Soviet doctrine implying the West's unilateral political disarmament. That anti-communist insurgencies were actually stirring in a number of these new acquisitions provided a nice opening to turn this perspective into policy.

Still, the Reagan Administration's inclinations on this score needed to be jolted into life. The opportunity came suddenly in the fall of 1983 in Grenada. Events presented the President with an easy opportunity to use American troops to topple a regime that looked thuggish and plausibly communist. Later, after the United States managed to inspect the files that overthrown Grenadian leader Maurice Bishop left behind, Grenada came to look like a textbook example of a helpless state on the way to becoming a Soviet tool.

At that point there was no American doctrine of supporting anti-communist insurgencies, and there was no anti-communist insurgency on Grenada for the United States to support. Nevertheless, the President counted substantial gains from his invasion. He had used force under an anti-communist banner and won plaudits in the political and diplomatic arenas, no small matter for an Administration eager to show that it was no Gulliver tied down by liberal Lilliputians.

More importantly, for the first time, communism—if you apply the label to the elements deposed in Grenada—had been shown to be reversible. This was a positively sparkling tonic for an ideologically minded Administration that had ached at the thought that communist regimes were considered locked in by history while non-communist regimes were regarded as open to capture. It also gave the Reagan team new courage to deal with its considerable frustrations in Nicaragua, where the insurgency that the Administration had organized late in 1981 was on the verge of wilting for lack of congressional support.

III

In his first term, Ronald Reagan had worked to restore to the United States a perceived strategic superiority. Public concern and the pressures of reelection had guided him back toward a posture of guarded readiness for accommodation with the Soviet Union in nuclear matters. In regional disputes, however, no similar willingness to compromise was evident. One can speculate that Reagan's relaxation of relations with Moscow on arms control had stirred a compensating hunger for ideological involvement. If it was necessary to pursue something suspiciously like détente in one sector, then it was necessary to keep the conservative faith conspicuously in another.

Yet in the key arena, Nicaragua, the prospect was bleak. The rationale Reagan was then stressing—that Nicaragua's backing of guerrillas in El Salvador justified his own backing of a contra interdiction force—seemed thin and evasive in view of the contras' evident determination to bring down the Sandinista regime. A more convincing argument was needed. In the grand tradition of American anti-communist pronouncements, Reagan moved to the high ground of moral principle. His remarks in his State of the Union address of February 6, 1985, remain the basic text of what others then began describing as the Reagan Doctrine (Reagan himself has never used this term: he apparently has wanted to preserve some flexibility). Said the President:

Freedom is not the sole prerogative of a chosen few, it is the universal right of all God's children. Look to where peace and prosperity flourish today. It is in homes that freedom built. Victories against poverty are the greatest and most secure where people live by laws that ensure free press, free speech and freedom to worship, vote and create wealth. Our mission is to nourish and defend freedom and democracy and to communicate these ideals everywhere we can. We must stand by all our democratic allies. And we must not break faith with those who are risking their lives on every continent, from Afghanistan to Nicaragua, to defy Soviet-supported aggression and secure rights which have been ours from birth.

Former U.N. Ambassador Jeane Kirkpatrick later noted dryly that the clarity of President Reagan's policy has been obscured by our practice of providing assistance to freedom fighters covertly, since covert policies are not explicitly defended by spokesmen of the government. But this is less than half of it. The President, after all, has not shrunk from defending his policy boldly in public forums. His policy is unclear because he has not clarified it.

His original rationale—that freedom is a universal right—is open and unlimiting; if freedom is a universal right, it must be wrong not to try to seat it everywhere, even in the Soviet homeland, no matter what the cost. The actual implementation of the Reagan Doctrine, however, has been confined to a relatively few places: one (Afghanistan) is on the Soviet border, but all the others are quite distant from the Soviet Union; the costs have been relatively modest. This gap between the doctrine's universal aspirations and its particular applications is a source of frustration to its more ardent advocates; to others it is cause for relief.

To the Administration, great strategic fruits are to be derived from a conservative foreign policy that starts with deterrence, proceeds through political, economic and ideological competition, and arrives at support for insurgents only as a last resort in the absence of openness to evolutionary change. National interest is regularly cited on behalf of the guerrilla movements the Administration assists.

To Secretary of State George Shultz, however, as to other official stalwarts, the stronger appeal lies in the "moral principles [that] compel us to support those struggling against the imposition of communist tyranny." A freedom fighter's use of force to resist tyranny is moral, he says, and is to be distinguished from a terrorist's use of force, which by Shultz' definition is intended to impose tyranny. He has broached the idea that aid to anti-communist insurgencies is a proper tit-for-tat rejoinder to Moscow's aid to Marxist insurgencies—a position implying a possible deal between the two great powers to swear off supporting insurgencies. His characteristic approach, however, has been to underline the moral, hence theoretically uncompromisable, aspect of the policy, even in Afghanistan, a country on the Soviet border that surely qualifies as strategic from a Soviet point of view.

Secretary Shultz and CIA Director William Casey say they have spotted a worldwide trend: an increase in the willingness of people to struggle against communist domination. They treat this phenomenon as one of spontaneous generation and do not calculate the contribution that American encouragement has made to inducing people to take up arms. Nor do they calculate the extent to which the United States accumulates a moral debt by its encouragement. Casey finds a moral argument for U.S. encouragement of anti-communist insurgents in what he characterizes as the illegitimate status of the Marxist-Leninist governments in question; these governments are illegitimate either because they are imposed (as in Afghanistan) or maintained (as in Nicaragua) by an outside power. He does not explain why the United States does not support attacks on unrepresentative governments friendly to the West, nor why the United States itself has kept afloat such unrepresentative governments. Nor does he explore the morality of the possibility that the United States, by its sponsorship of guerrilla war against a leftist Third World government, may in effect contribute to that government's decision to seek Soviet maintenance.

Shultz takes a further step. He lumps together communist aggression and tyranny, although the former refers in his usage to a regime installed by the Red Army and the latter to a regime seated mainly by its own efforts—quite a difference. He suggests that assistance to the foes of either one can be a lawful form of collective self-defense, which in turn seems to mean that, in the name of fighting communism, almost anything is allowed.

This is not to say all restraint has been cast to the winds. The Reagan Doctrine was not applied to Angola until early in 1986, a delay that pained, among others, Jeane Kirkpatrick. Once liberated from government service, she shed interesting light on internal debate in the Administration she formerly served, complaining that the State Department's Africa bureau, in pursuing negotiations with the Angolan Marxist regime, had kept the Angolan rebels at arm's length and had actually bestowed a big Export-Import Bank loan upon the Luanda government.

Conservatives invoking the Reagan Doctrine against a reluctant Administration are still trying to start up aid to the anticommunist opposition in Mozambique. There, however, Reagan is making a calculated effort to show Marxist President Samora Machel that Washington can supply, more effectively than can Moscow, the two basic commodities Machel needs: protection from South Africa and economic progress. Mozambique remains the best example of a situation in which the Administration, having a good guerrilla card to play, has not played it, choosing instead to try to wean the local Marxists over to the American side.

Ethiopia is a bit different. Some have urged the Administration to take up the cause of the Eritrean and other guerrillas fighting the Marxist government there. So far the Administration's answer has been no, on grounds that the rebels are not only secessionists but Marxists themselves. Meanwhile, through its immense food program Washington sustains the otherwise hostile government of Mengistu Haile-Mariam and trolls for the favor of the Ethiopian people. Here, again, is evidence that pragmatism is not dead in the Reagan Administration.

In fact, the Administration makes a pragmatic case for the Reagan Doctrine: it is containment-plus, on the cheap. The annual dollar amount of each current operation is in the several tens, or at most the several hundreds, of millions: not a big budget item even at the higher estimate and certainly far cheaper than the use of comparable American forces would be.

Reagan Doctrine partisans acknowledge the risks incurred by local friendly countries (Pakistan, Honduras, perhaps Thailand, conceivably Zaïre) that provide or may provide sanctuary for American-financed guerrillas. To minimize these risks the United States advertises its role as the sanctuary's guarantor and—though this somewhat undercuts its military purpose—keeps the level of military conflict within bounds. The further risks that might lead to the introduction of American forces arise only in Nicaragua, where a surge by the Sandinistas, a collapse of the contras or some kind of accident or provocation might necessitate direct U.S. intervention. Though the Reagan Doctrine is designed to obviate the need for the use of American forces, the moral commitment from which the doctrine springs would not expire simply because the guerrilla proxies had foundered. Besides, there is a subtle but unmistakable sense in which Washington hopes that the Sandinistas will disbelieve its insistence that it will not send in American soldiers; so disbelieving, the Sandinistas will be the readier to relent. For this theory, it should be added, there is not yet any proof.

IV

Republicans and conservatives were real or likely converts to the Reagan Doctrine from the time of its inception. The idea of supporting guerrillas was, after all, central to what the Heritage Foundation has described as the Reagan agenda: a new economic theory, a return to traditional values, the strengthening of national security and a rebirth of national optimism. The idea was put into practical effect during the President's first term (although it was actually under Jimmy Carter's Administration that the CIA began working in Afghanistan), was given a fresh mandate by his reelection, and was endowed with a broad conceptual thrust as his second term opened.

It remained only for holdout Democrats and liberals to climb aboard. Not only was such a turn critical to the evolution of Administration foreign policy, given the majority that the Democratic Party retained in the House (253 to 182) even after the Reagan presidential landslide and the G.O.P. Senate victory of 1984; it was also critical to the process of party politics, given the distance and nature of the terrain many Democrats felt the party had to traverse to bring their policy closer into line with public opinion.

Since the summer of 1985, the relatively few liberals who had held their ground on these questions have derided the shift in the stance of most Democrats, laying it to a mood of frustration and political panic created by passing events in the spring of that year. Terrorists had seized a Trans World Airlines flight in Athens, killed a passenger and then escaped with impunity. The Walker family spy ring had been exposed, and marines had been gunned down in El Salvador. The spirit of the anti-communist movie crusader Rambo had been everywhere taken as a sign of the times. Commemorations of the 40th anniversary of Allied World War II victories over Germany and Japan were popularizing the idea of the legitimate and successful use of force to vanquish tyranny. Little wonder that Nicaraguan President Daniel Ortega's (eighth) trip to Moscow, following hard on the heels of an April House of

Representatives vote to withhold aid from the contras, sent Congress into a spasm of embarrassment and rage.

Yet plainly, deeper forces were at work. The conservative brief had sunk in: strategic factors matter, liberty matters, the world is hostile, the United States must fight back. And liberals are politicians too. "We have created the impression that we are too divided to govern," confessed Representative Stephen Solarz (D-N.Y.), a leading party voice, in mid-1985. "If Democrats are going to regain the confidence of the American people and recapture the White House, we will have to develop a new and more toughminded consensus on foreign policy."

Already the party was moving, if fitfully, toward national security positions long espoused by southern and Jackson Democrats. The latter, identifying with the late Senator Henry M. Jackson and the Committee for a Democratic Majority, had furnished Jeane Kirkpatrick and other anti-communist notables to the Reagan foreign policy team (and in some cases to the Republican Party). The Soviet invasion of Afghanistan had pushed Carter Democrats rightward on the core issue of the basic perception of the Soviet Union and on defense spending. The first Reagan term saw important Democratic Party figures taking more security-minded positions in arms and arms control, for example on the MX. As the second Reagan term opened, the intervention debate spurted and Democrats were inevitably drawn in. The House floor debates on aid for Nicaragua, Cambodia, Angola and Afghanistan provided the absorbing spectacle of minds being changed, and of national policy actually being made, before the public's eyes.

A year earlier a narrowly divided Congress, resisting the President's effort to build a bipartisan consensus around the Kissinger Commission's Central America findings, had cut off the program for the Nicaraguan contras that the CIA had begun in 1981. Private and foreign funds had sustained some 10,000 or more of the contras; on June 12, 1985, the issue was again joined. The House was openly asked to offer direct aid ($27 million in "humanitarian" assistance) to a military force bent not simply on interdicting Nicaraguan supplies to Salvadoran guerrillas but, by the contras' own admission, on overthrowing the Sandinistas. Administration supporters stated that aid would break the military stalemate, put the democratic political resistance back into play, and prevent a direct American intervention. Opponents claimed aid would deepen the failure of an already bankrupt policy, isolate the United States in the region, align Americans with the wrong Nicaraguans, and tempt a wider war and perhaps an eventual American part in it.

In a series of votes, 50 to 80 Democrats ended up voting for the aid, although in a package that modified the original Administration proposal with the aim of encouraging negotiations. It was some distance from a full Reagan victory, but the most hesitant element of the American political system had at least decided to vote funds to keep an armed guerrilla force in the field. By February 1986 Reagan had been emboldened to come back to Congress with a request for four times as much in outright military and economic aid.

The subsequent House debate on Cambodia that opened on July 9, 1985, touched the very quick of the Vietnam syndrome—shrinkage from involvement—though only symbolically, since a mere $5 million was at issue and there was not the remotest chance that American troops might be drawn in. Not only had Cambodia, like Vietnam, gone communist. It had been lost, in one perspective, by the votes of mostly Democratic liberals in the 1970s. Now one of them, Solarz of New York, argued that the issue was help to repel a foreign invasion. He led an appeal for military aid, to be given not to the Khmer Rouge but to their lesser non-communist partners in the fight against the Vietnamese occupiers of Cambodia. He was acting to demonstrate, not least to American voters, that the Vietnam syndrome no longer held American policy in check.

Completing the sense of topsy-turviness on the House floor, a Republican, Jim Leach of Iowa, made the argument—once typically Democratic—that aid in the small amount contemplated could not possibly accomplish the large mission to which it was assigned, and that it would only stiffen occupying Vietnam, invest American prestige unwisely and put a distracting American stamp on an Asian cause. Do not rush to "assuage our national guilt over our past involvement in Vietnam" just to show we are not "paralyzed," said Leach, picking up the theme on everyone's mind.

The Administration said military aid was "not necessary or appropriate now." Eminently pragmatic in this instance, Reagan officials saw no advantage in poking publicly into a hornet's nest where the CIA was already quietly providing nominal nonmilitary aid to the non-communist rebels, and where the dominant Pol Pot group seemed bound to benefit most from any further aid to the insurgent cause. No committee hearings had been held. There had been nothing faintly resembling a national debate on Cambodia. In a few hours on the floor, however, Solarz prevailed by the margin of 288 to 122, with 132 of 236 Democrats voting in favor of military aid. At once, Secretary Shultz said the Administration would avail itself of the amendment's option to make the aid humanitarian, not military.

The next day, July 10, 1985, the House turned to the Clark Amendment, the country-specific ban—named for former Senator Dick Clark (D-Iowa)—on aid to Angolan insurgents enacted by Congress nine years before in a surge of anti-executive branch, anti-CIA, anti-Vietnam War feeling.

In the intervening years, guerrilla leader Jonas Savimbi of UNITA (the National Union for the Total Independence of Angola) had impressed many legislators with his charisma, his professions of democracy, his staying power and his promise to topple or at least bloody the Cuban-supported MPLA (Popular Liberation Movement of Angola) government in Luanda. In earlier years the Reagan Administration, while following its predecessors in favoring a repeal of the Clark Amendment, had not lobbied hard for it. Repeal, with its implied corollary of support for Savimbi, had seemed inconsistent with the part of the Reagan "constructive engagement" policy aimed at negotiating matching withdrawals of South African forces from Namibia and Cuban troops from Angola—especially since South Africa was Savimbi's chief supporter.

By the summer of 1985, however, constructive engagement had lost much of its momentum in the region and much of its support in Washington. It was left to a few Democratic liberals like Representative Howard Wolpe (D-Mich.) to defend an embattled Republican policy on Angola. Since the House was building up a head of steam behind sanctions against South Africa at the same time it was voting to repeal the Clark Amendment, it seemed an odd moment for the United States to step into a pro-Savimbi policy parallel to South Africa's. But the House, caught up by the scent of an easy anti-communist vote, casually opened the way to reintervening in Angola's civil war. Sixty Democrats joined the majority in the 236 to 185 vote for repeal. By early 1986, support to Savimbi had been approved.

On July 11, 1985, the House arrived for the first time at open consideration of a congressional request for funds for the Afghan resistance. A covert program had been begun soon

214 THE REAGAN FOREIGN POLICY

after the Soviet invasion of 1979: brushing off Moscow's claim that it was merely tending to an intolerable eruption on its border, Jimmy Carter had accepted the geopolitical explanation that the Kremlin was moving in on the Persian Gulf. News reports subsequently told of what became an aid flow of several hundred millions of dollars a year. A congressional resolution sponsored by then Senator Paul Tsongas, a liberal Massachusetts Democrat, endorsing "material aid to help [the Afghan people] fight effectively for their freedom," had passed unanimously in 1984. The State Department, fearing further exposure of Pakistan's role as sanctuary, persuaded Congress to change the operative phrase to "effective support." By July, admiration for the valor and anti-communism of the guerrillas had carried to the House floor an amendment earmarking $15 million for Afghan humanitarian relief. A brief colloquy avoided all issues of tactics and strategy and produced an uncontested voice vote for the measure. Congress had kept faith with the mujahedeen.

v

What is the record in Nicaragua and Afghanistan and the other places where the Reagan Doctrine is being tested? The President's defenders say he is performing a moral duty and fulfilling a strategic purpose and doing so prudently, without undue cost or risk to the United States. But this is too simple. The President, without conveying a clear sense of purpose, has pointed the country more deeply into open-ended conflicts with major geopolitical implications on three continents. In each of these places he states an intent to produce a negotiation leading to reconciliation, democracy and civil peace. No such result has yet come about, and a pack of nagging questions snaps about his heels.

There is the matter of resources. The costs so far are modest enough for the United States. But are we offering insurgents enough to compete effectively or, as critics on both right and left charge, "only enough to die"? Reagan met that criticism, rhetorically, in the 1986 State of the Union address, pledging a degree of moral and material assistance "not just to fight and die for freedom but to fight and win freedom."

Really? In Afghanistan, Nicaragua, Angola and Cambodia? Even if the other side escalates its aid? Having claimed the moral high ground, Reagan risks being marooned there. He is hard put to deliver enough "to fight and win" but he cannot promise less without exposing himself to principled reproach. It would not do for him to say, as some of the shrewdest supporters and critics alike say of the Reagan Doctrine, that its purpose is simply to bleed the Russians, to add to their costs of empire. That is a rationale of realpolitik, and one that imposes the heaviest costs, real costs, on those struggling for freedom, since they are likely to struggle on but not to reach their goal, to fight but not to win. It is an ironic twist to a policy supposedly devoted to a higher purpose. We can comfort ourselves by saying we are merely supporting their decision to struggle. We can say that any form of anti-communist struggle, no matter how costly, is moral. But the burden is borne very unequally, not in a manner that a careful moralist would boast of.

There is the matter of the democratic quotient and political ambition of the "freedom fighters." Few Americans seem to question the credentials of the geographically and culturally remote Afghan rebels, though the Islamic fundamentalism many of them espouse would arguably produce a political order closer to the one found in current-day Iran than to that of the United States. They are freedom fighters in the sense of combating a foreign occupation but not in the sense conventionally indicated by the use of the term "freedom." There are experts, moreover, who assert that the particular Afghans receiving U.S. support represent elements selected by Pakistan for its purposes, not by the United States for its own. In short, there is little reason to believe that these Afghans support either the ongoing U.N. talks, of which they are not a part, or the idea of negotiations outlined by President Reagan at the United Nations last fall.

Of Nicaragua it is perhaps enough to say that the inner politics of the contras hinges on a struggle between democrats and remnants of Somoza's old National Guard, and that American military support tends to put cards in the hands of the latter. In Angola the United States has now thrown its weight behind a tribal leader whose professed commitment to democracy must be set against, among other things, his reliance on South Africa and his training in Mao's China. The two Cambodian factions to which we are offering token aid are so weak and dependent that our assistance to them risks becoming, in effect, aid to the dominant resistance group led by the genocidal Pol Pot. Fighting communism, one might say, is one thing; building democracy is another.

Then there is the matter of a protracted stalemate or the

threat of defeat. In reviving aid to the Nicaraguan contras, Congress swallowed its misgivings that, eventually, the American government might itself join the Nicaraguan battle out of frustration. But such frustration is not beyond imagining and the circumstances would find some Americans arguing that we had a commitment to keep, prestige to uphold, resolve to demonstrate—the considerations commonly invoked when the national security value, the feasibility or the popularity of a given intervention is in question. In other circumstances, the United States might respond to stalemate and frustration by plodding on. The existence of a doctrine generates pressures to honor it. It does not prevent a decision to cut losses but it can make this course more difficult to carry out.

There is a further doubt about the President's stated goal of a negotiated solution. The logic of his position points to a more ambitious intent to dislodge the local regime in question and humble its Soviet patrons: to "win." This is vexing. The Contadora plan for negotiations, which would involve lowering the temperature of the Nicaragua dispute, smothering it in external concern and drawing the internal parties into a political process, fares poorly. The negotiating track in the other Third World conflicts is bleak, too. So those who lean to "negotiations" are not well placed to insist that they have the answer. To be honest, they need to ask themselves whether the rational liberal premise that negotiated solutions are possible has any greater objective merit than the darker conservative suspicion that they are not. Certainly all of us would feel better if we could locate a successful model or precedent in which a civil war between communists and anti-communists, both with great-power patrons, had been peacefully resolved.

But President Reagan has a winner-take-all bent that hardly appears more promising. He believes, again not without reason, that Marxist regimes have an inner dynamic that drives them beyond the limits of reliable power-sharing. That belief pervaded the "regional peace process" he offered at the United Nations last October. In it he asked the Soviet-backed regimes in Afghanistan, Nicaragua, Cambodia, Angola and Ethiopia to sit down with the anti-communist guerrillas and prepare to submit their hard-won power to popular approval. Moscow and Washington would then "verify elimination of the foreign military presence"—which amounts to elimination of Soviet-bloc presence. Each country would then be "welcomed back [sic] into the world economy," that is, the Western fold.

The same puristic devotion to "freedom," or to "winning," marked Reagan's rejection of the Nicaraguan elections of November 4, 1984. The disagreeable choice—and Marxists will always tend to present disagreeable choices—was whether to accept a flawed election and work from there in a difficult political context, or to reject the election, as Reagan did, and work in what has turned out to be an even more difficult military context. Supporters of the Reagan approach say he is patiently strengthening his bargaining position. Realists reply that the Reagan Doctrine has so far brought him the worst of both worlds: political failure and military frustration alike.

Somberly, one must ask how the Reagan Doctrine and, no less, its Soviet counterpart fit the goal of improved relations that the two powers accepted at the Geneva summit in November 1985. Reagan went there insisting that Soviet global conduct was the number one issue; Soviet leader Mikhail Gorbachev retorted that only arms control was on the table. The two positions appeared to pass like ships in the night.

There is a difficult history here. Nikita Khrushchev declared wars of national liberation "sacred." The tendency to take such words seriously was one reason the United States intervened in Vietnam. Fortunately Moscow, despite its slogans, did not have the reach in the 1960s to go much beyond its commitments to Hanoi and Havana. In the 1970s the Soviets, seeking American sanction of their claim to great-power parity, and the Americans, hoping to regulate a burgeoning superpower competition in the Third World, experimented with devising rules within a framework of détente. The project for a code of conduct collapsed, partly because the Kremlin could not resist new targets of opportunity, for example in Angola.

Now the big insurgencies are anti-communist. The shoe is pinching Moscow's foot, and Washington is enjoying Soviet discomfiture. President Reagan, in his tender of a regional peace process, offered local Marxist "warring parties" (his term for the five Soviet-sponsored governments) and Moscow itself a role, but a loser's role. Believing as he does in freedom, it was a natural gesture. Yet it strains credulity to think that Gorbachev would accept this Reagan approach to the Third World any sooner than Reagan would endorse Gorbachev's views on class war.

VI

So far the President has not raised the level of American commitment in any of these insurgencies to any degree that

truly threatens the Soviet position. In that sense the bark of
the Reagan Doctrine is worse than its bite, and this supports
the comforting proposition that Reagan can have his insurgencies without losing his access to Moscow. To the extent that
the President satisfies the claims of prudence, however, he
undermines the claims of ideology. Strategic considerations
may rationalize a policy of keeping the pressure on Moscow.
Moral considerations and the political pressures they generate
will keep pushing the President toward escalating and trying
to win. The Afghanistan and Nicaragua interventions are in
their seventh and fifth years respectively, and the longer they
drag on—without success for the United States—the closer
they will bring Washington to the choice of escalating or cutting
losses, each with its own calculus of costs and risks.

In some American minds it is as though we had a right to
roll back Soviet power from all the new places it penetrated in
the 1970s; then the game would be more or less even and the
two sides could strike a deal. But politics is not a game with an
agreed baseline. If we know one thing about great-power
politics, moreover, it is that action breeds reaction. The Soviets
pushed too hard for American patience in the 1970s, creating
extra strains that neither détente nor arms control could with-
stand, and in the process moving politics and policy in the
United States notably to the right. Now the possibility exists
that Washington, in a heady mood, could push too hard for
Soviet tolerance in the 1980s. A new leader in the Kremlin,
one may speculate, could have more to prove on this front.

Where is the pressure point? The American role in Cambodia
is too small for Moscow to stew about. In Angola the Kremlin
may be prepared to exploit an American involvement easily
depicted as a partnership with South Africa. Nicaragua is for
the Russians ultimately a geopolitical throwaway, where American engagement serves certain Soviet ends and an outright
American victory might do no special harm. But in Afghanistan, on its border, the Soviet Union has much to lose: if it
does, the Soviets may be driven to make the United States pay.
Bringing further pressure on Pakistan would be one way;
putting some aspect of bilateral relations with Washington on
the line would be another. Yet it is not only conservatives but
also liberals who leap to the cause of the Afghan freedom
fighters—Jimmy Carter was the first to apply the term to them.
The Administration is not reckless, but it is letting itself be
pushed into a situation where there is no consensus on whether
our purpose is victory, negotiation or simply the infliction of

pain on the Russians, and where there is too little calibration of how Moscow might someday respond.

Finally, the Reagan Doctrine forces us to go beyond the specifics of regional situations and their effects on great-power relations and to weigh what kind of a world we are trying to shape. Is it a world of sovereign states that accept certain obligations and common rules, or one in which precedence goes to the pursuit of values that are larger than nations?

I would argue that a world of states has its limitations but its considerable comforts, too. The impulse to freedom is strong among us but it can produce a romantic policy. A country with our pervasive international interests has a great investment in the ways of world order. Our readiness to ignore conventional forms of respect for national sovereignty, and to bolster forces that oppose governments, inevitably reinforces a like readiness by governments and forces hostile to us. And in that kind of competition, a government that is accountable to a democratic public opinion in a society ruled by law is inevitably going to be at a comparative disadvantage.

Many of us affirm the cause of freedom. We are eager to support this impulse in certain circumstances. But the last, liberal, Administration did not need a doctrine to fall in behind the mujahedeen. The best thing about the Reagan Doctrine is that Ronald Reagan himself has resisted pressures from his own core constituency to make him apply it indiscriminately.

The issue finally facing us is not simply the measure of devotion to our ideals. It is the wisdom and value of American involvement in foggy conditions and the question of how best to preserve American influence over the long haul. One does not have to be a Pollyanna to believe that the desire of struggling new Third World regimes to maintain their independence and to modernize effectively will tend to pull most of them away from the Soviet orbit as time goes on. To the extent that the Reagan Doctrine is prudently managed, it fails in its stated purpose of liberation. If it were to be managed with an eye to achieving prompter local successes, it could too easily slip out beyond the circle of acceptable costs and risks. This is what must temper our impatience to load up the guns of July.

Leonard Silk

THE UNITED STATES
AND THE WORLD ECONOMY

The year 1986 severely tested the ability of the United States to provide the leadership needed to prevent a threatened breakdown in the ever more closely integrated world economic and financial system. Dangers to the system have resulted from the high volatility of exchange rates, huge imbalances in trade and growing protectionism; these have been compounded by the inability of developing countries to meet their debt obligations, continuing fears of inflation in the midst of sharp declines in oil and commodity prices, sluggish growth in the industrial and developing countries alike, persistent overcapacity and unemployment. Aggravating the strains of clashing national interests were uncertainty and conflict among the major nations of the West over the right policies for solving this complicated set of problems.

If solutions are to be found, it is crucial that the leading industrial nations come to a common understanding of how to avoid repeating the mistakes that caused the Great Depression and the political disasters that flowed from it.

After World War I, and the inflations released by it, the major countries adopted highly restrictive monetary policies, which by the end of the 1920s choked off economic growth. The trend toward world deflation was reinforced by countries' mistaken foreign-exchange policies. In Britain the pound sterling had fallen to $3.44 in November 1920, but it was restored to its prewar dollar parity of $4.86 when Britain returned to the gold standard in 1925. Britain felt compelled to adopt excessively tight money to hold it there. The results were falling prices, economic slump, climbing unemployment and "the dole." In France, by contrast, the franc was undervalued after the war, and the large inflow of gold and foreign exchange put intense pressure on other countries, including the United States. In the United States restrictive tariff legislation was passed, especially the 1930 Smoot-Hawley Act, which hurt

---

Leonard Silk is Economics Columnist of *The New York Times* and Distinguished Visiting Professor of Economics at Pace University. Copyright © 1987 by Leonard Silk.

other countries and forced them to engage in severe deflation to maintain the exchange rates of their currencies. The Great Depression stemmed from the postwar boom—and from the deflationary measures some countries adopted to maintain their exchange rates.

Today there are some similarities to that earlier crisis, but there are important differences, including exchange-rate flexibility, an awareness of the danger of thrusting the world into a deflationary spiral, a recognition of the destructiveness to the system that unbridled protectionism would bring, and an understanding that fiscal and monetary policy can be used to stimulate the recovery of a national economy. But, despite some intellectual and political progress, divisions persist over how each nation can best pursue its self-interest—whether by holding down inflation and keeping its currency sound or by promoting economic expansion for the system as a whole. After the long post-World War II boom that lasted until the early 1970s and was followed by oil shocks, inflation and stagnation, the world economy is again suffering from overcapacity and high unemployment. Economists and politicians are searching for a way out of the dangerous bind—a way that can bring economic recovery without rekindling the inflation that compelled them to take the disinflationary steps that have led to the present unemployment. In a closely integrated world it is risky for any single nation, even the largest economy in the world, acting alone, to pursue a strongly stimulative policy without weakening its trade position and its financial structure—and without posing a threat to the international system.

II

The threat to the system was intensified by the United States' large and growing "twin" deficits in the federal budget and in foreign trade, and hence by the nation's growing foreign debt and dependence on the massive inflow of capital.

In fiscal year 1986 the U.S. budget deficit reached a record $221 billion, raising the national debt above $2 trillion, double its level in 1981 when President Reagan took office. The reasons for the vast increase in the public debt during the Reagan years are by now all too familiar: (1) the failed theory that so-called supply-side tax cuts would generate such an upsurge of national growth and tax revenues as to provide for expansion in both military and social expenditures; (2) the failed theory (or ideology) that curtailing the growth of federal revenues would force a curtailment of the nonmilitary activities of government (sometimes denominated "the Reagan Revolution"); (3) the rapid military buildup, and (4) the shortfall of revenues resulting from the unexpected and steep recession of 1981–82 and from the overall slow economic growth, with real gross national product increasing at an average rate of only 2.4 percent per annum during the first six years of the Reagan presidency.

While the budget deficits have been the focus of public and congressional anxiety, the strains on the American economy and the international system have been exacerbated by the less noticed growth of private debt. Business borrowing has grown rapidly, much of it to finance highly leveraged mergers and acquisitions, and so has borrowing by farmers, real-estate investors and consumers. Total American debt, private and public, has grown to nearly $9 trillion, more than twice its level at the start of the decade. Debt in recent years has grown much faster than the national economy. For two decades before 1982 total debt had held steady at 160 percent of the rising gross national product; in the past four years the ratio of total debt to GNP has leaped to 200 percent. This means that large numbers of business firms and individuals have put themselves in a more difficult position to repay debts if the economy turns down.

The rapid growth in private debt during the late 1970s and early 1980s was based on inflationary expectations; borrowers believed that the rising value of the assets they acquired and the declining value of the money they would use to repay their loans would more than justify the high interest rates they had to pay. Lenders and investors took big risks in the belief that inflation would bail out even unsound loans and investments. But the drop in inflation resulting from the sharp American and world recession of 1981–82 revealed the dangerous overborrowing that had gone on in the inflationary era.

The drop in inflation is doubtless the greatest achievement of the Reagan Administration. It resulted chiefly from the restrictive monetary policy pursued by the Federal Reserve under Paul A. Volcker, a policy which the Administration sometimes criticized as the cause of the recession but essentially supported. In 1986 the inflation rate as measured by the rise in consumer prices fell to 1.5 percent, its lowest rate since 1964, when the Vietnam military buildup was not yet in full sway. But the victory over inflation has been a costly one, and in 1986 the costs of both the inflation and stopping the inflation were still being paid. In the past year many farmers and oil producers were severely hurt or ruined when commodity and oil prices fell. Some 1,500 banks—about one out of every ten in the nation—were on the regulators' list of financially troubled institutions. One hundred and fifty banks failed in 1986, more than in any year since the Great Depression. Hundreds of technically insolvent savings and loan institutions were being kept afloat by regulators who did not want to exhaust the reserves of the Federal Savings and Loan Insurance Corporation.

Despite anxieties over the weakened financial structure in real estate, agriculture, energy, mining, manufacturing and banking, the wave of debt creation rolled on in 1986. What kept it rolling were the vast debts incurred, often through so-called junk bonds—high-interest, high-risk bonds—to finance mergers and acquisitions, as well as the debts incurred by corporate managements to fight off hostile mergers or acquisitions. As 1986 drew to a close, the revelation that the well-known arbitrager Ivan F. Boesky had agreed to pay $100 million in settlement of charges of insider trading brought by the Securities and Exchange Commission dealt a shock to Wall Street and the nation.

But "junk bonds" and such defensive devices as "poison pills" and "shark repellants" were only part of the reason total debt in the United States continued to grow rapidly in 1986; the growth was also fed by aggressive lending by financial institutions seeking to achieve a positive spread between their current rate of return and their current cost of money, by the drive of banks and thrift institutions to lend at floating or variable rates, pushing interest-rate risks onto borrowers, and by the interest-rate bargains or "buy downs" offered by auto companies and home builders seeking to make sales in a time of weakening consumer demand. Many businesses, unable to finance repairs, replacements or current operating costs, increased their debts simply to stay afloat. The drive to expand mortgage credit, much of it on a minimum down-payment basis, brought on a big increase in delinquencies and foreclosures on both homes and commercial properties as real-estate prices declined in many parts of the country, such as Texas and Oklahoma, which were hard hit by the slump in energy and farm prices.

A 1985 study by the New York Stock Exchange concluded that the health of American corporations had been endangered by excessive debt.[1] During 1986 nearly 70 percent of all corporate borrowing was short term; this is an extraordinarily high level. The "quick" ratio (liquid assets as a percentage of short-term corporate liabilities) fell to its lowest postwar level. The "interest coverage" ratio (pre-tax corporate profits to interest payments) was at a historically low level.

The danger is that if the United States' financial structure is further weakened by a worsening of the ratio of debt to gross national product, the outcome could be an increase in business failures (already at their highest postwar level), especially if the economy turned down. If, on the other hand, the monetary authorities were to go too far in trying to prevent a downturn, then inflation, high real interest rates and an overvalued dollar would continue to hurt American competitiveness in world markets.

III

The nation's internal and external economic problems are closely connected. The huge and growing public and private borrowing has pushed real interest rates above those in other competing countries. High interest rates, while essential to attract foreign capital given the inadequacy of saving by Americans, made the U.S. trade deficit worse. The capital inflow, by bidding up the value of the dollar, hurt American exports and import-competing industries, and caused the loss of many American jobs—some estimates run as high as two million—by forcing lay-offs and plant closings at home and shifts of production to foreign locations. The overvaluation of the dollar has not only helped to keep unemployment up but has also augmented the shift of jobs from goods to service industries, and in many cases to lower-paid jobs.

There are other factors involved in the job losses and job shifts, including the relatively high level of American wages, the spread of medium- and low-technology industries to other countries (including poor, developing countries) and the failure of American management to modernize as rapidly as foreign competitors, particularly Japan and the newly industrializing countries of Asia. Added to these problems are the low rate of national savings, the high cost of capital and the low return on

[1] "The Financial Health of U.S. Corporations: An Update," New York Stock Exchange Economic Research, July 1985.

capital investment in the face of worldwide overcapacity in steel, chemicals, minerals and other basic industries.

Throughout the world the problems of sluggish growth, financial instability, Third World debt and trade imbalances are interlocked—and lie at the heart of America's problems. As Nobel laureate Lawrence R. Klein has put it, both the U.S. budget and trade deficits and the related problems of sluggish growth, overcapacity and unemployment are "endogenous" to the world economic system. It now appears that these problems cannot be solved by the United States alone but must be solved within the context of that wider system.

The orthodox solution for a nation's problems of insufficient growth, overcapacity and unemployment—orthodox, that is, since the Keynesian revolution—has been for the government to increase the demand for the goods and services that a nation has the capacity to produce, and hence increase the derived demand for labor. And the prescription for increasing demand has been to cut taxes, step up government spending and enlarge the budget deficit. This prescription, crowned by the enormous deficit-financed war effort in World War II, ended the depression of the 1930s; it has been used, in combination with an accommodative monetary policy, under both Republican and Democratic administrations in arresting and reversing all the postwar recessions—including the steep recession of 1981–82. Some economists still consider the Keynesian macroeconomic approach for combating the business cycle the right prescription.

But the huge buildup of budget deficits and total national debt, along with the nation's increased dependence on international capital inflow, makes it difficult and even dangerous, perhaps impossible, for the United States to escape its burdens simply by increasing total demand through still greater increases in public or private borrowing. The harvest could be heightened inflationary pressure, a slowing inflow or actual outflow of foreign capital, a decline in investment, a further loss of international competitiveness, more people out of work and a worsening of protectionism, with ominous implications for the world economy and polity.

What do these new conditions and dangers imply for economic policy? The greatest change required appears to be that the unit for policy thinking must become the world economy rather than the national economy, although this flies in the face of traditional national politics and economic pressures.

National policymakers must be concerned with the wider community of interests, thinking not only about conflicts with adversaries but about mutually supportive relations with allies and trading partners as well. Whether or not the current U.S. Administration is able to tackle the problems facing the world economy, the challenge is of such magnitude that it will be with us for some years.

IV

Since the end of the Second World War the United States has assumed the leadership of the free world and the primary responsibility for rebuilding and integrating the world economy. But Charles F. Kindleberger, in his presidential address to the American Economic Association a year ago, said the United States has lost its appetite for providing the world with what he called "international economic public goods."[2] These are goods and services which benefit the entire international community but for which individual consumers, businesses or nations are not necessarily willing or able to pay, such as open markets for the goods of other countries in times of glut, supplies in times of acute shortage, steady flows of capital to developing countries, international money, the coordination of international economic policy, and a willingness to be the lender of last resort in times of financial crisis.

Without a nation strong enough and responsible enough to play the role of leader, the international financial system is in peril. The need for an international lender of last resort, a role played by Great Britain through most of the nineteenth and early twentieth centuries, is greater than ever today with more massive flows of capital and goods, instantaneous communications and shiftability of funds, a plethora of transnational banking and industrial organizations, and the buildup of Third World debt to the trillion-dollar level. Unless the United States regains its ability and willingness to sustain nations in danger of default or builds a collective defense with Japan and others, there could be a financial disaster comparable to those of 1873, 1890 and 1929, or an even greater one.

One reason for the current danger is that the United States, like Great Britain after 1890, has lost economic power relative to the rest of the world. Although it remains the largest and

[2] Charles F. Kindleberger, "International Public Goods Without International Government," *American Economic Review*, March 1986, pp. 1–13.

most important economy in the world, a relative loss of power has been causing the United States to turn inward and focus on its own imperiled interests. "The contraction of concern from the world to the nation," said Mr. Kindleberger, "is general, and applies to economists as well as to politicians and the public."[3] While there had been a recent upsurge of interest in the international dimension, the focus of this interest, he maintained, had been almost exclusively on what the connections mean for U.S. interest rates, trade and industrial policy, growth and wealth.

Nevertheless, even within these economic constraints and the pressures of American interest groups that feel themselves adversely affected by foreign nations, the Reagan Administration, under the leadership of Treasury Secretary James A. Baker, has been struggling to play the role of leader and provide "international economic public goods." The Administration has sought open, or at least partially open, markets in a time of gluts; enhanced flows of capital to developing countries in a time of anxiety among banks about their existing overexposure; international money in a time when the dollar is overvalued and the American trade position and balance of payments are extremely weak; and policy coordination among the major industrial countries in a time when other governments, like the United States, are increasingly preoccupied with their own problems and, in some cases, have begun to regard "coordination" as inimical to their national interests. A critical concern for the future is to make sure that the United States, or some group of nations including the United States, is prepared to play the role of lender of last resort should an international financial crisis develop.

Secretary Baker's difficult task is to advance American interests by pressing other countries to share the responsibilities and burdens of providing international public goods. Since the Plaza meeting of September 22, 1985, of the Group of Five— at which Japan, West Germany, Britain and France agreed with the United States that the dollar needed to be lowered against their currencies—the U.S. Treasury has been pursuing a dollar-devaluation policy in order to cut the trade deficit, restrain congressional protectionist pressures and force monetary support for the United States on Germany and Japan.

The dollar did come down sharply, at least against the

[3] Ibid., p. 9.

German mark and the Japanese yen. But as 1986 wore on, it became less clear whether the U.S. dollar-devaluation policy would fit in with the aim of reviving stronger and more stable world economic growth or whether it might even be harmful—especially if it wound up sending the dollar into a free-fall.

After the middle of the year Japan and West Germany resisted further depreciation of the dollar: Japan feared the loss of export markets and Germany worried about the regeneration of domestic inflation. The United States urged both countries, if they wished to avoid further dollar depreciation against their currencies, to use fiscal and monetary policy, especially cuts in interest rates, to spur the growth of their domestic economies, to help increase the demand for American exports and sustain the debt-ridden developing countries.

On the eve of the September 1986 meetings in Washington of the International Monetary Fund and the World Bank, a dispute surfaced between Treasury Secretary Baker and Federal Reserve Chairman Volcker over the need for further dollar devaluation. In congressional testimony, Mr. Volcker said he thought the dollar had declined enough and that other policy measures were needed to reduce America's trade deficit, but Mr. Baker seemed to be threatening further dollar devaluation unless the Japanese, the Germans and their European partners did more to stimulate their economic growth. Mr. Baker's pressure evoked a heated response from the European finance ministers and central bankers, meeting in Gleneagles, Scotland, who warned that, to prevent a further dollar decline, they would intervene in the currency markets. At the IMF meeting in Washington, President Reagan reinforced Mr. Baker's warning that the dollar would sink further unless the other industrial countries took action to accelerate their growth. But the stalemate continued.

The Europeans insisted that the problem of global imbalance in trade and exchange rates was the United States' fault, a consequence of its huge and continuous budget deficits. They contended that the United States had failed to deliver on its part of the Plaza agreement—bringing down the budget deficit as the Europeans and Japanese accepted the further depreciation of the dollar. Indeed, the American budget deficit had swollen further in the year since the Plaza agreement, and the other governments blasted away at this failure.

President Reagan sought to deflect this criticism by declaring that he would act more strongly than ever to get rid of the budget deficit. His "highest task," he said, was "curbing the growth of our government's spending." "No nation," he declared, "can survive if Government becomes like the man who in winter began to burn the wall boards of his house to keep warm until he had no house to keep warm." His Administration had "made progress against those who would condemn future generations to pauperdom." His main weapon against them, he declared, was the Gramm-Rudman-Hollings law, which mandated a steady course to a balanced budget in 1991. "I pledge to you," he declared to the 151 nations assembled at the IMF meeting in Washington, "that I will do all in my power to stop this fiscal death march."

Yet, as the fiscal rhetoric escalated, foreign disbelief that the United States would act to cut its budget deficit deepened; it was believed that the United States was instead trying to put the burden of readjustment on other countries by urging them to reflate their economies and reduce their competitiveness.

The Germans were particularly adamant in refusing to play "locomotive" for the world economy; they maintained that they had taken on that role once before, in response to the blandishments of the Carter Administration, but had weakened their economy in the process and would not do so again. Chancellor Helmut Kohl and Finance Minister Gerhard Stoltenberg insisted that the German economy was already growing quite fast enough. They said that the problem of unemployment—the jobless rate was hovering close to nine percent—was mainly a structural, not a cyclical, problem; it needed to be solved from the supply side, through greater mobility of labor and flexibility of capital. The president of the Bundesbank, Karl Otto Pöhl, resisted American urgings that the German central bank cut its discount rate and step up the growth of the money supply, asserting that the money supply was already growing too fast in Germany.

The Japanese were more responsive to Secretary Baker's campaign for greater cooperation in the interests of world economic stability and growth. In late October, Mr. Baker and Finance Minister Kiichi Miyazawa worked out a bilateral agreement stating that action by the key industrial countries was "critical to promoting world economic growth, reducing imbalances, and resolving international debt problems." As part of the accord, the Japanese government agreed to cut the discount rate of its central bank and to submit a more stimulative budget to the Diet. But less than two months later, on

December 25, 1986, the Japanese government approved the smallest spending increase in three decades. "It is hard to find revenue sources for more public works projects," said Miyazawa.

V

As the American initiatives vis-à-vis Japan and West Germany demonstrate, the United States in 1986 adopted a policy of "aggressive bilateralism," which was intended to promote its own economic interests but at the same time to forge coalitions that it hoped would keep the world economy stable and growing. In defending the pressure that the United States was putting on Japan and Germany to expand their economies more rapidly, Secretary Baker insisted that this policy was not aimed primarily at expanding the market for American goods but at preventing a breakdown in the world economy. "We feel that we are engaged in a life or death struggle here to preserve the world economy," he said. And, in the wake of the November congressional elections in which the Democrats gained control of the Senate, Mr. Baker said that the election outcome should prove to the Germans, the Japanese and America's other trading partners that "we were not crying wolf" in warning that a mood of populism, isolationism and protectionism in the United States posed an increasing danger to the world economy.

The effort to make bilateral deals with key partners represented a shift from the multilateralism that had characterized U.S. international economic policy during the period when it led the way in the construction of the great postwar international economic institutions, including the International Monetary Fund, the World Bank and the General Agreement on Tariffs and Trade. But aggressive bilateralism also marked a shift from the go-it-alone tendencies of the Reagan Administration during its first term, founded on an exaggerated view of America's economic strength. During his first term, President Reagan and his then secretary of the treasury, Donald T. Regan, hailed the capital inflow to the United States as a tremendous vote of foreign confidence in the American economy and regarded the rising dollar as evidence of the nation's vigor and the Administration's successful policies. In the second term, however, with Mr. Regan moving to the White House as chief of staff and Mr. Baker taking over as secretary of the treasury, dollar machismo gave way to a policy of dollar devaluation. But the policy of dollar devaluation as a means of stabilizing and regenerating world economic growth ran into problems in 1986.

Mainly as a result of the 40-percent fall in the dollar against the yen, Japan suffered a severe slowdown. Its export industries lost profitability and sales, especially to its competitors in South Korea, Taiwan and other newly industrialized countries, which had prevented their currencies from falling significantly against the dollar. The Baker-Miyazawa agreement was achieved because Japan recognized that, to safeguard its export markets, it needed to halt further dollar devaluation against the yen. Germany, feeling less threatened by the loss of the American market (a minor part of its export sales) and relatively secure within the European Common Market (where the bulk of its exports go), rejected the American threat of further dollar devaluation.

Within the U.S. government there were differences of view, especially between the Federal Reserve on one side and the Treasury and the White House on the other, on how far to push dollar devaluation. The Fed tended to worry more about inflation and the danger that the dollar would fall out of control and cut off foreign capital inflow, while the Treasury and the White House pressed for what were known as "pro-growth" policies, fearing that recession posed a greater danger for the United States and the world economy than inflation. The world could live with inflation, they reasoned—it had done so through the 1970s and early 1980s—but serious recession could trigger a collapse of the world debt structure and bring on deflation and depression.

Another problem troubling policymakers last year was that the U.S. trade deficit continued to worsen despite the depreciating dollar and falling oil prices. It ran at about $175 billion in 1986 compared to $132 billion in 1985. Most economists thought the widening trade deficit reflected the normal lag in the so-called J-curve. During the initial period after a currency devaluation, according to this theory, import costs rise and export earnings decline as foreign competitors, determined to hold on to market shares, are slow to raise prices. But, as their profit margins are squeezed, they do eventually raise prices, causing a drop in their sales as cheaper domestic goods are substituted for imports, and the trade deficit shrinks. Late in 1986, following declines in the trade deficit in August, September and October, the consensus view of private and official economists was that the J-curve was at the turning point and that 1987 would see a marked improvement in the trade deficit, which would help keep the economy growing. But a huge jump in the trade deficit in November to a record monthly level of $19.2 billion shook confidence that a more favorable trend had begun.

At best, the improvement in the trade deficit was expected to be slow. Japan and other foreign competitors, despite the currency devaluations, were still holding down their export prices in a world suffering from unemployment and overcapacity. The outlook was for sluggish growth in the world economy to continue, thus limiting the demand for American exports; and other countries had invested heavily in facilities to serve the American market and would not readily give up. Major U.S. trading partners, including Canada, Mexico and other Latin American countries, had not allowed their currencies to rise much, if at all, against the dollar and were unlikely to swell the demand for American exports. A policy problem facing the United States was whether to press these other countries to accept dollar devaluation against their currencies; but their own unemployment and depressed industries and agriculture implied strong resistance and possibly worse political relations, increasing the risk that further dollar devaluation would be counterproductive.

There was the further risk that, unless the United States moved more decisively to eliminate the budget deficit, the trade deficit would persist anyhow. As Clayton K. Yeutter, the U.S. trade representative, put the problem at the Congressional Summit Conference on World Debt and Trade in New York in early December: "We have contributed mightily to the trade imbalance by allowing our Federal budget deficit to outgrow our total available savings." Warning that Congress might lack the "political patience" to await a trade turnaround, Mr. Yeutter warned: "We seem poised as a nation to shoot ourselves in the foot just as our trade situation is beginning to improve."

President Reagan, politically weakened by the Republicans' loss of the Senate and by the Iran/contra affair, could have greater difficulty in staving off protectionist legislation from the new Congress. Legislators, however, were looking for ways to avoid naked protectionism that would virtually force retaliation, and so were foreign governments. The hope was that ways could be found to reduce trade imbalances by a positive "market-opening" approach that would enable the United

States and others to increase their exports of services, high technology, intellectual property, agricultural products, and trade-related investment.

Belief that this market-opening approach might be possible was encouraged by the meeting of the GATT contracting parties at Punta del Este this past fall, launching the Uruguay Round of Multilateral Trade Negotiations. Although the meeting at Punta was more successful than had been expected, it left two major issues unresolved—agriculture and services. Worries remain that it will be a long and hard struggle to contain and reverse protectionist forces.

In the strained world economic environment, many governments will be hesitant to rush into the Uruguay round and commit themselves to an extension of tougher trading rules on agricultural products and other goods and services. The United States itself is in an ambiguous position. In recent years at economic summit conferences and in other forums it has pushed hard for another GATT round; yet it has itself adopted protectionist measures and is resorting to an aggressive bilateralism toward its most important trading partners. At the end of the year, the Administration said it would impose a 200-percent tariff on a broad range of agricultural exports from the European Common Market; Mr. Yeutter said the purpose was to force the Europeans to settle American claims of $400 million resulting from losses on grain sales due to the entry of Spain and Portugal into the European Community.

Other countries are also trying to decide whether bilateral or multilateral approaches, or some mixture of both, are more likely to best serve their interests. Canada, for example, has sought to initiate bilateral negotiations with the United States to create a wider "free trade zone." But finding the Reagan Administration by turns inattentive, sharply critical of particular areas of Canadian protectionism, and more than ready to take countermeasures against them, Canada appears to be wavering between bilateral and multilateral approaches to the trade problems.

For the world system as a whole, multilateralism offers greater efficiency and equity and the prospect of policy coordination among the industrial countries, and between them and the developing countries. As Sylvia Ostry, Canada's ambassador for multilateral trade negotiations, has argued, coherent development of Secretary Baker's plan for increasing the flow of public and private capital to the developing countries requires not only enhanced cooperation between the IMF and the World Bank but also the contribution of GATT, so that trade in financial services can become a key element in the development process.

During 1986, its first full year in operation, the Baker plan made only slow progress, but enough to show the critical contribution that a coherent multilateral approach can make. A money package supported by the IMF, the World Bank and commercial banks was quickly put together to help Mexico, which was thrown back into economic crisis by a severe earthquake, falling oil prices and government mismanagement. The World Bank negotiated policy-oriented loans for eight major debtors for a total of about $3 billion, and discussions were under way with 11 countries for an additional $4.7 billion. The IMF negotiated standby programs and surveillance arrangements with 11 major debtors. The commercial banks, still reluctant to increase their exposure in the debtor countries, did make a few new loans, completed multiyear reschedulings with the Ivory Coast and Yugoslavia and launched rescheduling talks with Bolivia, Morocco, Nigeria and Uruguay. New money packages were under discussion with Mexico and Nigeria, and an oil facility loan for Ecuador was nearly completed. Colombia raised $40 million through an eight-year bond issue in the Japanese market. And a number of countries were moving to adopt debt-equity swaps with foreign lenders. Secretary Baker, while cautioning that it would take time to achieve lower debt service ratios for the debtor countries, noted that they had been helped significantly by the more than five-percentage-point decline in interest rates since 1984, which would save the major debtors $14 billion annually.

The most important change introduced by the Baker plan was its stress on growth rather than austerity as the crucial strategy for rescuing the debtor countries. But the Baker plan's critics insisted that, while this growth strategy represented a significant conceptual advance, it was not supported by enough new money from the industrial countries or by strong enough measures for bringing down interest rates, converting debt to equity and forgiving part of the Third World debt.

The United States, however, is not ready to go much beyond the original Baker plan, feeling strapped for funds to do more and unwilling—perhaps unable—to lean harder on the private banks and international agencies. Some American businessmen, led by James Robinson, chairman of American Express, have been urging Japan to do more to aid the developing countries; indeed, Mr. Robinson has proposed that Japan, now the world's biggest creditor, launch a "Marshall Plan" for the developing countries. At the start of the new year, Japan, after running a trade surplus in 1986 of nearly $90 billion, announced a multilateral aid program of about $9 billion over three years. But neither Japan nor any other country seems ready to shoulder the burden of aid-giver comparable to that which the United States assumed after World War II on behalf not only of its allies but also of its wartime enemies, Japan and Germany. Indeed, with memories of the Japanese and German bids for world dominance during World War II still very much alive, there is ambivalence in the United States and other Western countries over how large an international leadership role Japan and Germany should be urged to play. In any case, neither country wants to take on those international responsibilities. Forty years after the war, the United States is still having the leadership role thrust upon it.

VI

How can the United States best perform that international role?

To do the job in a world in which the line between domestic and international economic policy has been rubbed out, the United States must set its own financial affairs in order. This means, first of all, tackling the structural deficit in the federal budget that has aggravated the trade deficit and made the nation so dependent on capital flows from abroad.

How hard and how quickly to hit the budget deficit is both a political and an economic problem. To hit it too hard in the economy's current state, with the economy growing so slowly as to be on the verge of a recession, might be to plunge it into the unwanted recession; some economists warn that all-out efforts to reduce the budget deficit would repeat the mistakes of the Hoover Administration and the early Roosevelt Administration, which, in futile efforts to balance the budget, raised tax rates and aggravated the depression.

But to fail to deal with the budget deficit at all might be to worsen foreign and domestic fears about the American debt and the fiscal irresponsibility of its political system, and to heighten the risk that foreign capital inflow would become a massive capital outflow that would reduce savings available for investment, force up interest rates and intensify recessionary forces.

The inflow of foreign capital to finance the trade deficit has thus far helped to sustain American living standards by enabling Americans to consume more than they produced. But the cost of amortizing and servicing the growing foreign debt is steadily rising. If the United States is to halt that rise, it must eliminate the deficit in its current-account balance of payments and even achieve a surplus that will enable it to repay or at least service its foreign debt.

How much damage to the American standard of living would result from eliminating the trade deficit would depend on whether the deficit is eliminated chiefly by raising exports or cutting imports, and whether it is done within a pattern of economic growth or stagnation. Eliminating the U.S. trade deficit chiefly by expanding exports would mean higher employment and output, thereby offsetting some or all of the costs of consuming less than the nation produces. To achieve that goal requires that America's trade deficit be wiped out within a pattern of domestic and international economic growth; in fact, it is difficult to believe that the world economy will go on expanding if the United States falls into a slump.

This takes us back to the problem of the federal budget deficit. Solving the budgetary dilemma—and it is a genuine dilemma, with the danger of undesirable outcomes from trying to cut it too much or too little—requires widening the frame of the problem. Domestically, that means that steps taken to reduce the deficit by cutting government spending or by raising taxes need to be offset by a monetary policy aimed at bringing down interest rates to help keep the economy growing.

For the United States, with its heavy dependence on foreign capital, to shift to a tighter budget and an easier monetary policy, aimed at increasing national savings and reducing interest rates, will require international cooperation, especially a willingness on the part of America's major partners to stimulate their own economies and to sustain world economic growth, which the United States has spurred but can no longer sustain alone. Specifically, the other major countries ought to bring down their interest rates as the United States lowers its rates, to prevent the dollar from plunging and inflicting worse disorder on the world monetary system. The aim of convergent monetary policies, however, should not be to keep the dollar where it is but to move it significantly lower while also easing the world economy into a "soft landing."

Theoretically an overall redesign of the world monetary system might be desirable, but practically the United States is likely to try to work bilaterally or with small groups of countries to solve its own problems and strengthen the international system, much as it has done in the past year and a half, starting with the Plaza agreement among the Group of Five in September 1985. This was followed in March 1986 by a G-5 coordinated reduction in central bank discount rates; in April by a second round of discount-rate cuts by the G-5 minus Germany; in May at the Tokyo economic summit by an agreement among the G-7 (the United States, Japan, Germany, Britain and France plus Canada and Italy) on new arrangements for closer policy coordination; in September by an agreement of G-7 finance ministers for a multilateral surveillance exercise; and in October by the Baker-Miyazawa agreement. "These six steps," said Mr. Baker, "are only a start. We need to build on them while keeping our expectations within reasonable bounds."

All this is certainly "reasonable"; it may even be the best that can be done in the existing circumstances. But the question is whether it is good enough, given the dangers facing the American and world economies, the persistent trade and exchange-rate misalignment, the spreading protectionism and the precariousness of the debt-ridden developing countries.

VII

In sum, there are no "technical" solutions to the economic problems the world is facing. What is most needed is political will—the will of the United States to deal more effectively with its own problems and the will of all the major industrial countries to work together for a common end. It is easy enough to say that, with the lessening of American dominance and the diffusion of economic power, Japan and Germany must accept wider international responsibilities and join the United States in efforts to prevent a crack-up after the greatest period of growth the world economy has ever experienced.

But if that cooperative spirit is lacking, a crack-up could indeed come, with severe political as well as economic consequences. The political consequences could include a cut by the United States in its military support for Europe and Japan, if their investors were to start unloading dollar assets and building their own regional redoubts, and that would mean a weakening of the defenses against aggression. In a sense, we have been here before. It is the knowledge of what could lie ahead if we fail to work together that may be the main reason to hope that we will not let it happen again.

The most important aim of economic cooperation in the year ahead will be to keep the world economy moving forward. For within a pattern of growth the serious problems of world debt, trade and currency imbalances can be contained, and progress can be made toward their solution.

At the end of the 1920s it was the resort by individual nations to unduly restrictive monetary and fiscal policies and to "beggar-thy-neighbor" protectionism, in the presumed self-interest of each, that caused the Great Depression. That blunder must not be repeated. The greatest change needed to preserve stability and growth is for the world economy, rather than the national economy, to become the unit for policy thinking. Despite the resistance of traditional national politics and interest-group pressures, the development of internationally integrated monetary and fiscal policies has become vital to the economic well-being of every country.

James Schlesinger

REYKJAVIK AND REVELATIONS: A TURN OF THE TIDE?

For much of its first six years, the Reagan Administration has cruised along in its foreign policy in a manner both serene and enviable. The errors in nuclear policy that had marred our relations with Europe in President Reagan's first year were attributed to growing pains. Mistakes such as the Euro-Siberian gas pipeline controversy with the Europeans and the Administration's initial hard line toward the People's Republic of China were repaired with little permanent damage. Even a major blunder, our ill-starred intervention in Lebanon, was terminated quickly—and our forces extricated with such tactical skill that little permanent damage was done (save to our prestige and influence within the Middle East). Certain other actions—our support of El Salvador, our move into Grenada and our attack on Libya—however controversial at the outset, turned out to be generally successful and much of the initial criticism died away.

Meanwhile the Soviet Union was passing through a time of troubles. International dynamics in a world still significantly bipolar reflect to a large extent a kind of counterpoint between the United States and the Soviet Union. Consequently, the position and prestige of one superpower tends to vary inversely with the gains or losses of the other. At least until the accession of General Secretary Mikhail Gorbachev, the Soviet Union appeared plagued by bad luck and unable to deal with its many internal and external problems. President Reagan had had the good fortune to come into office as the Soviet Union went through three succession crises in a row. In addition to its internal drift, the U.S.S.R.'s policies were also marked by a series of blunders—from the walkouts at the INF (Intermediate-range Nuclear Forces) and START (Strategic Arms Reduction

James Schlesinger is Counselor, Center for Strategic and International Studies, Georgetown University, and Senior Adviser to Shearson Lehman Brothers, Inc. He has been Secretary of Defense, Secretary of Energy, Chairman of the Atomic Energy Commission and Director of Central Intelligence.

Talks) negotiations in Geneva, the heavy hand and threats directed against Western Europe, and the shooting down of a Korean Air Lines passenger jet. For much of the early 1980s, therefore, the Soviet Union wore the black hat in international affairs—and the United States benefited correspondingly.

Much, perhaps too much, has been made of the Soviet geopolitical offensive of the 1970s, but the Soviets did make significant gains in the Middle East and elsewhere. And, indeed, a geopolitical tide had been flowing toward the Soviets, at least since Watergate and perhaps since our earlier entanglements in Southeast Asia. Whatever its origins, throughout the 1970s American institutions had been severely challenged and the society had lost its self-confidence. One of President Reagan's greatest accomplishments was his contribution to the restoration of America's self-confidence, which resonated among America's allies, who had been troubled by the faltering United States of the 1970s.

In short, during the 1980s, the geopolitical tide that had been flowing toward the Soviet Union in the 1970s was reversed—and began to flow toward the United States.

In the sixth year of the Administration, in part reflecting the more effective stance of the Soviet Union under Gorbachev and in part reflecting simply the law of averages, the Administration's foreign policy was suddenly beset with difficulties. Even before the embarrassments of November—the revelations that our anti-terrorist policy had been undermined by secret sales of arms to Iran and that the proceeds of those sales had in part been used to fund the operations of the anti-Sandinista guerrillas in Nicaragua (in clear defiance of a congressional ban)—our foreign policy had been marred by both a sense of drift and serious blunders.

I shall here concentrate on two issues: East-West relations, particularly as affected by the Reykjavik summit; and White House mishandling of Third World security problems, particularly as revealed by the Iran/contra affair. There have been, however, additional problems, if subsidiary ones, that have further reduced the Administration's stature. The dramatic override of the President's veto of the South Africa sanctions bill indicated a misreading and a mishandling of congressional sentiment. The Administration had fallen too far out of touch with the congressional mood. The brief flap over the disinformation program directed against Libya's Muammar al-Qaddafi reduced the credibility of the Administration abroad, but also at home. The shooting down of an American cargo plane over Nicaragua (perhaps inevitable) with an American crew and an American survivor (certainly not inevitable) added to the Administration's vulnerability. Finally, the loss of Republican control of the Senate, particularly in light of the President's unprecedented campaigning, presaged further difficulties for the President.

The November revelations implied something far more serious than the normal lame-duck deterioration of an administration in its final years. They suggested a weakened executive—at best on the defensive, and quite possibly crippled. The fabled Reagan luck apparently had run out. The question now is quite simply: Has the tide that had flowed toward the United States in the early 1980s started to ebb?

II

The summit at Reykjavik represented simultaneously the culmination and the collapse (at least temporarily) of realistic hopes for arms control. To say that the summit was ill prepared is to indulge in classic understatement. Indeed, the entire performance at Reykjavik underscored the continuing validity of the diplomatic adage that leaders should go to summits not to negotiate, but to ratify what has already been agreed to. The President was led astray by an exaggerated faith in his powers of persuasion. There are indications that the summit's hasty design reflected the all too common domestic political priority: the quest for an arms control "success" before a midterm election. Not only was the summit ill prepared, it was quite badly executed with spur-of-the-moment proposals followed by spur-of-the-moment despair. It combined the worst aspects of earlier summits. It was as ill conceived as the Vienna summit of 1961; it had the worst outcome since the blowup of the Paris summit of 1960; and it rested upon utopian expectations not seen since the Yalta conference of 1945.

Nonetheless, the environment for a serious arms control agreement was the most favorable since the early 1970s. The auspicious environment had been created by the enhanced bargaining position of the United States, due to the Strategic Defense Initiative; by Mr. Gorbachev's strong desire to focus on improvements in the stodgy Soviet economy; and by the deep-seated Soviet wish to avoid a technological competition in arms with the Americans. At long last, the Soviet desire to avoid another turn of the screw in the arms competition seemed to have overcome their long-term inclination to try to extract marginal advantages in such negotiations. The Soviets were prepared to offer sharp reductions in their bloated strategic offensive forces, which represented the potential for a serious agreement, if the United States had been adequately prepared to exploit it. Yet, finally, it all turned into nothing. Reykjavik represented a near disaster from which we were fortunate to escape. It has quite likely forfeited the possibility of a major arms control agreement for the balance of the Reagan term. Perhaps the summit's only useful result is that it has changed what had been the universal European clamor for an arms control agreement into a keen European awareness that such agreements might seriously damage their security interests.

At Reykjavik the American negotiators appeared to have been little informed either on the exigencies imposed by Western deterrence strategy or on several decades of discussion and debate regarding both the possibilities and the limitations of nuclear disarmament. Nuclear weapons remain the indispensable ingredient in Western deterrence strategy. For a generation the security of the Western world has rested on nuclear deterrence. Its goal has been to deter not only nuclear attack but also massive conventional assault from the East. Failing to achieve the force goals outlined at the Lisbon conference in 1952 and the subsequent "New Look" of the Eisenhower Administration, the Western alliance came almost to embrace its conventional inferiority. Indeed, with the trip wire strategy of the Eisenhower years, conventional forces were stated to exist solely to determine the proper moment for unleashing the Strategic Air Command. It was taken as axiomatic that the West could not match "the Soviet hordes." Whatever its limitations, that strategy worked as long as the nuclear threat was primarily unilateral and until the Soviets began to develop an adequate counterdeterrent.

Attitudes began to change in the 1960s with the move toward flexible response. By the mid-1970s the European allies had come to accept the importance for deterrence of a stalwart conventional capability. Perhaps that capability would not be sufficient in itself to protect Western Europe against an all-out conventional assault, but with the mutual reinforcements provided by the strategic and theater nuclear weapons (the other two legs of the NATO defense strategy), it could provide a comfortable level of deterrence. There NATO doctrine has rested for the past decade. Despite the bitter controversies regarding new deployments, nuclear weapons provide the glue that has held the Western alliance together. Indeed, the controversies themselves reflect an unstated acknowledgment of this critical role.

The American position at Reykjavik seems to have reflected no understanding of these simple fundamentals. Indeed, at one point in the negotiations the President had accepted Mr. Gorbachev's proposal that both sides eliminate all strategic offensive arms by 1996. Happily, the Administration has now backed away from this breathtaking proposal and insists that it represents only a long-term goal. But that impulsive, if momentary, agreement underscores the casual utopianism and indifferent preparation that marked Reykjavik.

Surely we must be more cautious in casting aside the existing structure of Western security before we are assured that an alternative truly exists. In the absence of the nuclear deterrent the Eurasian continent would be dominated by that nation with the most powerful conventional forces. The President may win plaudits from the National Conference of Catholic Bishops or from the National Committee for a Sane Nuclear Policy or even from the left wing of the British Labour Party when he holds out his vision of "a world without nuclear weapons," but it endangers Western security and seriously weakens alliance cohesion.

Secretary of State George Shultz has expressed his confidence that, given their greater economic resources, the allies can create conventional forces superior to those of the Warsaw Pact. But such a view simply ignores the psychology, the long history, and even the geography of the NATO alliance. With serious economic strains, adverse demographic trends (sharply falling birth cohorts, particularly in Germany) and no draft in the United States, will the allies do in the 1980s what they were unwilling to do in the prosperous 1960s and early 1970s? Should we risk Western security on so flimsy a hope?

Even if we attribute the aberration of negotiators consenting to the elimination of all strategic weapons to their being swept away by the enthusiasm of the moment, what are we to make of the main American proposal to eliminate all ballistic missiles by 1996? It was put forward not on the spur of the moment but after some, albeit not very deep, reflection. It appears to have originated in the Department of Defense (under some suspicion of disingenuousness, in that the Soviets could never accept it and that it would "play well in Peoria"). The proposal was included, in a general way, in President Reagan's July letter to Mr. Gorbachev without any suggestion of timing—more as a long-term aspiration than a concrete proposal. For that reason the Joint Chiefs of Staff did not take it very seriously. But at Reykjavik it was—without prior consultation with the Congress, the allies or the Joint Chiefs—put forward as a concrete proposal to be achieved in ten years' time. Although the President and Secretary Shultz have backed away somewhat from this proposal, it is still supported by some senior Administration officials and remains a part of our proposal in Geneva. While, happily, it lacks the quixotic heedlessness of the elimination of all strategic nuclear weapons, it raises very serious questions and has been subject to no serious analysis. Indeed, the National Security Decision Directive calling for the study of the military implications of the elimination of ballistic missiles was not circulated until several weeks after Reykjavik.

For a quarter of a century the value of the nuclear triad (bombers, intercontinental ballistic missiles and submarine-launched ballistic missiles) has been taken as axiomatic for America's military posture. Annually reiterated in the posture statements of various secretaries of defense, the value of the triad reflects not only the special features in targeting of each of the elements of the triad, but the desire to avoid putting all the principal deterrent eggs in one basket. As recently as 1983 the President, in accepting the report of the Scowcroft Commission, embraced this concept. The report pointed out that the triad would complicate any Soviet attack plan and would dissipate Soviet resources that might otherwise be concentrated against a single deterrent system: "Thus the existence of several components of our strategic forces permits each to function as a hedge against possible Soviet successes in endangering any of the others." The report went on to say, "the different components of our strategic forces would force the Soviets, if they were to contemplate an all-out attack, to make choices which would lead them to reduce significantly their effectiveness against one component in order to attack another." Space does not allow the spelling out of these technical details. Suffice it to say that at Reykjavik the Administration suddenly jettisoned 25 years of deterrence doctrine and the President's prior embrace of the Scowcroft Commission report. Without warning, without consultation with Congress or its allies, indeed without any prior analysis, the Administration proposed the abandonment of two of the three traditional legs of the triad.

Does no one in the Administration recall the days before ballistic missiles and the deep concern regarding the vulnerabilities of our bomber force, then deployed at only 55 Strategic Air Command (SAC) bases, susceptible to surprise attack? (That concern, needless to say, deepened with the initial Soviet deployments of intercontinental ballistic missiles.) The inevitable result, then and now, is the call for an airborne alert of the bomber force to limit its vulnerability on the ground. Does anybody in the Administration recall the lengthy dispute between the Congress and President Eisenhower, as the Congress pressed additional money on the Administration for airborne alert and the President argued that all it would lead to was "worn-out bombers"? A hypothetical bomber force of the 1990s would consist of many fewer bombers than in the 1950s, probably located on an even smaller number of main bases. Can anyone doubt that the concerns of the 1950s about its vulnerability would rapidly revive?

The ability of such a bomber force to penetrate Soviet air defenses would cause similar introspection and concern. The Administration itself has steadily emphasized that the Soviets invest far more than we do in "strategic defense." Most of that vast Soviet investment is in air defense. (By contrast, the United States, having accepted that Soviet ballistic missiles have essentially a free ride, has maintained only a skeletal air defense.) In the 1990s could our bombers be assured of penetrating the hundreds of radars, thousands of interceptors (with a lookdown, shoot-down capability), and tens of thousands of surface-to-air missiles that will then constitute Soviet air defenses? Moreover, the Soviet air defenses would likely be even more formidable if we were to "share" our strategic defense technology with the Soviets, as the President has promised. How assured would we feel under those conditions?

For more than 20 years we have been confident that submarine-launched ballistic missiles (SLBMs) were invulnerable. At Reykjavik we proposed to dispose of this leg of the triad. Do we really want to rid ourselves of what we have regarded as the invulnerable part of our deterrent—and depend wholly on air-breathing vehicles? The Administration argues that submarine-launched cruise missiles could to a considerable extent maintain some degree of invulnerability, as we eliminate the SLBMs. Do we seriously want to reduce radically the range at which our submarines can operate, forgo the advantages of long range embodied in the Trident ballistic missile and force our submarines to operate close to the Soviet Union with all the inherent increase in vulnerability? Do we want to depend on the capacity of cruise missiles to penetrate substantially enhanced Soviet air defenses?

Under the proffered conditions, the bulk of our retaliatory force would rest on bombers, located at a small number of bases and vulnerable to surprise attack. Would we really want to depend upon a surviving force of cruise missiles going against Soviet air defenses? Surely an administration that originally came into office stressing "the window of vulnerability" for our strategic forces should appreciate that under such conditions concern about the survival of our deterrent would once again escalate.

Finally, one must consider the budgetary consequences. Bombers, with their heavy requirements for manpower and fuel, tend to be quite costly, particularly if they are required to fly often in airborne alert. As we are procuring and operating this deterrent force of the future, and simultaneously rebuilding our air defenses and creating a ballistic missile defense, what portion of a relatively fixed defense budget would be absorbed? To what extent would our conventional military capabilities unavoidably be sacrificed—at the very moment that the need for further improvements in conventional defenses is being acknowledged throughout the alliance? At a minimum, it would appear that we should await the result of the belatedly ordered analyses before we press forward with the proposal to eliminate ballistic missiles.

One of the anomalies at Reykjavik was the contrasting treatment of the nuclear deterrent and the Strategic Defense Initiative. In Western strategy the nuclear deterrent remains the ultimate and indispensable reality. Yet at Reykjavik the President was prepared to negotiate it away almost heedlessly. By contrast, the Strategic Defense Initiative was treated and continues to be treated as if it were already a reality ("the key to a world without nuclear weapons") instead of a collection of technical experiments and distant hopes. The President proposed to deploy SDI in 1996. But by 1996 only a most rudimentary defense, based upon kinetic-kill vehicles, could be deployed. None of the well-advertised exotic defenses, including lasers and particle beams, could possibly be available until well into the 21st century. Thus, the proposed early deployment of this rudimentary ballistic missile defense would occur in the same year that the possession of ballistic missiles would no longer be permitted. That would, of course, ease the problem of making the ballistic missile defense effective. (There is always a hypothetical ballistic missile threat sufficiently limited that it can make even a rudimentary defense effective.)

Even with the threat of ballistic missiles nominally eliminated, the President argues that an early deployment of a rudimentary strategic defense system is necessary as insurance against Soviet cheating. It would be very costly insurance indeed, and one may well wonder whether or not the resources invested in such a rudimentary defense would not be better invested in other military capabilities. However, the stakes would be high, much higher than the Administration understood at the time of Reykjavik. If we were actually to eliminate ballistic missiles and return to a retaliatory force based primarily on bombers located on a small number of SAC bases, our main retaliatory force would be extremely vulnerable. Even if the Soviets were to cheat only to the extent of hiding away a very small number of missiles, our main U.S. retaliatory force would be placed at risk.

One may be bemused by the President's preoccupation with SDI. At Reykjavik he was prepared apparently to sacrifice our entire strategic nuclear armament, but unprepared to compromise on outside-the-laboratory testing of SDI. One finds it hard to believe that preserving the freedom to test SDI is by itself of sufficient importance to determine whether to jettison or salvage the Western system of security based on nuclear deterrence. Nonetheless, we must accept the astonishing irony: it was the impasse over SDI that saved us from the embarrassment of entering into completed agreements from which subsequently we would have had to withdraw. Thus, SDI may already have made an invaluable contribution to Western security—not for the bright, if somewhat evanescent, future regularly proffered to us, but rather by preserving the elements of nuclear deterrence from our Administration's recklessness at Reykjavik. For that we must be permanently grateful to SDI—irrespective of the still uncertain outcome of the research and development effort.

To be sure, the preoccupation with SDI, plus Gorbachev's tactical blunder in failing to seize upon the President's acceptance of the notion of total strategic nuclear disarmament, saved us at Reykjavik. But one should pause and examine what might have been. For more than a decade we have sought to control the grossly inflated Soviet offensive forces, which in-

248 THE REAGAN FOREIGN POLICY

corporate a major counterforce capability. Gorbachev offered
to reduce Soviet strategic offensive forces by 50 percent. If the
offer was genuine—and that could only be determined by
extensive negotiations—it might have achieved the true goal
of arms control: enhanced stability in the military postures of
the two sides. To Gorbachev's predictable demands that the
1972 Anti-Ballistic Missile Treaty be strengthened (can we
really have been surprised by his insistence on this point after
all the Soviet statements of the past three years?), we should
have responded by seriously addressing his legitimate concerns
about the scope of SDI testing, rather than pursuing the tack of
eliminating all ballistic missiles by 1996, which led the discussions down the grandiose, if futile and dangerous, road toward
total nuclear disarmament.

What have been the reactions to the events at Reykjavik
since the summit? Reykjavik may have been a marginal electoral
success for the midterm elections, but it has been a foreign
relations disaster. On the first point the Administration seems
to have been quite satisfied by its mastery of the political
technique it calls "spin control." White House Chief of Staff
Donald Regan commented: "We took Reykjavik and turned
what was really a sour situation into something that turned out
pretty well." What that says quite simply is that the public
relations impact on the American electorate is all-important,
while the substance of arms control and foreign reaction are
of negligible importance.

In Europe, however, the reaction was one of consternation,
as the substance and process of the negotiations at Reykjavik
became better understood. The Europeans, needless to say,
were vastly disturbed to discover that such revolutionary
changes in the Western security system affecting Europe could
be proposed and negotiated without any prior consultation.
But they were perhaps even more disturbed by the sudden
realization that the American negotiators apparently proceeded at Reykjavik without the slightest understanding of the
basis of the system of Western security. At a more specific, and
perhaps lower, level of concern, there was exasperation at the
casual proposal to eliminate the missiles placed in Europe after
so much political travail. We had made the argument that
missiles in Europe were essential to deterrence by linking forces
in Europe to the larger American strategic deterrent. While
one can argue that the Euromissile issue is more symbolic and

psychological than military, still it is hard for us to abandon the initial rationale.

Amid considerable distress, a hasty round of conferences was held. Soon British Prime Minister Margaret Thatcher, bearing a portfolio for all the European allies, appeared at Camp David to deliver a *reclama* on Reykjavik. The outcome, which set priorities for arms control, was highly satisfactory. It was agreed that priority should be given to major reductions in intermediate-range nuclear forces and a 50-percent reduction in strategic offensive weapons, and in the context of the elimination of conventional disparities, a ban on chemical warfare and a reduction in shorter-range systems within the European theater. Perhaps most significant, the long-standing strategy of NATO was reconfirmed.

Once again, as with the earlier rhetoric of SDI replacing (immoral) deterrence, Mrs. Thatcher helped save the Americans from their own folly. The selection of priorities, while sensible, was rather belated. The normal procedure is to establish priorities *prior* to negotiation—just as the normal procedure would be to study the consequences of eliminating ballistic missiles *prior* to making such a proposal. The Administration does appear to have backed away from its breathtaking discussions at Reykjavik in a manner equally breathtaking. For that, at least, we should be grateful.

Nonetheless, the consequences of Reykjavik remain serious. Though allied governments have been eager to put as good a face as possible on the summit, beneath the surface of public support they remain deeply disturbed at both the substance and the procedure of the Reykjavik negotiations. Their confidence in American leadership has been significantly weakened. In the immediate aftermath of the summit some began to cast around for alternative methods, other than American protection, to provide for their security. Although the initial alarm has now diminished, some residue remains.

With our allies we have gotten the worst of both possible worlds. On the one hand, the confidence of West European governments in the capacity of American leadership to protect the general interests of the alliance in negotiations has been seriously damaged. On the other hand, the publics and much of the press in Europe have been excited by the promise of major arms control agreements, and particularly the elimination of the Soviet intermediate-range threat directed against Western Europe. They have been persuaded that the elimination of the dreaded SS-20 threat would have taken place had it not been for the American obstinacy about SDI. While the Soviets will remain unsuccessful in the near term in changing attitudes of governments, they have been given a fertile field to sow in the battle for public opinion.

Perhaps even more important in the long run, the President's embrace of the goal, both utopian and dangerous, of a world without nuclear weapons will inevitably weaken support for the strategy of nuclear deterrence upon which the defense of the West continues to rest. This is particularly true in Western Europe. It has already been seized by the British Labour Party and by the Social Democratic Party in West Germany in the run-ups to their respective elections. But it is also true in the United States. Once again, as with SDI, the President has been destructive in his judgment on deterrence. He has clearly done more to weaken deterrence than did the U.S. Catholic bishops in their 1983 pastoral letter.

The full effects of Reykjavik will probably never be known, as the summit has been wholly superseded in public discussion by the issues of arms for Iran and the illegal funding of the contras. Admittedly, these latter events appear more dramatic and have a greater impact on the public mind. They do constitute a serious embarrassment for the United States and provide the potential for a major diplomatic setback. Nevertheless, their inherent weight is much less than the negotiations at Reykjavik. They cannot significantly alter the military balance or significantly weaken Western security. By contrast, Reykjavik had the potential for upsetting the military balance, for suddenly vitiating Western military strategy, and for destroying the cohesion of the Western alliance. It is a pity that the more consequential shall have been overtaken by the less consequential if more dramatic. Reykjavik was a near disaster, and we should learn from it all that we can. Perhaps the best that can be said about the summit is that it was a *near* disaster. As the Duke of Wellington remarked after Waterloo: "It was the nearest-run thing you ever saw."

III

The tangled affair that falls under the rubric of the "arms scandal" has rocked both the government and the country. There has been public confusion regarding what our policies really are and a stunning drop in the President's approval rating. It has weakened and may cripple the Administration far beyond the lame-duck status normally occurring at this stage in an administration. I do not intend here to attempt to disentangle the precise relationships among people and events, the contradictions and the illegalities; that is the task of the congressional review committees and the independent counsel. I shall instead attempt to examine the implications for American policy in the broadest sense and the impact upon our international position.

Whoever allowed this combination of events to proceed could not have designed his work more destructively. The combination of weapons supplied to the regime of the Ayatollah Ruhollah Khomeini (on the scale of the American public's dislikes, Iran ranks well above the Soviet Union), the ransoming of hostages (not only were arms traded, but ransom money was raised explicitly for that purpose), and the illegal diversion of funds to the contras (for whom public sentiment has varied between indifference and hostility) was put together in a package and planted in the White House complex. It was a ticking time bomb, ingeniously contrived and placed close to the President. It was only a matter of time before it detonated.

The origins lie well back in the Administration's reading, strongly touched by ideology, of recent history. The setbacks that the United States experienced in the 1970s were attributed in no way to the limits of American power, but simply to the lack of will. The solution was equally simple: American strength and American will. Be determined. Overcome all obstacles. A cult of toughness became the norm. There was a widespread failure to understand the real restraints on American power and the American public's deep-seated ambivalence about the use of force, including the disguised use of force.

In the long run, heroic posturing is as unsatisfactory a basis for foreign policy as is moral posturing. Some in the Administration seemed to view *Rambo* not just as a highly implausible adventure tale, but rather as a profound political treatise. Administration policies were shaped by ideologues who lacked familiarity with American politics and what the American people are prepared to accept. Covert operations were not just a tool, useful if somewhat distasteful. Instead they were regarded as a noble instrument, a righteous cause—of which one could be proud in public—almost a crusade. There was frustration with the restraints placed upon presidential control of foreign policy. There was resentment of the new oversight requirements that Congress had imposed upon intelligence operations.

From its earliest days the Administration appeared willing to run roughshod over congressional prerogatives and sensibilities in these matters.

The CIA's violation of the first Boland Amendment, which precluded actions to overthrow the government in Managua, and most particularly the mining of Nicaraguan harbors, led to the second Boland Amendment, cutting off military aid to the contras. With the CIA at least ostensibly removed, responsibility for directing Central American operations came to reside in the White House. The National Security Council staff was not an "agency" under the Boland Amendment (or so it could be argued) and staff members could be protected by executive privilege. Former National Security Adviser Robert McFarlane commented, "We cannot break faith with the contras," from which one might infer that the Administration felt less constrained in breaking faith with either the Congress or the law. For several years NSC staff members, notably Lieutenant Colonel Oliver North, raised money, provided intelligence and directed operations, all to sustain the contra effort and morale.

In order to avoid congressional oversight of the Central Intelligence Agency and to evade the intent of the Boland Amendment, these secret operations were effectively placed in the White House, close to the President. A generation's admonitions to keep all covert operations as far from the President as possible were discarded. The President himself seemed happy with the situation, ready to discuss the presumably covert operations in Central America. The borderline between overt and covert, sometimes difficult to define, became wholly obliterated. Also obliterated was the distinction between the permissible and the impermissible.

The seeds of the secret shift in policy toward Iran were sown in 1984 with the kidnapping of Americans, most notably William Buckley, whose abduction aroused the CIA. To the call to extricate our hostages was added the persuasive voice of Israel and the vague longing for a longer-term relationship with Iran. The massive political victory of the President in 1984 reinforced the frequently encountered White House hubris and further weakened a sense of limits to what the President could accomplish or what he was permitted to do. White House hubris was reinforced by a set of successes from Grenada to the *Achille Lauro*.

The selling of arms to Iran started in 1985 through the

Israelis, apparently in the belief that such transactions could remain secret. By 1986 weapons were being removed directly from service inventories for shipment to Iran. And then North and others on the NSC staff, already heady with past triumphs, truly went amok, diverting the bulk of the proceeds through a variety of secret bank accounts in Switzerland and the West Indies to the illegal support of the contra operation and perhaps to other beneficiaries, possibly including sympathetic politicians in the United States. The notion that this extensive network of operations, spanning at least 11 countries, could be kept secret reflected a touching, if naïve, faith in clandestinity.

The consequences hardly need to be spelled out. The nation is in an uproar. The Administration is in disarray. Its energies will be directed in large degree, at least until October 1987 (when the Senate says it will finish its investigation), toward attempting to control the damage. It has lost control over the national agenda. Public confidence in the President has been seriously eroded. The question remains whether the Administration can partially recover or whether it will be permanently crippled.

It should be noted that the principal damage in the public's view resulted from the shipment of arms to the despised ayatollah and the trading of those arms for the hostages. For the American public, this has counted far more than the "illegalities" associated with the diversion of public resources. Why?

America remains a nation with a strong idealistic bent. It does not believe that it is right to profess one policy, to press one's allies and others to follow that policy, and then in secret to do the reverse. The President, upon coming into office, asserted that terrorists should recognize that "retribution would be swift and effective." Countless voices have asserted that we will "never negotiate with terrorists." The public was urged to believe that this indeed was our policy. And here we suddenly are dealing with the hated ayatollah—with an Iran branded by the President as the principal example of those "outlaw states . . . run by the strangest collection of misfits, looney tunes and squalid criminals since the advent of the Third Reich."[1] Worse than that, here we are paying ransom,

[1] Address to the Annual Convention of the American Bar Association, July 8, 1985. The address was given a week or so before the President gave oral approval to the sale of arms through the Israelis. Apparently the President's speechwriters were not apprised of the prospective shift in policy.

arms for hostages—something that we proclaimed we would never do and have urged all others to refrain from doing. The public's shock was unavoidable. The diversion of funds appears far less reprehensible to the public.

A president must be true to his image. He is allowed a great deal of running room so long as he does not break an implicit social contract with the public: that he is a man who will not violate the public's deepest convictions, which he has come to personify. President Carter, rated high among presidents for his honesty, was sharply rebuked for his few fibs, which in sum were a fraction of those tolerated in other presidents. Why? Because the conviction that he conveyed to the public in 1976 was that he would restore goodness in Washington and never lie to the American people. Similarly, no one would ever expect President Reagan to be sending weapons to the ayatollah in exchange for hostages, or that his staff would be raising ransom money while the Administration proclaimed the need to stand up to terrorists. President Reagan was elected to be strong— to stand up to the nation's enemies. Trafficking with terrorists was not his image. It was not precisely Standing Tall.

The irony is that the President had both betrayed and been felled by that cantankerous American patriotism he had done so much to foster and had come to exemplify. The Republican governor of South Dakota, William Janklow, expressed it simply: "There are not five people out there who want to send arms to Iran. The only way we want to give them arms is dropping them from the bay of a B-1 bomber." Perhaps it was best put by a Chicago lawyer and Reagan appointee: "It's like suddenly learning that John Wayne had secretly been selling liquor and firearms to the Indians."

Much, far too much, has been made by the President's defenders of Roosevelt's trading overage destroyers to the British in 1940. It is a misleading parallel. This nation has moved beyond the Wilsonian notion of open covenants, openly arrived at. It accepts, although it is not happy with, the reality of secret diplomacy. But secret diplomacy in this country must be an extension of and in spirit with its open diplomacy. It cannot be the reverse of what we say publicly, especially (as in the Iranian case) when the secret action is in all-out opposition to what the American people want. Illegalities, which may excite the lawyers, although secondary in terms of public response, certainly do not help. All these marked the Iran/contra affair. The public outcry was scarcely surprising.

By contrast, none of this applies to Roosevelt's trading of overage destroyers to the British. Roosevelt had made no secret that he wanted the British to survive (and win!). His announced policy had been: all aid to the Allies, short of war. Nor had he made much of a secret of his loathing for Hitler's Germany. That had been clear since his "Quarantine the Aggressor" speech in 1937. Moreover, his foreign policy goal was one approved by the American people. The nation certainly preferred the Allies and disliked the Axis; it just did not want to become involved in the war. Finally, though no doubt of lesser importance, we got precisely what we traded for. We received bases that all admitted were valuable for the defense of the western hemisphere. That the Iranians conned us on the release of the hostages simply added insult to injury.

Finally, there is the national attitude toward clandestinity. While the country has moved well past Henry Stimson's "Gentlemen do not read each other's mail," it still remains deeply uneasy about clandestine operations, especially those originating from within the White House. Those who are fascinated by clandestinity, from the time of the White House plumbers to the time of Colonel North's operations, have failed to understand this deeply held public attitude. The public is prepared to accept clandestine activities, but only when they seem clearly required. Wholesale clandestinity brings to the surface all of the public's deep-seated ambivalence.

Adequate public support is fundamental to the carrying out of foreign policy in this society. The need for any secret diplomacy to be consistent with our open diplomacy and our publicly expressed goals is accepted by the American people, is manifest. The need to be circumspect about clandestine operations—and not to give way to the impulse of the "cowboys"—is essential for retaining public support. Those who advise any president, including Mr. Reagan, otherwise do not understand the spirit of the American democracy or the exigencies for carrying out foreign policy in this society.

IV

We must now assess the consequences of the arms scandal at home and abroad.

In the first place, the President has been dramatically weakened. His diminished credibility, with the Congress and with American elites generally, means that he will be able to provide little positive leadership in foreign policy for the balance of his term. His proposals will be greeted with skepticism at best. Moreover, his standing with the public can be only partially restored—and then more in terms of affection than high regard for his leadership. One of the truly astounding reactions to the arms scandal was reflected in the response to one question in a recent *New York Times*/CBS poll: "Whom do you trust more to make the right decisions on foreign policy— Ronald Reagan or Congress?" The public chose Congress over the President 61 percent to 27 percent. The public may have its difficulty with the practical and constitutional questions involved, but it is a truly stunning judgment on the capability of the executive branch.

Yet the impact on foreign policy may be modest. Congress is firmly under the control of the moderates. American foreign policy thus should remain quite stable—perhaps too stable. The wilder blades of the Watergate Congress have been removed or have "matured." There will be little repetition of the bizarre attitudes and turbulent debates of the early 1970s. Nonetheless, it is equally clear that Congress is hard-pressed to provide useful new initiatives. Thus, American policy over the next two years will likely turn out to be a holding pattern.

The controversy regarding the arms scandal has acquired a momentum of its own. It will roll on, even to the point of public boredom. White House attempts to suggest that Oliver North "acted alone" or that rogue elephants at the NSC were out of control will prove ineffective. First, whatever their excesses, Poindexter and North clearly were responding to the policy vibrations within the White House. Second, to suggest that no one knew what the President's staff was doing is perhaps even less reassuring than that this activity was authorized. The "explanation" that the President's staff was out of control is a rather desperate alibi; its only utility is to obviate the charge of complicity in illegalities. After all, just who was nursing this would-be Ludendorff in the basement of the White House?

Finally, and perhaps most important: clearly it was the President who authorized the arms for Iran and the trading of arms for hostages. The rest, including the raising of ransom money and the illegal diversion and use of funds, may indeed have been extracurricular. But the propitiation of the ayatollah's regime (under the guise of working with Iranian moderates) and the willingness to ransom hostages—both in conflict with our stated policy—are acknowledged to be the President's responsibility. Those are the issues about which the public is concerned. For the public the diversion of funds is a rather recondite legal point. Consequently hopes for a Reagan recovery—other than as a grandfather figure—would appear modest at best.

The consequences abroad complement those within the United States. The loss in credibility of American foreign policy has been serious. It will be a long time before any American attempt to obtain backing for an anti-terrorist policy will be regarded as more than a pretense—or will elicit as much support as derision. In Europe the distress over the inept performance of the Americans at Reykjavik was reinforced by the belief that the Americans had been both weak and deceitful in selling arms to Iran and in their stance against terrorists. Unlike Reykjavik, however, these matters do not seriously undermine Western European security. Confusing, irritating, embarrassing they may be, but they scarcely impinge on Europe's vital interests. As a consequence, the initial European response—unlike that after Reykjavik—was a mixture of scorn and irritation. After all, Europeans are not above a touch of schadenfreude when the Americans are making fools of themselves—so long as it does not threaten European security.

Europe's initial anger and contempt, however, rapidly turned into deep concern as it became evident that the United States was going into a serious political crisis, different from but perhaps as severe as Watergate. It suggested that the United States might be preoccupied with internal matters for two more years and that, at best, it could provide little international leadership and at worst might be entirely diverted from its international responsibilities. So the initial smugness has given way to serious alarm. But Europeans do tend to exaggerate the impact of a political crisis in the United States on its ability to function internationally. The separation of powers is regarded by foreigners as the bane of the American political system. There is little understanding of the beneficial aspects of the separation of powers or of how Congress to a large extent can substitute for and provide stability when the executive is in crisis.

The post-Watergate experience is misleading. American foreign policy will proceed largely unaffected. There will be no innovations, but there will be no drastic changes. But the perception of American weakness and political stalemate may be as important as the reality—especially coming after Reykjavik. Loss of confidence in the United States will certainly lead to some loss of alliance cohesion and may lead to unwise actions by several of the European states.

The effect in the Middle East may be more far-reaching. In so volatile a region, it would seem hard to increase instability. But we may just have turned that difficult trick. The government of Israel has been embarrassed. The governments of the moderate Arab states (excepting Saudi Arabia) are angry and dismayed. The American position has been weakened throughout the Arab world, including Saudi Arabia, which was itself involved with the propitiation of Iran. Iran's and Khomeini's prestige have both been increased. (That has not helped the moderates, such as they are, within Iran.) The position of Iraq has been weakened—with all that this implies for control over Middle Eastern oil. If it has been our purpose to terminate the Iran-Iraq war, we have succeeded only in lengthening it.

Saudi Arabia has been encouraged to turn toward Teheran. Iranian influence in Riyadh has grown. The dismissal of Saudi Oil Minister Ahmed Zaki Yamani and the movement of Saudi products across the Persian Gulf to assist their hereditary enemy against their Arab brother bear witness to that. Within OPEC, Iranian influence has grown; this may be unimportant for now, but potentially highly significant in the 1990s.

As the political difficulties in the Middle East increase, we should be more aware than we are of the accelerating dependence of the United States on the oil fields of the Persian Gulf. Low oil prices—in the absence of any effort to sustain the domestic oil industry—are taking their toll. American production is falling by roughly half a million barrels a day each year. The rig count is off from its peak by more than 80 percent. By 1990 it appears that we will be importing more than 50 percent of our oil, over nine million barrels a day. And the decline in U.S. production will likely accelerate as we hit the decline curve at Prudhoe Bay. As we gradually, and more or less heedlessly, increase our dependency upon the Persian Gulf— and all that that implies in terms of reduced leeway for American foreign policy—we may have additional reasons to regret this series of actions that has further damaged our credibility in the Middle East.

V

The Reagan foreign policy record has no monuments like the breakthrough to China, the Egyptian-Israeli peace agreement or an effective arms control agreement. Until now it has been characterized as "no hits, no runs, no errors"—although the last phrase must now regrettably be dropped. The great accomplishment of Ronald Reagan has been much more psychological and political. He has presided over, and through the ebullience of his personality contributed to, the restoration of American self-confidence and public confidence in our institutions, particularly the presidency. Abroad he has presided over a sharp rise in American prestige (and therefore perceived power), reinforced by a sharp decline in Soviet prestige during its recent time of troubles. These were major accomplishments, but they are now seriously threatened. Public confidence in our institutions has been shaken once again. There are signs of a return of public cynicism. Although one should not expect a return to the mood of the 1970s, none of this can help national strength and unity. Internationally our prestige and influence have received a serious blow, though perhaps more from Reykjavik than from the arms scandal. The great accomplishment of the Reagan years has been reduced, even if it has not been brought low.

The tide that began with the Soviet invasion of Afghanistan and increased in force in the early 1980s has now ceased to flow toward the United States and has begun to ebb. To what extent will that benefit the Soviet Union? To what extent will the tide flow strongly in the Soviet direction? No doubt, the Soviet Union will benefit. But the Soviet image has been badly marred by its blunders, by its relative technical backwardness and by its economic weaknesses. As a consequence, the Soviet Union fortunately does not now appear to be in a position to take full benefit from the regrettable setback to America's prestige.

INDEX